CHILDHOOD AND DESTINY

THE TRIADIC PRINCIPLE
IN GENETIC EDUCATION

CHILDHOOD AND DESTINY

THE TRIADIC PRINCIPLE
IN GENETIC EDUCATION

JOACHIM FLESCHER, M.D.

Published in co-operation with the
Dual Therapy and Research Bureau

INTERNATIONAL UNIVERSITIES PRESS, INC.

New York   New York

FIRST EDITION

All rights reserved

Copyright, © 1970 by Joachim Flescher, M.D.

Library of Congress Catalog Card Number: 73-107509

Printed in the United States of America

TO

PARENTS WHO
'KNOW NOT WHAT THEY DO'
TO THOSE WHOSE DESTINY
THEY ARE SHAPING—
WITH UNDERSTANDING
AND A PORTENT
OF NEW HOPE

ACKNOWLEDGMENTS

I want to express my appreciation to Barbara Hunt for her help in correcting and polishing my manuscript, as well as to my daughter Sylvia, who has shown an early interest and gift for this field and for whom English is the mother tongue.

Finally, my heartfelt thanks to my wife Anna for her patience in typing the many drafts of this volume.

TABLE OF CONTENTS

INTRODUCTION

This is not the first book ever written, and for that matter not even *my* first book, on the prevention of neurosis (Italy, 1945, 1948, U.S.A., 1951). In my last one I have claimed, probably with some presumption, to have presented "all that is known" about mental prophylaxis. For about two decades since that time, because of external events involving the lives of millions of people—one day I may reveal how they touched me most personally—I have been engaged in the study of the *role of aggression* in human psychopathology (1945, 1951, 1953, 1955, 1959) and especially of the relevance of aggression to the problem of mental hygiene in general.

Why I have suspended editing my rather advanced work on the topic of man's destructiveness in order to concentrate on making public the results of my research on prevention is easily explained: The present social and political scene proves most cogently that it is less urgent to describe the ways by which the psychic forces have brought about mankind's predicament than the means of ameliorating it, provided that these exist. I hope that I will be able to convince my readers that in fact they do exist and are within our reach.

A new and most decisive incentive to formulate an integrated ideology for an analytically-oriented mental prophylaxis was provided by my experience with "dual therapy" and the philosophy of "genetic psychoanalysis" on which it is based (1966). In my present attempt to define the principle of genetic prevention, I resolved to document my conclusions even more thoroughly than is my habit. For the suggestions advanced here, I anticipated, are likely, for reasons which will become clear in the course of this writing, to arouse unconscious and even open resistance in parents.

In the present volume further evidence will be offered to the effect that psychoanalysis has greatly suffered from failure

1

to include in the methodology of analytic treatment the central and most crucial discovery of Freud. I ascribe it without hesitation to a specific and deeply entrenched resistance of analysts which has survived their own analysis. It is, I must state most emphatically, the same resistance which accounts for my colleagues' (with extremely few exceptions) unwillingness to apply the genetic approach in analytic therapy. This is the more bewildering and significant because a wealth of clinical material has been made public over a number of years about the success of the application of the triadic principle in psychoanalysis (Flescher, 1958, 1966, 1968). What is pertinent here, however, is that the emotional factor responsible for such a striking *psychological blind spot* is the same one that has made *effective mental prophylaxis impossible*. Only a painstaking exploration of the shortcomings of classical analysis on one side, and of the present state of preventive education on the other, could document and explain adequately the following fact: After over half a century of application of the unique tool for the exploration of the human mind we are still unable to assist either the individual or the masses in obviating the consequences of mental disorders.

To avoid being misunderstood by hasty readers, I would like to state explicitly that without the discoveries of classical analysis, the genetic modification proposed by me would not have been conceived and this book would not have been written. Clearly I am not joining the chorus of those who celebrate the demise of psychoanalysis. On the contrary, I am drawing attention to its still untapped potentialities, in the conviction that genetic prevention, if applied at least to the extent to which we practice the most elementary rules of physical hygiene throughout the world, will ultimately preserve future generations from crowding psychiatric wards, hospitals and prisons, as well as save countless victims of *collective irrationality* from ending their lives in death camps, mass graves and military cemeteries.

To document the validity of my views, I felt that I had to bring persuasive proof that a parallel exists between a destructive parental influence—by commission or omission—and the analyst's countertransference response which prevents his therapeutic effort from being successful. Equally compelling appeared to me the task of explaining convincingly the basic principle from which the "practical rules" were ultimately derived. All this seemed necessary because in the matter of child rearing, which is much more than instruction, it is well known that one should not expect, as in other fields, an unquestioning automatic adherence to guiding rules and prescriptions offered by "experts." To bring compelling proof and to be convincing, however, inevitably entailed presenting a greater bulk of material.

Regarding precisely this aspect, the counsel of some friends and well-disposed colleagues—among them Dr. Martin Grotjahn—seemed to merit consideration. Their advice was to the effect that it is not a good policy to publish voluminous books if one aspires to be read by many. In view of the dwindling patience of the average reader and the growing habit even among intellectuals of preferring magazines and digests over books, this opinion cannot possibly be lightly dismissed. Still I was unable to depart from my conviction that, as I have maintained on a previous occasion, short of analysis, *only the weight of the evidence can induce an interested and inquiring parent to change his attitude toward his children.* Hence I have decided to publish each of the two major works—the present one on *psychic prevention,* and the other on *aggression*—in two volumes, the first dealing with the *individual* and the second with the *group.* The close interrelationship between normal and abnormal individual psychology on one side and collective mental and behavior patterns on the other will, I trust, safeguard sufficiently the logical coherence between the two volumes on each topic.

I would like to prepare the reader for the likelihood of finding in this writing what may appear to him repetitious. Upon closer scrutiny, however, he will discover that the new context aims at highlighting a fresh and what I deem an essential facet of an already mentioned concept, mechanism or process.

In the chapter "Theoretical Foundation," there are delineated the basic premises on which the presentation of the results of my investigative efforts rests. I apologize for the rather tightly knit conceptual framework used as my point of departure. Its terseness will be made up for, I hope, by the relatively easier to follow subsequent chapters and even more so by the many illustrations, drawn chiefly from my practice of dual therapy and from that of my staff. Actually only the psychologically more sophisticated parents—their number is fortunately growing—may want to study carefully the theoretical chapters. The less demanding may simply start at the chapter on "The Triadic Principle" or the one on "Genetic Scripts." Still others, motivated by trust or by impatience, may want to confine themselves to skimming the chapter on "Genetic Child Rearing" and to a thorough assimilation of the "Practical Rules."

The iterative resumption of themes already dealt with permits readers to begin the book at any of the chapters mentioned. I foresee, however, that not a few fathers and mothers will be challenged by the suggestions offered them and will work back to the basic premises on which these are founded.

I should also like to mention here the controversy about parental "responsibility." With increasing frequency, books appear which implicitly or explicitly try to free the parents, especially mothers, of responsibility for the emotional difficulties of their children. While this view bears out the charitable attitude of the authors, it violates a fundamental truth for the following reason:

The ancestral past of man, whether it is deposited in chromosomal potentialities or in archetypal disposition, is ultimately referable to more or less long-standing influences impinging on our progenitors. These latent assets or liabilities are mediated through the last and closest link of the child with that very past, his parents. To the ancestral (inherited, constitutional) foundation of assets and liabilities the parents add their own (environmental) personality-shaping psycho-

4

logical influence. On the strength of this, one indeed could free parents from the responsibility with which the modern genetic view is inclined to burden them. After all, they could not be held accountable for the past, which they are only mediating and to which they are merely the last contributors. How could the parental influence of a few years compare with the eons of time during which all the innumerable generations of ancestors have borne up under the influence of nature and man?

Yet the truth is—at least my experience compels me to believe—that *this last link overshadows in its destiny-shaping influence all the ancestral past.* This is evidenced by two observations: First, the nature of the difficulties to which the child has fallen victim clearly points to specific traumatic interventions and omissions by the child's parents. Second, it is only the analytic *recall or reconstruction* of the parents' detrimental influence, and the psychological *correction* of that same influence, which brings about a lasting cure. To close one's eyes to this truth, as do those who engage in "exculpating" parents—although it can be of transient comfort to them, deprives us of the benefits of effective therapy. Even more fatal, it also makes dependable mental hygiene impossible.

In conclusion, it is most pertinent here to recall the moving legend about a Child born to save the world from misery and perdition by promoting peace and love among men. The psychological truth of this religious lore rests, however, on the fact that even such a Child cannot be born in a vacuum, that is, without a past which shapes man's personality and destiny. Only what parents positively instill in their children through acts, words and feelings—those of which they are aware and those hidden in the deepest recesses of their minds —will accomplish the longed-for miracle: the freeing of coming generations from all the heartbreaks which abbreviate our already too short abode here. Only then will man be able to live out his days in security and dignity, and to draw to the fullest from the infinite sources of physical and spiritual enjoyment open to his sensitivity, unique among living creatures.

5

CHAPTER ONE

THEORETICAL FOUNDATION

Whatever may be the experts' view on the ways in which improper behavior and attitude of parents bring about emotional problems in their children, the following has been established beyond any doubt: the emotional (genetic) environment of the family by far overshadows any other physical or mental influence on the future of the young. In the analysis of many thousands of patients since Freud, the connection between their suffering and their childhood experiences was meticulously studied and reconfirmed. The psychic injuries (traumata) inflicted upon the children have been shown to be brought about either through *deprivation* (lack of stimuli) or through *overexcitement* (excessive stimuli). The importance of this latter source of traumatization is in my view not yet fully appreciated.

If we add to this the body of knowledge which psychoanalysts after Freud have accumulated concerning the *changing* needs and vulnerabilities of the child during his development, the following question could be raised: Why is it that after more than half a century of application of the psychoanalytic method to the study of normal as well as abnormal psychic phenomena, no integrated and effective philosophy for the prevention of neurosis has been developed? All attempts so far to apply one or another guiding principle gleaned from the empirical findings and theoretical deductions of psychoanalysis have yielded only minor or, more frequently, deeply disappointing results.

Hand in hand with this (the logical connection between the two will soon become clear), an objective observer of public as well as professional opinion must notice that the reputation of classical psychoanalysis, even as a therapeutic method, has long since lost its original luster. More and more its effectiveness is questioned—and not merely, as in the past, by unenlightened and rabid opponents of psychoanalysis. Actually Freud himself was the first to show signs of such a tendency. Not only did he reiterate that psychoanalysis is effective solely in "classical" neuroses, but he would almost proudly indulge in the habit of "confessing" that he always avoided becoming a victim of therapeutic fervor. This attitude of the founder of psychoanalysis, the most dramatic breakthrough in psychiatric treatment, is by no means either self-explanatory or to be taken lightly. Did not Freud originally seek, and think he had found, a causal therapy for all neuroses which had hitherto been impervious to the therapeutic efforts of the physicians of his time?

Without going further, at least at this point, into the evidence and cause of the waning reputation of psychoanalysis, I shall state that it is my conviction, grounded in the very foundation of psychoanalytic theory, that a surrender of therapeutic aspirations on the part of those using the Freudian method is uncalled for. What follows will explain my position.

Role of Unconscious Conflicts

It has been demonstrated beyond the shadow of a doubt that psychic disorders owe their existence not only to past traumata, but to current (unconscious) conflicts which ensue from them. As we now understand, these traumata have disrupted the orderly course of the child's development (Flescher, 1951, p. 135) so that the resulting immature impulses and inclinations inevitably have to clash with more healthy aspirations of the individual or with the demands of society. But precisely the fact that psychic pathology is constantly dynamically refueled by conflicts[1] *currently* prevailing in the unconscious explains its reversibility. Hence the known theo-

---

1. Even the clashes with society do not engage primary impulses, but only their conflict-determined derivatives.

retical axiom that *if analysis succeeds in solving the underlying pathogenetic conflict, it also eliminates the attending pathology.*

Reversibility of Psychic Disturbances

Given the two premises—that there is a causal connection between childhood trauma and immediate or delayed psychopathology, and that whatever is psychic in origin and nature is reversible—the following conclusion seems warranted: if analytic therapy has not yielded satisfactory results commensurate with these premises, it must simply be due to the fact that *we have not yet found the right approach* for reversing psychic disorders. To remedy this, it stands to reason that we have first to see if we can identify the factors responsible for the frequent inadequate results or complete failures of psychoanalytic treatment and even, as Freud himself has pointed out, aggravation of the patient's condition.

That neither the theoretical basis of the Freudian method nor the principle of reversibility of psychic pathology can be questioned is proved by the simple fact that therapeutic failures are only frequent but still far from regular. The two above tenets are sufficiently borne out by innumerable cases which have been, with the help of analysis, that is through resolution of conflicts rooted in infantile constellations, freed from anxiety attacks, obsessional phenomena, and functional and psychosomatic maladies. The frequently sporadic, episodic and seizure-like nature of psychic symptomatology and even the occasional spontaneous suspension of manifest psychoses also testify to the potential curability of even the most severe mental disorders.[2]

---

2. This holds true even for many especially recidivant psychosomatic disorders. If one succeeds in eliminating the underlying psychic conflict, the recuperative forces of the organism become more effective. I myself had a few gratifying therapeutic experiences in cases of stomach ulcer, colitis and asthma.

Corrective Experience

It was obvious from the start that the source of error, in spite of its generic nature, would not be found in the theoretical core of psychoanalytic methodology which rests on a solid basis of empirical data. It must then be traced to the methodological *technique* applied in analytic therapy. The essence of this technique can easily be gleaned from what is the ultimate goal of analytic therapy: while the immobilizing conflicts are being resolved, the analyst learns how and in what sense the patient's psychoinstinctual development has been disrupted. By affording the patient a *"corrective experience"* of the traumata suffered, the impasse in his development is eliminated and ultimately the forward movement of the maturational process is recaptured and carried to completion. These are the cardinal steps leading to the cure of psychic disturbance or its somatic equivalents.

But before we begin the inquiry about the technical obstacle which may account for the therapeutic disappointments of those who receive and provide psychoanalytic treatment, let me introduce a new factor in our field of observation, a third source of traumatization of the child. Though it is most significantly intertwined with each of the two former traumatic factors, I have found, it overshadows by far their importance. In fact it is this last source of psychic injury which seems to endow the first two (deprivation and overstimulation) most decisively with their pathogentic influence. I have elaborated upon it on another occasion (Flescher, 1966). Here I shall only broadly outline this third factor and indicate a few of the major investigative steps which led me to draw some final conclusions about its pertinence to the problem of mental prophylaxis.

Transference

We know that *transference* plays an essential part in the process of analytic therapy. For that matter, it is within the transference, that is the reliving in the "analytic situation" of past relationships with parents or closest substitutes, that the patient's "resistance" and "defenses" display their full force. It is through the analysis of transference alone that they become, or at least should become, accessible to analytic scrutiny and resolution. We know, and we teach our analytic candidates, that in transference to the analyst the analysand's past experiences with his mother and father are relived and the pertinent conflicts activated. This means that mostly under the influence of *repetition compulsion* the patient has a tendency to structure the analytic situation so as to approximate, if not to make it identical with, the genetic situation of his childhood. It is precisely this fact—the activation of the past conflicts—which provides the unique opportunity *to undo the very pathogenetic traumatizations* from which they draw their dynamic roots. In order, however, to bring about a repetition of this genetic, i.e. personality-shaping past, it is inevitable that the patient greatly distort in his mind the perception and evaluation of his analyst. It is therefore crucial in analysis that the therapist be attuned to the elements in the material brought by the patient that *mirror his genetic past.*

Countertransference

But regarding transference, Freud himself had already discovered that analysts are far from capable of the proverbial "professional objectivity." Powerful emotional factors operating within them greatly impair their objective evaluation and understanding of the patient. Indeed for the subjective distortions of the therapist himself, that is his own irrational contribution to the interaction with his patient in the psychoanalytic situation, Freud coined the term *countertransference.* Since then many studies have appeared on this source of disturbance of the therapeutic process. Thus far, however, there has been no systematic inquiry into this phenomenon even from a typological viewpoint. An initial step in this direction was made when I tried to classify and dynamically qualify the most frequent countertransference phenomena (1953).

Reactive Countertransference

I distinguished first a countertransference response which is simply *reactive to the transference of the patient*. It bears witness to our general human vulnerability, in the sense that emotions, attitudes and actions of another person impinge on us in any close interpersonal relationship and modify our own feelings and thoughts. To recognize early such an inclination within ourselves entails the surrender of the flattering but unsubstantiated image of the analyst as an absolute "objective" observer, i.e. impervious to the pleading, clinging, seductive or threatening verbalizations or attitudes of the patient. The easily demonstrable, though often well-concealed, at least from his own awareness, responses of the analyst to the patient's transference I proposed, therefore, to designate as *reactive countertransference*.

Defensive Countertransference

The second type of emotional contribution of the analyst to the analytic situation, was found to be to a large degree, though not completely, independent from the transference of the patient. It is less related to the patient but rather represents a response to the analytic situation as such, and hence is discernible with many if not all patients of the same analyst. Here the countertransference is rooted in the *defenses* operating in the therapist himself and thus deserves to be referred to as *defensive countertransference*. It is expressive of emotional problems of the analyst, which his own personal and didactic analysis has failed to solve.

Suggestive Countertransference

For the third type of response on the part of the analyst I proposed the term *suggestive* or *induced countertransference*. It results from the subtle *empathic* interplay between the analyst and the analysand. The phenomenon is, I believe, generally observable when two individuals are engaged in an intense emotional relationship of some duration. Under the influence of *suggestion,* a factor psychologically still obscure, each party takes over to a variable degree, and often alternately, some role assigned him by the unconscious of the other (1966, p. 78).

It was in the process of further study of countertransference manifestations that I came to recognize the role which the *objective sexual identity* of the analyst plays in determining the nature and intensity of the transference-countertransference interplay. In reference to the well-known "neutral screen" of the analyst on which the patient is supposed to project his fantasies and distortions, I felt that the following question could not be left unanswered: Is what the patient brings in terms of verbal or non-verbal communication into the analytic situation not influenced by the sex of the analyst? An answer to this question was the more compelling as it was axiomatic that in analysis the *patient is reliving traumatic situations involving not only one parent but each of the two parents.* Indeed, the terms *maternal* and *paternal transference,* for many years adopted in psychoanalytic literature, refer most explicitly to this very fact.

Paternal and Maternal Transference

In perusing from the above viewpoint my own clinical material, that of my psychiatric trainees, and also that published by my colleagues, the conviction grew in me that by offering the patient only one analyst as a so-called "neutral screen" we are expecting from him the accomplishment of a rather difficult task: we are straining the necessary distortion of reality on the part of the analysand by compelling him to direct both maternal and paternal transference onto the one and only available figure of the analyst. In other words, while the screen is in fact not "neutral" at all, but vulnerable to the sway of often complicated emotions which we are only now beginning to understand, it is expected to function adequately as the object of conflicts and defenses pertaining to both mother and father. In light of this, the requirement of "neutrality" evidently now assumes the meaning not only of objectivity but of irrelevance as to the sexual gender of the double transference object.

Analyst as Parent and Educator

The tremendous complications deriving from this intermingling of maternal and paternal transference cannot possibly be overlooked by any observer who is willing to see what is really going on in the analyst-patient interaction. How can the intricate psychic processi be followed and, what is more important, corrected and reversed, if we enforce within the transference, i.e. the reliving of the patient's past, a mixup of genetic occurrences which have or at least should have been once separate? (Flescher, 1966, p. 399, 1966a, p. 421). How can the single analyst implement optimally the task which Freud so cogently defined in his last writing as that of "an authority and substitute for his (the patient's) parents, as a teacher and educator?" (1938).

The implications of Freud's view are so pertinent to the ideology of genetic psychoanalysis that I have used it as an introductory motto in my previous volume (1966). The latter details the philosophy, the technique and the indication of "dual therapy" as the prototype of triadic therapies derived from genetic-psychoanalytic theory. The *triadic principle* to which the methodology of genetic psychoanalysis adheres, is rooted in the proposition that a *child is not only the biological but also the psychological product of both parents*. It being so, I have presented, at the Orthopsychiatric Meeting of 1954, the theory and a preliminary report on the results of a modification of analytic therapy which reflects the *genetic triad* (mother-father-child) also in the therapeutic set-up (1958, p. 46). In dual analysis the patient is seen alternately by a male and a female therapist; this then allows the therapists to deal separately with the maternal and paternal transference. For the other therapeutic set-ups based on the same triadic principle I have to refer the reader to the above-mentioned volume (p. 507ff.).

Let us resume the presentation of the steps which led me to the introduction of triadic therapies.

I had also to raise the following question: If the patient is afforded only a male therapist how can the (transference) relationship with a male analyst reflect events and repercussions which have taken place between a patient and his mother without seriously taxing his capacity for reality testing? Moreover, how can a *triadic* occurrence in the patient's past, that is, a traumatic event or a long-lasting detrimental pattern involving *both* parents and the child, be relived and worked through *emotionally* in a relationship with only one analyst?

To take a typical example: A girl has been seduced by a parent, older brother, cousin, uncle or neighbor. She has concealed the event from her mother and this has caused, as it always does, deep-seated guilt feelings which made any relationship with the opposite sex impossible for her. When she comes into analysis she needs to be relieved of the guilt feelings. How can she be made conscious, within the transference, of the guilt-ridden fantasies and be helped to correct experientially the past trauma with one transference figure who at once stands for both father and mother, male and female, seducer and confessor?

A mother notices her little daughter annoying her father, absorbed in reading an important letter. Halfheartedly (as she recognized during her analysis) she says to the child, "Stop it." This naturally has no effect whatsoever. Finally the father loses patience and pushes the daughter firmly away from him. A piercing scream is not the only reaction of the child. When her mother comforts her, the little daughter exclaims: "Daddy is just like one of those cave men who pull their wives by the hair." This mother must have had good reasons of her own not to put an end to this acting out of the child's oedipal conflict (the wish to attract father's attention and yet at the same time show mother that she only wants to be a nuisance to him). If these reasons are not eliminated, the daughter very likely will be compelled many years later to provoke her husband into physical violence only to have the opportunity to complain to a compassionate female friend about her cruel monster of a husband. In the traditional dyadic analysis, at best only an intellectual admission on the part of the patient can be arrived at, because the role of the love object and of the one to whom one had to bring the alibi cannot be kept separate.

But still another consideration of principle is appropriate here: If therapy ultimately consists in helping the patient to recapture the progression toward maturity, how can this be achieved when only one transferential parent is available? Do we not know how deleterious the physical or emotional absence of a parent is for the child's development? The experiential reliving and the lifting of amnesias and reconstruction of the past are indeed only a part of the analytic process. Hand in hand with the undoing of repression and the removal of other defenses, we know that still other changes have to occur in the patient to obtain significant and lasting therapeutic results. If the patient's emotional maturity is to be furthered, not only must his general sense of identity be restored but also a *clarification and consolidation of his sexual identity* must definitely take place. In view of the known bisexual constitution and the pursuant psychological bisexuality of both men and women, this is by no means an automatic occurrence during analysis.

Here is a short presentation of the pertinent steps in the development of the child.

First (Feminine) Nucleus of the Ego

The first nucleus for identity, the foundation for the ego, is provided by the mother. This "maternal" and therefore also feminine core of the Self in children of both sexes has hitherto not been sufficiently explored. The core of the ego is only in the girl bio-syntonic. It is known that improper mothering accounts for very serious repercussions and disorders. These must not manifest themselves, though they often do, immediately but can appear only many years later. The identification with the mother is actually nothing other than the residuum of the psycho-physiological *unity* which the infant forms with his mother prior to and, with decreasing intensity, after birth. The demarcation in the child's mind of the Self puts an end to this unity. This process of *individuation* does not, however, nullify the consequences of this historical truth *in both sexes:* they come biologically from the mother, they are for the most vulnerable period of their existence utterly dependent on the mother and they become individuals only by severing their Self from the Gestalt of their mothers. If it is true that the ego core in the child is mother-derived and feminine, only one conclusion can be drawn: this core has to be overlaid by something more definite, deriving from another source entirely, if a clearly defined and stable *bio-syntonic sexual identity* in the boy and in the girl is to be established.

Sexual Identity and the Oedipal Phase

Such a different source is provided in the *oedipal* phase. To achieve a solid and psychologically unambiguous sexual identity, the *streamlining of the sexual needs for love toward the parent of the opposite sex* in the oedipal phase is essential[3] as well as the (sexual) *identification of the child with the parent of the same sex.* The orderly completion of this bi-directional process is predicated upon the successful resolution of the *Oedipus conflict* in its two known variations:

In the *normal* oedipal constellation, the child loves the parent of the opposite sex and hates and fears the other parent. (The boy's sensual wishes have as their object the mother. The father in this context is hated and feared as a rival. The opposite obtains in the case of the girl.)

---

3. The influence of heterosexual attraction on the psycho-sexual maturation of the child has its biological counterpart: the mere physical proximity of opposite-sex animals, though in separate cages, has been found to accelerate their sex-hormonal maturation.

In the *inverted* oedipal constellation the contrary is the
case: the same-sex parent is loved and the obverse-sex parent
experienced as a hateful and dangerous rival. (The girl
wishes to possess the mother exclusively and to eliminate the
father. The opposite holds true for the boy.)

Superego and Ego-Ideal

A third most essential step in the child's development is
that of building the psychic structure which is destined to
carry the codes of behavior and the moral standards, i.e. the
conscience of the individual. Those values which are conformed to or accepted on a "you ought to, lest . . ." basis,
that is, values enforced by fear of punishment, are derived
from the introjection of the parents and their demands and are
governed by the *superego*. Those values which the child instead strives for by emulating his parents out of love and
admiration, are at the core of the psychic structure referred
to as *ego ideal* (Flescher, 1951, p. 110). The latter values
are more dependable behavior-regulators because they have
been accepted and adhered to by the ego via *identification*
with the parent on the basis of a mutually *gratifying* relationship. It is this kind of relationship that provides the "love and
admiration" as spur for the genuine espousing of parental
standards. Both these structures, the superego and the ego
ideal, are carriers of religious and ethical values and underlie
man's highest aspirations.

"Corrective" Identification

From the above it is evident that well-defined processi of
identification with parental figures, i.e. the transferential
equivalents of the real parents, are indispensable to achievement of clearly defined sexual identity. Hence we need an
answer to still another question: how can either of these psychic
mechanisms come into play in the one-to-one relationship with
the analyst when he plays the hybrid composite figure of both
mother and father? Do we expect a boy who during some

years of his development lives only with his mother, to bring about the miracle of identifying with his absent father? Or vice versa, in the case of a girl deprived in her crucial years of a mother? If the objective sex of the analyst does play a role in the transferential experiences of the patient, as more and more investigators are inclined to concede, we will encounter an insuperable obstacle when this boy is analyzed in the traditional setting by a woman analyst and this girl by a male analyst.

Sexual Identity and Sexual Attraction

But it is not only identification with the parent of the same sex that is indispensable for the development and consolidation of a clear sexual identity. As the oedipal phase, we have maintained, contributes a most important motive for the wish to be psychologically what one is biologically, the availability of a heterosexual object, that is, a parent of the opposite sex, is also essential. It is on him that the bio-synotonic component of the bisexuality, i.e. the masculine component in the girl and the feminine component in the boy, is *projected*. This is basic to a genuine heterosexual attraction, and this is, as dual therapy makes compellingly evident, a most potent stimulus for the filtration of one's own sexual identity. If so, the sexually ambiguous transference role of the single analyst cannot possibly suffice here. If one accepts the view that the objective gender of the analyst is of pre-eminent importance in the therapeutic process, then how can a male analyst be an object of heterosexual attraction to a male patient and a female analyst to a female patient?

There is still another requirement for normal psychoinstinctual maturation: it is not enough that each parent is both physically and emotionally available to the child. The nature of the *relationship prevailing between father and mother*— always clearly sensed if not directly observed by the child— should be such as to make him wish to imitate the parent of the same sex in his attitude toward the opposite sex. I have

seen the failure to supply the child with such an experience
(when he instead observes constant baiting, defiance, verbal
or physical fights) destroy not only the child's capacity but
even his very *will* to search for happiness in love with the
opposite sex. If the analytic situation has to "correct" this
specific deficiency in the genetic past of the patient, can the
dyadic nature of the relationship with one analyst make it
possible? How much opportunity of "sensing" the analyst's
basic attitude toward the opposite sex and inducement to
emulate it is offered the patient in the classical analytic
situation?

One could argue that in certain cases a neurosis may have
developed exclusively or predominantly because only one parent did not live up to his responsibilities toward the child. In
such a case it would be logical to accept also the possibility
that an analyst of the same sex could undo the consequences
of the genetic disturbance which has ensued. Why such a
solution is helpful only to a limited degree is pursuant to the
problem of countertransference, as will be borne out by what
follows.

Social Context

Analysts have a tendency, though they are on the whole
alert and capable of empathy, to be strikingly often remiss in
seeing the patient in his *social context*. The most typical situation is that of the patient complaining to his analyst about
his wife, his parents, his relatives, his friends, his boss, etc.,
and inducing the analyst to side with his grievances and
criticisms, contrary to the myth of the analyst's "objectivity"
and "neutrality." A direct and forthright confrontation of the
patient with his distorted comprehension of the attitudes, actions and reactions of others is as a rule only half-heartedly,
if ever, undertaken. The same can be said regarding the patient's own contribution to his unhappy experiences. In other
words, the human tendency to find a comfortable "modus
vivendi" with those with whom we are in contact exerts its

influence also in the analytic situation. Is it not more comfortable to agree with a patient's grievances and complaints than to analyze them within the framework of his psychological makeup? The mechanism of ambivalence clearance,[4] that is, of shifting whatever hostility may appear in a relationship between two individuals outwards toward a third (scapegoat) party or the external world as a whole is the most frequently used defense. It is also most generously employed in the analyst-analysand interplay.

Deflected Hostility

But still another factor enters here. The analytic situation has its inherent and inevitable frustrations. Many relevant complaints against the therapist are not expressed by the patient but only suppressed and ultimately disposed of through repression. The resulting hostility is then (unconsciously) deflected outward ("displaced") with the *analyst's own self-protective needs* automatically facilitating such a deflection. This occurrence gives credence to the more or less explicit recrimination of relatives about the analysts' tendency to alienate patients from their families. Some might want to explain it by the analysts' need "to keep the observational field confined," that is, to concentrate on the "intrapsychic process" rather than on the nature of the patient's relationship with others. Such a view may imply that it is easier to study a patient when his emotional investment is not multiple. (As if not following in analysis the vicissitudes of the patient's emotional engagements would prevent them from existing!)

Dyadic Monopolization in Analysis

The mentioned tendency seems to gain another (theoretical) support from the belief that the *intensity* of transference and

---

4. See chapter on "Ambivalence Clearance" in Flescher: *Anxiety, Guilt and Aggression*—A Dualistic Inquiry Into Human Psychopathology (in preparation).

its analysis on a "here and now" basis is most essential to analytic therapy. Much can and will be said to show this to be simply rationalization. For the moment, however, we shall only advance that it is the analyst's own unresolved infantile needs, subsumed, as explained, under the concept of *defensive countertransference,* which are operating here to the detriment of the course of analytic therapy. I hold that the tendency to *monopolize emotionally the analysand,* made possible and indeed promoted by the dyadic nature of the analytic situation, should especially command our fullest attention.

To analyze a patient consists, as said, in giving him a new chance to correct the detrimental influences to which he has been exposed as a child. The least one could expect is that the patient *be spared exposure to influences of the same type which laid the foundation for his neurosis.* By now it is also common knowledge that the parents' ubiquitous tendency to damage their children psychologically is not an expression of some inborn viciousness on their part. No parent decides consciously and with premeditation to shape the future of his child so that he becomes an intellectual or emotional cripple or else dangerous to himself or to others. If a parent disturbs the orderly process of the child's development it is only because he is compelled to do so by his own *unresolved childhood conflicts,* still operating in his unconscious. How true this is, we have learned first in child guidance settings when through various changes in the therapeutic approach the dovetailing of the parents' psychological disturbances with that of the child's was most strikingly confirmed. I have had the opportunity for first-hand experience with this since 1950 while working at the Madeleine Borg Child Guidance Clinic and the Linden Hill School for Emotionally Disturbed Children. But the most incontrovertible proof is contained in the process and summary recordings of about twenty thousand genetic psychoanalytic sessions in the files of the Dual Therapy and Research Bureau.

Also the therapist can, and very frequently does, via his defensive countertransference, disrupt the orderly evolution of the analytic process, which we have defined as aimed at the belated completion of the patient's maturation. Paradoxical and regrettable as this fact is, it offers us a sort of feedback, i.e. the invaluable opportunity *to study, via the repercussions of faulty attitudes of the analyst,* the *detrimental influences of the parent on the child.* It is this feedback on which our views on genetic-psychoanalytic prevention rest and against which, we believe, any hypothesis about mental prophylaxis must be tested. This is because the psychological mechanisms through which neurotic constellations of parents and therapists translate themselves into difficulties for their charges, have revealed themselves to be essentially identical. The mentioned tendency of analysts to monopolize the patient emotionally by integrating him into their own psychic economy makes it likely that the same factor appears also in the psychological constellation of a parent whose progress towards maturity was disrupted. In other words, the extremely frequent disinclination of psychotherapists to support benignly a gratifying involvement of the patient *outside* of the transference-countertransference interplay, alerted me to the observation of a similar phenomenon *within* the genetic triad, i.e. the mother-father-child interrelationship.

Conditioning in Traditional Education

But before we continue on this topic, let us first take a glance at what essentially distinguishes progressive from traditional education.

"The younger the twig, the easier it is bent." This axiom was and still is the basis of traditional education. It is supported both ideologically and pragmatically by modern theories of *conditioning* and learning. Traditional pedagogy to be effective had to be inherently stern, inflexible and consistent throughout. Any other attitude would impair the conditioning process. How the discoveries of Freud demolished the belief in the desirability of this type of child-rearing insofar as mental prophylaxis is concerned can be presented briefly as follows: it is true that the child's prolonged dependency on the parents makes it relatively easy for them to enforce, if they wish, conforming behavior on the part of their offspring. For this they are endowed with more than enough physical and moral power. However, not only are the results undependable, but the price paid by the child in psychic health reveals itself, immediately or many years later, as too great to justify this approach.

Conformance and Self-control

To take only the achievement of moral behavior and social concern for others as a first example, the unreliability of an inflexible pedagogy is apparent to anyone who does not close his eyes to group behavior of adults forced rigidly into conformity as children. Typical here is the known German method of child-rearing, which uses intimidation and severe punishment to obtain blind acceptance of parental standards. Individuals brought up in this manner are likely to throw overboard, in group situations, under certain conditions of leadership and by "mutual induction," all self-control and to engage collectively in most patently destructive and inhuman acts. Such experiences, for which through the centuries of our history millions have again and again paid with untold suffering and with their lives, prove this beyond the shadow of a doubt: insofar as correcting *latent disposition* toward antisocial behavior is concerned, traditional education at best writes in water and at worst aggravates the problem.

At other times "conditioning" child-rearing fails, even in the early stages of development, to bring about in the child a compliance to educational norms. His unwillingness to conform appears then in the form of more or less serious *conduct and habit disorders*. Most, if not all, infantile impulses which the child normally gives up or sublimates appear in all their primitive cruelty and destructiveness in *manifest behavior*. In such cases, constant clashes between the child and his parents or parent substitutes testify to the failure of forcible education.

Soon the boy or girl becomes an object of frustration, anger and anxiety for the family. The almost inevitable disciplinary measures of retaliatory kind only add new impetus to the child's defiance and disruptive behavior. Ultimately the young rebel grows up to become, when joined with other peers of similar genetic backgrounds, a serious liability to the community. The difference between the two groups, the superficially conforming and the openly rebelling, is basically not as great as may seem at first sight. Often the first is actually only a variation of the second, overlaid by a very brittle façade of conformity. The dangerous outbreaks of criminal violence in seemingly soft-spoken, overconforming individuals, who are generally thought of as harmless, is an extreme example of how little manifest behavior can be relied upon for predicting the future actions of someone brought up with the conditioning method of traditional education.

Neurosis as Price of Conformity

There is still a third alternative, again not sharply demarcated from the two groups previously described. In this group the drawbacks of traditional education do not reveal themselves by unstable results. The moral codes seem integrated and solid and the behavior of the individual congruous with them. Moral conscience may in certain cases be even more sensitive, and even morbidly heightened. The failure of education, however, appears in the fact that the price which the "dependable" compliance exacts from the conditioned individual consists of a marked predisposition to develop distressing symptoms together with a neurotic restriction of the capacity to love, to enjoy one's work and life in general. The inevitable rebellion against the restrictions imposed on man appear then not in open clashes or even feelings of rebellion against the environment, but mostly in silent subterranean *intrapsychic struggles*. It is indeed chiefly the analytic therapy of this last group of victims of "neurosis" which has provided the analyst with the opportunity to achieve in our century a breakthrough in our understanding of the operation of the human mind.

The intensity of those inner conflicts and the existence of certain constellations determine a) how long they are kept in abeyance, b) whether negativistic or directly destructive impulses against parental and external authority, i.e. social environment, break through immediately or decades later and c) whether new self-affecting ("auto-plastic") valve mechanisms are activated for release of tension. In this last case, neurotic or even psychotic *symptoms* appear. These are thus in essence discharge phenomena, with the known defenses of the ego (repression, introjection, projection, displacement, denial, reversal, and I am particularly stressing, ambivalence clearance) acting as channeling and direction-giving factors. Phobic, hysterical or hypochondriacal anxieties, obsessional thinking or compulsive rituals, depressive moods, suicidal impulses, sensory or ideational misconceptions of the external world then crowd the mind of the affected individual. At other times neurotic mechanisms may invade the physical sphere, leading to disturbances of bodily functions (as in conversion symptoms of hysteria) or to reversible or irreversible organic (psychosomatic) changes.

Dynamic Psychiatry

It was, as just mentioned, precisely the recognition of the causal connection between, on one side, the occurrences in the years in which the child is "educated" with traditional methods mostly by his parents and, on the other, the resulting neuroses, that originally offered the hope of eliminating and preventing mental disturbances. Under the influence of psychoanalytic discoveries, such factors as "psychic economy," "level of tension" and its changes through direct or indirect energy discharges, or through the lack of them, began to be considered. The attention paid to phenomena subsumed under the term "psychodynamics," which led to the foundation of what soon became known as "dynamic psychiatry," ultimately influenced the search for preventive measures. Those who hoped that what we have learned about causation of psychic disturbances may also assist us in preventing them, began to look for alternatives to the traditional educational approach.

To put it more simply, the heavy price in neuroses which humanity seems to be forced to pay for the acquisition of culture (Freud, S., 1930) compelled a radical rethinking of educational philosophy in terms of the inherent capabilities, resourcefulness and vulnerability to stress of the human mind. Interesting questions were being raised at the same time as the focus of observation shifted from the one to be educated onto the educator. Were the antisocial and uncontrollable impulses of the children perhaps not merely a result of educational inflexibility? Might inflexibility result simply from the educator's inclination to repress his own instinctual pleasure-seeking needs, his compulsive rigidity enforced by his fear of losing his own control? The experience that an instinctual impulse is more likely to be channelled toward a substitute activity and aim—that is, to be *sublimated*—if a less coercive educational approach is used, began to be taken more consistently into account.

It was only logical that the acknowledgment of the traumatic role of deprivations and frustrations in determining emotional maladjustment should lead to the following conclusion: the avoidance of those traumatic experiences may be sufficient to ensure a healthy development of the individual. The vision of "dammed-up" or "pent-up" instinctual energies which may—actually must inevitably—one day "explode" began to haunt the minds of those studying the problem of prevention of neuroses, as well as the minds of parents who anxiously were expecting guidance and counsel in their educational task from the new but rapidly expanding science of psychology. Every newly acquired radical insight, however, carries in itself the germ of exaggeration. So it was with the modern view about the parents' function.

As previously indicated, the excessive *frustration* of the child's needs, whereby he is not given the opportunity to release the psychic tensions generated by his instinctual and emotional needs, is only the first source of psychic stress to which he can be exposed by his environment. An opposite type of detrimental influence derives from *overstimulation* of the child. Here the environment strains the child's psychic resources by overexciting him and increasing his tension beyond tolerance. In consequence the child's development can be disturbed, halted ("fixated") or reversed ("regressed") by overstimulation, just as it was by deprivation. At closer observation, the two traumatizing conditions reveal themselves to be less different than they seem at first.

Deprivation Through Overstimulation

Overstimulation, such as excessive fondling, kissing, tickling and so on, *increases* tension instead of releasing it as gratification does. Especially in children, who in their most important years of psychosexual formation lack the capacity for adequate orgastic release, the threshold of maximal tolerance of tension is quickly reached. Thus a deprivational condition is created analogous to the previously described one in which the child is traumatized through lack of gratification. It is indeed astounding that such an easily accessible observation has not been understood by students of the problem of prevention. The reason for this, I suggest, is to be found in one essential aspect of psychoanalytic theory and practice: Freud brought forth the most compelling evidence that a causal relationship prevails between repression of sexual impulses and inception of neurosis. This led to the glib conclusion that in order to prevent neurosis the parent as educator should restrict as little as possible the child's instinctual life. Here lies the basic reason why the slogan "freedom of expression" was coined to convey the hope of safeguarding man's psychic balance imperiled by the restrictions of culture.

Relations Versus Relationship

The truth is that the frequency with which lack of emotional relationship goes hand in hand with unrestricted and even excess sexual activity should have dampened the zeal of those who propagated the philosophy of unlimited sexual indulgence. Indeed, it can hardly escape the attention of any physician or marriage counselor, that "satisfactory" physical relations between marital partners are often found to coexist with a total lack of communication between both. Nothing illustrates more frequently and, as we shall see, more significantly this lack than the following: even urgent problems of their children are either not discussed, or only in a way that results in utter frustration and violent clashes between the parents.

It is precisely the absence of meaningful communication which leads to the most fatal disruption of family life in seemingly "sexually well-adjusted" marriages. (We shall see later the reason why it can, and often has to be so.) But even enjoyment of sexual life per se is not in store for those adults who as children were exposed to overstimulating experiences by their parents.[5] On the contrary, as the young, in order to cope with overexcitement, have to resort to repression and other types of defense mechanisms, both the sexual function and/or pursuant subjective pleasure in physical love are seriously curtailed. Another important source of error, harking back to the confusion between overstimulation and gratification, is the fact that intercourse is initiated in foreplay and brought to completion through stimulation. The impression thus is engendered that all that happens before and during the act gratifies the sexual need simply insofar as it gives intense pleasure.

The above phenomenon, incidentally, made Freud raise a question which until now has remained unanswered: If, as psychoanalysis has maintained, gratification of a sexual need consists of release of (sexual) tension, why is the increase of tension during the sexual act experienced as pleasure? I my-

---

5. Personal convictions about the nature of one's sexual life are often not matched by the objective conditions. This is partly explained among others by the difficulty to evaluate sexual orgasm, where simple physiology is overshadowed by the intensity and the specific nature of the subjective experience. This invalidates many of the findings of the Kinsey report.

self would be inclined to ascribe some importance to the
anticipation of the *forthcoming release* (in orgasm), similar
to the exhilaration normally experienced when one finally sits
down to a well-laden dinner table.[6] The distressing feeling or
even pain of hunger has no reason to disappear, as nothing
has yet been ingested. For the overstimulated child such an
anticipation, as mentioned, has very little realistic basis. In
addition to the unrelieved sexual tension, the burden of moral
conflict on the child's psychic condition has to be considered
here: the conflict about the nature of his wishes. The child
cannot help becoming anxious and guilt-ridden, for he has
learned or senses that his wishes will arouse objections from
his parents.

Excitement, Anxiety and Guilt

The reference to the role of *anxiety* and *guilt* in connection
with the problem of how the child copes with tension increase
seems to me to justify the following consideration. It is my
impression that another contributory or actually more decisive factor overlooked by students of the present issue is due
to a *too narrow interpretation of the principle of tension release.* We may discover that tension due to unreleased excitement, the nature of which is not recognized by the subject, is
to be sharply differentiated from an increase in excitement
which accompanies those organ changes preliminary to and
encumbent on the actual act of release. In the latter case—
shall we call it "organ excitement?"—the individual *knows*
and accepts his wishes because they *do not enter into conflict*
with the standards of the environment or with his own. In
such a condition, mounting excitement is not interfered with
by feelings of anxiety and guilt as well as of shame and disgust.
The subjective feeling of pleasure mounts with every step
which brings the individual nearer to orgastic release. In the

---

6. I found the "anticipation pleasure" this time associated with the
"proxy" mechanism in some young women, who, though being on rather
rigid diets, delight in cooking and baking for others.

case of an overstimulated child the psychic forces (for example, rooted in the incestuous taboo) which oppose his conscious (i.e. undistorted) perception of bodily changes also prevent the shift of excitement towards the executory organs and the concomitant "preliminary" pleasure sensations. To give a concrete example: if a child witnesses parental intercourse in the so-called "primal scene," the excitement is only exceptionally perceived as arousal. Not only does the incestuous taboo prevent the child from *feeling* sexually aroused, but also his sexual organs are not in a corresponding state of tumescence. What appears instead consciously is an attack of anxiety as the third link of the sequence: overstimulation → frustration aggression → anxiety (and/or guilt feelings) (Flescher, 1951).

Trauma and Psychic Conflict

The considerations just advanced, which in essence enlarge the scope of theoretical inquiry into the dynamics of a trauma beyond the narrow alternative of tension increase or release, point up again the importance of *intrapsychic conflict*. We recall that to resolve the conflicts underlying the psychic disorders of whatever nature, they (the conflicts) have first to be made conscious. This goes on concurrently with a constant integration of warring forces in the individual, mainly in the sense of opposing or securing implementation of objectionable wishes in face of *anxiety* and *guilt* reactions of the patient. Paradoxically, these two reactions also prevent the patient from perceiving consciously the nature of his conflicts and thus resolving them. Yet by this same fact they (anxiety and guilt feelings) perpetuate themselves, because as long as the wishes are repressed, that is confined to the unconscious, they constantly refuel anxiety and guilt. This is because the unconscious has no capacity for reality testing and a wish is deemed, in this sphere of our mind, to be identical with its completion: *what is merely imagined is reacted to as if it had been carried out in action.*

In view of the above it is not surprising that, in the process of lifting the conflicts from repression, the ego again must face the very emotions which made it resort to the defense of repression in the first place, i.e. anxiety and guilt feelings (referred to often as superego anxiety). As no "corrective experience" is possible without the solution of unconscious conflicts, it is evident how crucial, for the outcome of the therapeutic process, is the way in which a certain treatment technique succeeds in overcoming anxiety and guilt in the analysand. We will have occasion to elaborate later on the implication of this aspect for the problem of prevention, and most specifically how parents can and why they should help their children not to fall prey to anxiety and guilt feelings.

CHAPTER TWO

FAILURE OF PROGRESSIVE EDUCATION

Freedom of Expression

The anxiety of parents and educators about predisposing the child to neurosis by compelling him to accept limits and bear frustration led to rather absurd precautions. Even the offering of rewards to make a child renounce gratification of an impulse was considered unwarranted intervention fraught with dire consequences. Instead "self-expression" was elevated to the rank of highest educational principle. Any restriction or setting of limits was seen as ultimately leading to the obfuscation of the child's intellectual brightness and to the blunting of his imagination and creativity.

> An eleven-year-old boy had remarked most casually to his parents that he saw a gnome sitting on the top of a passing car. When a friend of his parents asked him what he meant, the parents chided the interlocutor in an anxious whisper: they didn't want anyone to interfere with the boy's creative imagination.

The new trend, however, was destined to lead to great disappointment. The application of the principle of "permissiveness," underlying what soon became known as "progressive education," failed in the first place because its promoters did not consider the *changing needs* of the child. A bias was immediately discernible which made the so-called "enlightened" parents choose one aspect of the psychoanalytic findings, while neglecting all the others. In becoming permissive they disregarded an achievement of Freud which was of no lesser credit to his genius than the discovery of the role of the unconscious

33

and of repression. He established the regular *sequence* of developmental "stages," or "phases" of psychosexual organization (oral, anal, phallic, genital), almost at the same time that he succeeded in tracing back the origin of neuroses to childhood experiences. Thus it was overlooked that permissiveness has a different effect on the development according to whether it involves a *phase-specific discharge* pattern or one which, according to the age of the child, should have been given up long ago.

Consequences of "Permissiveness"

One by one, cases began to be reported where the non-interference of the adults had not spared the child anxiety states, uncontrolled general autoerotic or specific genital activity (masturbation) or uninhibited display of aggression. In other words the avoidance in child-rearing of "repression" and of "damming-up" in order to offset later instinctual "explosions" did not seem to do the job. It was therefore not merely a matter of avoiding enforced conforming behavior. Along with the absence of self-confidence and self-control in "permissively" raised children, it was noticed that the acquisition of certain skills was lacking and learning in general left much to be desired. School performance, a fairly good index of the child's psychological health, did not seem to benefit at all from "liberal" education. The avoidance of frustrating the child resulted also in not a few paradoxes. Thus for example, while the child's aggressiveness was given complete freedom, the educator's restrictive, ostracizing and disciplinary intervention was completely throttled. Hence a confusing picture of two different standards regarding expression of anger and hostility was conveyed to the child. The fact that the educator (in order to promote "freedom of expression") was expected not to react with anger to the child's uncontrolled display of hostile behavior, to his use of foul language and to his unlimited indulgence in sexual activity could have only one result: the parents merely suppressed the *external* (verbal or physical) manifestations of anger but could not possibly decree such feelings out of existence. It is indeed surprising that psychoanalytically enlightened students of the problem of education have overlooked the fact that unexpressed feelings have a tendency, because of psycho-economic necessities, to discharge themselves in conscious or *unconscious* radical hostile fantasies. By way of *empathy* the child invariably perceives them and cannot help but be deeply affected by the contradiction inherent in this most common example of a "double bind" impinging on him from the parents: on the one side the manifest attitude of the parental figure conveys "go ahead, I *really* don't resent what you are doing or saying," on the other side, the empathic perception signals to the child parental anger and malevolence with (unconscious) fantasies about bodily damage and even with death wishes.

"Liberal" Sex Education

In view of the important implication for the theory of prevention of past experiences in this area, it behooves us to delve a little more into the vicissitudes of the "liberal" trend in child-rearing. Parents, at least certain of the more sophisticated ones, accepted the injunction to refrain at all costs from controlling or even merely commenting on the whole gamut of the child's pleasure-seeking addictive needs like thumbsucking, interest in excreta (his own and others'), exhibiting himself and looking at others' (naked) bodies. None of the autoerotic and masturbatory activities and attempts at intercourse of the child were interfered with. Furthermore the focus shifted from simple sexual enlightenment and non-intervention to direct encouragement of the child's sexual activities. From the increasing diffusion of knowledge about the Oedipus conflict and the incumbent dread of punishment (castration anxiety) the conclusion was drawn that such "liberality" might *protect the child from castration fears*. In the hope of sparing him such fears he was exposed freely to the sight of his parents' bodies, to their exchange of physical caresses and to direct or indirect[1] observation of parental intercourse. It did not occur to those advocating this approach that these measures were likely to be experienced by the child as seduction and that the consequent overstimulation would precisely *increase* the child's *castration anxiety,* which Freud saw had the function of acting as a *barrier against incest.* (Unconscious oedipal fantasies have been found to be the source also of unrelenting *guilt feelings* and of an ensuing need for punishment by oneself or by others.)

In order to "prevent repression," analytically indoctrinated parents did not refrain from "interpreting" the child's impulses to him without consideration for the limited psychic resources of the infantile ego. *Active* exploration of the children's sexual curiosities, doubts and concerns became a habit of parents who failed to realize that they were probably indulging their own unsatisfied curiosities and lingering uncertainties. In the area of sex education, answers frequently went beyond the questions raised by the child. The resulting overstimulation of the child was either overlooked or disregarded. In all these patterns the parents' unconscious need for exhibitionism to minors seems to play an important role. Such a need usually prevails in adults who are greatly handicapped in their physical relations with adults. With children, such grownups take advantage of the fact that they are in control of the situation. At other times the parent will employ the "proxy" mechanism, i.e. unconsciously delegate to the child the mastery of a trauma which he (the parent) has not yet worked through himself.

Also, the most uncontrolled and violent expression of sibling jealously was not curtailed. There was in general a careful avoidance of disapproval and of anything which could be construed by the child as withdrawal of parental love.

---

1. Indirect observation in such case is insured by parents who through conscious or unconscious intention do not prevent the child from having free access to their bedroom on this occasion. On the role of such an "oversight" on the part of parents for the "primal scene" experiences of their children, see *op. cit.* p. 21.

Thus the parents refrained from expression of authority and the imposition of restrictions because these could appear to the child as cruel and again—engender castration anxiety.

A Puzzling Omission

As Freud's discoveries about infantile sexuality, the ones which were both the most original and the most shocking, centered on the ubiquitous operation of the *Oedipus complex,* it was only natural that the question of how the principle of permissiveness was applied in the corresponding developmental phase should particularly attract my attention. Surprisingly, references to this problem are extremely scarce, and even when present, are insubstantial and incomplete. A typical example is the W. Hoffer paper on "Psychoanalytic Education" (1945, p. 391). He observed that in progressive education "much stress was naturally laid on the management of the Oedipus situation." But what follows refers only indirectly to the oedipal issue: "Masturbation was not restricted; expressions of jealousy were encouraged; the parent's bodies were not hidden from the child's sight; curiosity, which we now believe was excitement, was satisfied and information willingly given; expressions of hate and discontent were never disapproved of." In any case this type of "management of the oedipus situation" must appear paradoxical, to say the least. How could such liberality be helpful to the resolution of the oedipal conflict?

Parents' "Interpretations"

Sometimes we find only tangential references on this topic. Thus E. Sterba (1945, p. 309), dealing with the problem of giving the child interpretations, took exception to the tendency of interpreting his oedipal wishes to him without consideration for his infantile ego. She felt, however, that in general the attitude of the interpreting parent determines the outcome. According to Sterba, interpretation, though its effect is more frustrating than mere forbidding or suppression, as-

sists the child in his struggle against the instincts and promotes sublimation. "In such cases"—she maintains—"interpretation will operate as a prophylaxis of neurosis" (p. 317).

Results of Liberal Education

In general, independently from the theoretical liabilities of
the liberal approach, the fact is as already mentioned that the
expected results were not forthcoming. While the children
appeared less inhibited, they also did not accept even minimal
limitations. Though they seemed brighter, their achievements
were marred by lack of consistency in effort and in engagement. There was in general a pronounced tendency to day-
dreaming. Toilet training was more arduous and the achievement of sphincter control was delayed for a long time—and
when finally accomplished, undependable. The latency phase
—in support of those who stress the influence of environment
rather than of concurrent biological decrease of sexual energies—seemed not to afford to these children's ego the expected
breathing spell. Normally, less harassed by instinctual demands, the ego has the opportunity to consolidate itself and
the child is able to devote himself more to acquiring new
knowledge and new skills. The pressure of instinctual demands
on children raised in an atmosphere of overpermissiveness,
however, did *not* decrease in latency. Sometimes psychiatric
help had to be enlisted because the children fell victim to
mounting anxieties and became uncontrolled and unmanageable. They had a tendency not only to disregard the injunction
of adults whom they experienced as inimical, but even to
rebel against group pressures. These children, seemingly "free
from conflicts," betrayed a surprising inclination to obsessive-
ness, to depressive moods and general irritation. Though anything which could be perceived as a threat was carefully
avoided by the parents, *castration fear in the boy and penis
envy in the girl were markedly present.* The child's capacity
to deal with his instinctual needs revealed itself to be minimal.
Thus the progressive approach, instead of promoting matura-

tion, seemed to foster infantilization, to inhibit the development of the ego, and to impair its essential functions.

In conclusion, sexual freedom and lack of restraint, as alternatives to the over-all suppression of sexual manifestations and the absolute submission to coercive educational control, not only did not bring about the intended results but, on the contrary, seemed to create more serious problems.

Discriminatory Child-rearing

But let us put aside for a moment the disappointing elements in progressive education, and rather turn our attention to some better studied and integrated observations that are more useful for the solution of the problem of prevention. The fact that the child has to pass through a sequence of overlapping developmental phases seemed to support the following conclusion: The child should be allowed a fair degree of satisfaction of phase-specific needs but also some leeway to fall back on previous discharge patterns. In other words, a sharp separation between one phase-specific behavior pattern and another should not be expected and should even be avoided. In the effort to engage the child in new habits and interests as well as to induce him to renounce the old ones, the enlistment of the child's own will and aspirations appears to be essential.

The changing role of the *primary objects,* that is the *parents,* in each developmental phase was to become much more comprehensible to the students of psychoanalytic education. Yet here again paradoxical findings were no exception. For example, while autoerotic activities seemed to make the young child less dependent on the mother, the child later showed greater difficulties in separating from her. The more intense the investment of the child in the mother, the more indispensable her company seemed to become, though his biological dependency on her was actually decreasing. Still, the child was also expected to outgrow this inclination in conformance with the transitory nature of the dependency phase. We shall

later see that an important factor enters here which, at that
stage of insight into the relationship between mother and
child, was not taken into consideration by the so-called "de-
velopmentalist" school. (The latter refers to educational
trends prevailing outside the psychoanalytic movement though
largely concurrent with and undoubtedly prompted by psychoanalysis.)

This school advanced the principle that training should
not transcend maturation. It promoted, in general, more flexi-
ble requirements and standards. Proponents of the develop-
mentalist view like Gesell and Dewey tried to reassure the
educator worried about the persistence of undesirable patterns
in the child. They encouraged him to rely with confidence on
the child's outgrowing his infantile patterns. They attempted
to date specific inclinations of children; they found, for example, that strong interests in odors prevailed toward the end
of the second year and concern for counting manifested itself
at the beginning of latency. Montessori also stressed the "sensitive" period of the child and its use for teaching by avoidance of direct pressure.

In conclusion, those who were attuned to the phase-specific
needs of the child were against "starting early and pushing
hard." Enforcing upon the child functions for which he is not
yet ready was to be avoided. In order to promote the child's
capacity to identify with an adult, some proposed the view
that parents see themselves as peers of the child, separated
from him only by age, maturity and experience.[2] If the parents
did not see themselves in this way it was felt they would be
inclined to treat despotically "the child as a toy or a puppy"
(L. E. Peller, 1946, p. 407).

Generalities about the Oedipus Complex

The same school paid somewhat closer attention to the
outcome of the oedipal conflict, though it also did not go be-

---

2. How one can preserve the role of a peer if one accepts this reservation
is not clear.

yond generalities which could not possibly help the parents in handling this developmental stage of the child. Thus the oedipal phase with all its frustrations was considered as one which the child has to go through in order to develop the capacity for solid and deep affections and attachments. The dissolution of the Oedipus complex was seen as reinforcing the need to be like the adults. What was ultimately to survive was a tender attachment to the parents and an admiration for them. This view did not take into consideration the known separation between the tender and the gross sexual impulses which analytic therapy finds to be in so many cases a most important and often unassailable defense rooted in the *unresolved* Oedipus conflict. Indeed a woman can retain a lifelong tender and admiring attitude for her father while all other men are objects of her hostile sexual exploitation.

Peller made also the interesting suggestion that because of the defeat of the child's sexual ambitions (evidently the oedipal ones) and the pressure of inescapable guilt feelings, the educators "should keep other tensions and deprivations at a minimum" (1946, p. 409). She rightly points up the difficulties with which a child has to cope when he has to adjust to repeated changes of parental figures. She is also keenly aware of the parents' own needs which are not necessarily attuned to those of the child. I can fully subscribe to her observation that "for every child who asks to be kissed or to be taken on the lap, there are at least three adults who want to invade the reserve of a three-year-old and bestow unsolicited affection upon him" (1946, p. 412).

We shall later see, however, that the erotic overstimulation of the child and the incapacity of his ego to cope with it is only *one,* and not even the most significant, aspect of the detrimental effect of such an indulgence on the part of the parents.

Return to Traditional Education?

To resume the topic of progressive education, it must be said that the observations made regarding its final outcome were so cogent and striking that a point was reached where it seemed perhaps the best thing that educators could do was to return to the time-honored, traditional measures of the past: return, that is, to early disciplinarian intervention, unquestioning submission to authority, in short, to procedures of automatic conditioning. Other voices expressed a general pessimism, or a sublimated (existential?) adjustment to what was considered an unavoidable human vulnerability to cultural requirements and the restrictions which society and the political forces, that determine its structure and govern it, impose on the individual.

On my part I did not think that we found ourselves in a sort of dead-end street because of the apparent incompatibility between the requirements for the mental health prophylaxis of the individual on one side and the social, cultural and political forces on the other. After all, within the same social, cultural and political structure, there were children who were not growing up to become delinquents, neurotics, psychotics, addicts or perverts. In addition it did not seem warranted to simply discard the psychoanalytically inspired principle of enlightened and more tolerant child rearing. Indeed the observed failures of progressive education could hardly invalidate the fact that analysis of neurotic adults has incontrovertibly confirmed the causative role of those traumatic experiences to which the patient was exposed as a child. Of even greater theoretical and practical significance was the fact that reconstructing, correcting and working through the psychic residuals of these detrimental (childhood) occurrences were absolute preconditions, if not the very essence, of the cure of our patients. On the other side, it was well known that, especially in the treatment of children with reactive behavior disorders (first studied by van Ophuijsen), firm restrictions and setting of limits were an inherent aspect of the therapeutic process. Yet we soon shall see why this approach, specifically used against a certain category of behavior disorders, was not an argument for a simple return to old pedagogical practices.

At this stage of the search for some guiding principle of preventive education, certain basic questions arose: If neither inflexible restrictions and early conditioning to frustration nor the opposite liberal and permissive approach did any good, what other choice was there? Should one fall back on the famous "golden rule" of the "middle road"? Is a compromise course, that is one of carefully steering between too much and too little freedom of gratification, applicable in view of the decisive role in mental etiopathology played by repression of specific conflicts?

In my earlier attempt (1951) to answer the question of gratification versus deprivation and restriction, I was inclined, as is evident from this writing, to draw too narrow a conclusion. I maintained that gratification is much less harmful than restriction, provided that it is not confused with overstimulation by the parent. Though I repeatedly stressed the latter reservation, I still feel the need to justify my past opinion or at least to explain through what kind of reasoning I arrived at it.

Dualistic View on Anxiety

My point of departure was the same which led me to the conceptualization of the "dualistic" view on anxiety (1955), i.e. that *deprivation* (frustration, rejection) as a rule is *aggression-provoking*. The dependency of the child on the adult usually leads to suppression of his "frustration aggression" sooner or later followed by its *repression*. According to the dualistic theory, anxiety is the most frequent consequence of the damming up of frustration aggression. The child deals with anxiety as he did with his anger: he represses it in its turn. Though repressed, i.e. unconscious, the anxiety is nevertheless dynamically effective insofar as it frequently causes excessive demands for affection and privileges on the part of the child. Apparently what the child requires from his parents has a defensive function: limitless affection, privileges and gifts have the purpose of assuring him against a breakthrough of

anxiety and its dynamic precursor, hostility. In this case, one
might be inclined to think it most reasonable that these demands be gratified by the parents lest the strain (of frustration) on the child exceed his psychic resources. But it is no
less evident that gratification alone is not sufficient to assure
the child permanently. The operating repression constantly
regenerates the danger of a breakthrough of the feelings of
anxiety and hostility which enforce the child's endless demands
for reassurance. It is as if the child could not trust the parents'
display of affection, because of his own hostility against them.

Overpermissiveness and Insatiability

Not only that, but the child's demands and insatiability
distinctly reveal the kind of hostile control and monopolization expressive of a pronounced ambivalence, justified by the
dynamic history of these demands. Thus it becomes inescap-
ably clear that, contrary to what an uninformed observer may
think, the child's excessive demands, *his lack of self-control
and his need to control the parental objects*—a most striking
and paradoxical combination this—are not simply fostered
by the parent's overpermissiveness and willingness to give in
to the child's requests. They are instead caused by the psychological repercussions of the original traumatic *frustration*
inflicted upon the child and relegated to the unconscious.

This being so, it is apparent that any advice given to the
parents as to how much to give in to the child's demands or
when to be firm is not only irrelevant but most likely completely misleading. We see from this alone how generalizations narrowly confined to the criteria of permissiveness or
restrictions are of no help in the education of the child. Indeed, even when we find that a very aggressive child has never
been restrained by his parents we must caution them not to
rush simply into setting limitations.

Anxiety- and Guilt-relieving Aggression

We first have to ascertain if his aggressive behavior is a
genuine one and not of *secondary* type. In the latter case, his

display of hostility and destructiveness may, for example, be expressive of anxiety-denying or guilt-induced aggressiveness, that is, *aimed at securing punishment*. Premature limitation in this case may be injurious to the child, as it is likely to exacerbate the already mentioned vicious circle of frustration aggression → repression → anxiety → anxiety-relieving aggression → repression → anxiety, etc. In the case of greater participation of the superego in the conflict about aggression, i.e. when the issue of aggression, manifest or not, brings the child into conflict no longer with his family but instead with his own moral standards, the dynamic sequence is as follows: frustration aggression → repression → guilt → guilt-relieving aggression → repression → guilt, etc. Any restrictive intervention must perforce exacerbate the unconscious anxieties and guilt feelings of the child beyond the limits of his tolerance. What is instead necessary in this case is to help him work through, either by verbal expression or by action in play, those original traumatic frustrations, the first historical link in the psychodynamic chain of cause and effect.

Still other factors enter here, which show that confining the issue to the counterpoint of permission and restriction is due to our tendency to conveniently simplify matters whether or not it is appropriate.

Let us consider a typical situation of a child who has displayed aggression through provocation and destructive behavior toward his environment, to the great exasperation of his parents. We may not find in the history of this child any exaggerated fears, at least not those of a directly observable kind. The impression we receive is of apparently "inborn" destructiveness. Still, in therapy we are obliged to set certain limits to the child's disruptive behavior, if only to create the minimal conditions for our working together. When we proceed to do just that, we make a startling discovery: The child is *able* to accept limitations and respond to them with ever-increasing *self-control*. Evidently he is not only willing but capable of doing what he seemingly could not in his home environment. One might then be inclined to assume that the parents have been "too weak" and actually disinterested in effectively opposing the child's provocativeness or destructiveness. In other words, such parents appear to pay only lip service to their desire to teach the child self-control.

"Spontaneous" Improvements

But how then can one explain the bewildering fact that children frequently improve during the interval between the parents' application for psychotherapeutic help and the actual onset of therapy? And why is it that a "stranger" is more successful in curtailing the child's uncontrolled behavior than are the parents on whom the child depends for all his basic needs? The spontaneous improvement of children when their parents turn to a child guidance clinic seems at first glance to be engendered by a greater alertness of the parents to the needs of the child. Was the latter perhaps the cause of the parents' turning for help in the first place? Another explanation could be a parent's fear of being found in default and hence his wish not to appear to have been neglectful, hostile, seductive, etc., with the child. Still even this explanation proves to account only partially for the change. Psychological scrutiny of the parent's psychic constellation (usually it is the mother who applies for help) reveals that the mere prospect of being assisted in her task, experienced as a fulfillment of her own dependency and other needs, hitherto kept in abeyance, immediately begins to alter her attitude toward her child to his benefit.

However, the most important factor ultimately found to explain the therapist's effective control of the unruly child is traceable to the absence of certain self-defeating motivations which accounted for the parent's failures. To gain an adequate insight into this aspect of the problem of prevention, certain basic facts must again be recapitulated:

Psychoanalytic findings restricted the crucial age of human development to the first 5 or 6 years of life, although experiences in the "latency" phase, and during and even after puberty, have been recognized to influence considerably the final outcome of the maturational process. The gross distinction of the psycho-sexual phases in the oral, anal, sado-masochistic, phallic and finally (after the latency period) the genital phase is here presumed to be of general knowledge. These phases are also considered not to be sharply demarcated but instead *overlapping,* so that in each stage traces of preceding stages can be found. To what degree psychoanalytic findings assist parents in handling their children according to which phase they are going through is naturally of basic importance to our inquiry and will be gone into soon in greater detail. Meanwhile we will have to keep in mind that excessive quest for attention, company, gifts and privileges on the part of the child are not the only possible consequences of privations, rejections and/or overstimulation by parental figures. From the same conditions, but with other constellations in the parent-child relationship, instead of demandingness there may ensue excessive indulgence in *autoerotic* (self-gratifying) pleasure- and relief-seeking activities.

In studying further the parents' contributions to the child's excessive needs for signs of acceptance, love, etc., or his excessive indulgence in sexual self-gratification, we discover a source of error due to our tendency to limit the observation of the parents to their *manifest* behavior or to those needs of the child that are particular to the *current* psychoinstinctual stage. Such needs may be gratified by the parents adequately or even more than adequately, and yet the child may still appear unable to limit his masturbation or equivalent activities of thumb-sucking, nail-biting, rocking, hair-pulling, etc. We may uncover the *secondary nature* of these uncontrollable impulses of the child if we look, for example, for traumata (from deprivation or overstimulation) which have impinged upon the child on developmental levels which he has more or less tentatively reached but from which he has withdrawn. We already have learned to know this mechanism as a defense and referred to it as *regression.*

Discharge Patterns in Regression

A castration threat proffered by the parent in the phallic or the genital stage may throw the child back to autoerotic activities typical of the oral and anal stage. For example, the child's stubbornness and unwillingness to abide by the rules of toilet training, his refusal or inability to adjust the eliminatory functions to exigencies of time and space, may ensue from a too harsh interference of parents or parental substitutes in the masturbatory activities of the child. The same problem may be brought about by the child's apprehension over the birth of a younger sibling; he may have thought or rightly perceived a change in the attitude of the parent toward himself in the sense of decreased interest, patience, acceptance and so forth.

The importance of the "attitude" of the parent toward the child attracted the attention of the students of preventive education in proportion to the recognition of the influence of the unconscious in interpersonal relationships. Indeed the progressive deepening of our insight into the wide gap prevailing between parents' conscious and unconscious impulses and inclinations has taught us not to rely too much on the first; what a parent unconsciously *feels* toward the child may nullify all that his conscious best-planned intentions are aimed at. Kisses, caresses, cuddling, gifts, concessions and dispensations bestowed upon the child can hardly undo, for example, the repercussions of feelings of rejection and resentment which parents harbor in their unconscious against the recipient of these overt signs of love and acceptance. No display of "love" can undo the reverberations on the child of those oscillations in mood in a parent laboring under the burden of some long-standing emotional problems of his own. This holds true also for the repercussions on the parents of some *current* occupational and economic frustrations caused by threats from current socio-political conditions and the like.

The first source of my familiarity with the *unconscious attitude* of parents toward their children was provided by the therapy of parents concurrent with that of their children, typically provided in a child guidance setting. As consultant and supervisor in treatment seminars, I have had plenty of opportunity to observe the immediate change in the children's attitude and release patterns following a parent's newly gained insight into some of his unconscious conflicts. Cogent as this sounds, it still does not do justice to the nature and intensity of the emotional interaction prevailing between a parent and his child. We shall see later that the *genetic* reconstructions in dual therapy have provided us with a new and unique source of information in this respect. For the moment, however, let us return to the history of the search for preventive principles prior to the formulation of the basic theory of genetic psychoanalysis.

Anna Freud's Observation

What a pre-eminent educational tool the child's attachment to an adult (parent or parent substitute) presents, was most compellingly illustrated by Anna Freud's work in residential nurseries (1943). There it was observed that when children were taken care of by a group of nurses indiscriminately, the children were unable to adjust, for example, to training for cleanliness. As soon as the children and adults were grouped into families, however, things changed radically. Though jealousies were observed, the development of the child and most specifically the training for cleanliness were accomplished, and also the progress in speech was strikingly accelerated. Evidently the establishment of a personal tie is indispensable for the child's capacity to identify with the adult. Otherwise the mere observation of the adult's behavior, which was available to the child before the grouping into families took place, would have had the same result.

Pleasure Principle Versus Reality Principle

From the viewpoint of basic principles governing the human mind, the process of maturation can also be described as consisting of a progressive replacement of the *pleasure principle* of the infantile psyche by the *reality principle*. The latter is predicated upon the capacity to tolerate tension engendered by delay, frustration and even prolonged deprivation of needs. To follow the reality principle means to be able and willing to interpose an act of judgment between an impulse or desire and its implementation. This act of judgment consists not only in the proper evaluation of present reality but also in mustering memories of similar experiences in the past and of the reactions and measures taken on those occasions. If an individual is capable of doing this, he is likely either to find better means for gratification in the immediate situation or to wait until more favorable conditions arise. He may also channel the impulse into aims and objects similar but not identical with the original ones, that is toward *sublimation*. Ultimately, considered reasoning may counsel definite and lasting renunciation of the given impulse. This occurs normally when the external conditions are absolutely forbidding or when the impulse is morally not acceptable to the individual himself even under the most favorable external conditions. Whether it is unacceptable to the individual because of his own values or because of conformity to the standards of his social environment or because of health reasons is, it has to be admitted, often unclear. In this context the role of reality deserves a few comments.

How Reality Is Mediated to the Child

Reality impinges only indirectly on the child's needs. Parental care cushions the child from the dangers and limitations of reality. The protracted biological helplessness of the child explains this role of the parents. It explains at the same time why the intensity of this emotional investment in parents overshadows in its importance all other areas of reality. As the most crucial state of helplessness is the one in which the infant depends on maternal care, it is the mother who in her emotional importance screens off and at the same time mediates the external world to the infant. In addition, the very concept of reality and even as we have seen the first delineation of the Self are formed within the relationship with the mother. It is she who is expected to provide adequate nutrition after birth as she has done since conception, as well as to fulfill the infant's need for love and security. The occasional absence or delay of these gratifying experiences together with the attending frustration teaches the child to distinguish reality from fantasy.

Hallucination, Fantasy and Perception

The child is for a long time unaware that in reality it is the father who usually provides security, shelter and food, thus mediating reality to the family as a whole. The far-reaching psychological and pathogenetic consequences of this simple fact about the human infant reveal themselves most strikingly in the setting of dual analysis.[3] The infant's imagination is stimulated so intensely by his needs, and his ego's perceptive, mnemonic and evaluative powers are still so undeveloped, that what he imagines overshadows what he perceives. Thus one speaks about the infant's tendency to *hallucinate* what he wishes. Because of this capacity to conjure up satisfying images, he experiences himself as omnipotent. But this feeling is labile and shortlived. The hallucinated satisfaction ultimately does not still the hunger, the thirst or the wish for closeness with the mother. Undoubtedly, her ministrations and her presence are more effective in bringing about a general feeling of satiety, security and well-being. This is why she is the first "non-Self," the first "object" who inherits in the child's mind the quality of omnipotence. From the state of helplessness in the face of his needs and the ill-defined reality which is full of dangers and discomfort to him, the infant can only be freed in the measure in which the repetitive, protective ministrations and loving care of the mother succeed in recreat-

---

3. This point is examined in greater detail in *Anxiety, Guilt and Aggression*, see note p. 21.

ing that original state of wish-fulfillment which is identical with the absence of any desire. Thus the mother's actions and attitudes decide how the child experiences himself and feels about himself. *His self-image, imperiled by the strain of his needs and longing, is repaired with each act of maternal care* which provides nutrition and general body care and conveys security, warmth and tenderness.

CHAPTER THREE

PARENTS' ROLE IN INFANCY

In outlining the role of a mother in the child's early life, the impression might have been given that her task is a very easy one. After all, the infant's needs and requirements seem to be simple. Actually we have most concretely learned only *after* Freud's discoveries that neither the actions nor the verbalizations, nor even the conscious feelings of the mother suffice to provide an optimal milieu for the child. This point can never be overemphasized: the *unconscious* attitude of the mother and the expectations she has regarding the child even *before* it has been conceived are factors determining the nature and outcome of this first relationship of the newborn.

Why Do Mothers Want Children?

Pertinent to this topic are the following observations: To a casually raised question of whether a mother wanted the child, she is usually inclined to answer, "Certainly!" The response is often accepted at face value, since motherhood is in general highly idealized—in fact overidealized—in our society. Yet when asked *why* she wanted[1] to have a child, a mother may surprisingly admit that actually for one or another reason she did *not* want the child. Another mother will disclose having changed her mind later, when raising the child;

---

1. In child guidance clinics a distinction is made between "wanted" and "planned" pregnancies, because the latter may occur without the first when a wife has let herself be persuaded to accept motherhood either by her husband or by her parents, or when another external factor (for example, worry about the military draft) provided the primary motivation.

the son or daughter became an unpleasant or even unbearable burden. Still another may recall having contended with many doubts and reservations about the impending motherhood. Finally there are those who not only thought of abortion but made more or less serious attempts to carry it out. And now a few illustrations of specific motivations which we found during analytic therapy of mothers who assured us that the child *was* wanted. For one mother it was important to have a child only because her parents exulted so much over her sister's children. Another, observing how her friend who was previously markedly thin "shaped up nicely" during her pregnancy, wanted to improve her own physical appearance. A third felt lonely because of the long absences of her husband and needed company.

Sooner or later these and similar expectations inevitably end in frustration. This is because they are not a goal per se but merely stepping-stones for further aspirations. Was the fuss over her child all that that mother needed from her parents? Whom did the mother who used motherhood as a cosmetic expedient want to impress—her husband? her parents? her female friends? Could a child's company substitute for the absent husband? Besides, there is a basic difference between an anticipatory fantasy and the reality of the care and ministrations that the existence of a child entails. Usually other complicating elements enter here, not the least of which is the fact that just because of the unusually long dependency of the child on his parents in the human species, parenthood is not an easy burden to carry.

Among the factors making the raising of a child more arduous than it is in itself, again unconscious conflicts residual from the parent's own childhood play an overriding role. Among these, *sibling rivalry* occupies the first place. Competition for care, attention and love in all its varieties, legitimate (parental) or illegitimate (incestuous), is known to disturb all parent-child relationships, though in varying degrees. The same is true for unconscious conflicts about the sexual gender of the offspring. These conflicts may sharply interfere, for example, with the acceptance of a girl by her mother. She may be considered an "inferior" product or else be assigned the role of a "phallic extension," in the fantasy of a masculine mother.

Child as an Enemy

The nurturing relationship between a mother and a child may be seriously disturbed by a specific "genetic" fantasy of the mother. As early as during pregnancy, fears of damage or destruction of her body by the pregnancy or anticipated childbirth may prevent a mother from developing or maintaining a positive attitude toward the child. Such neurotic fears, as I am elsewhere illustrating (see *op. cit.,* p. 21), are no exception to the general rule that they have the function of denying unconscious *wishes:* one seems to fear what one actually would like to happen. (I refer to them as "wishful fears.") They are as a rule rooted in the parent's past rage against *her own mother's* pregnancies and deliveries. In this case (I am greatly simplifying here) the own ego is confused with the object image of the mother.

A patient's childhood was marked by a repetitive breaking of his limbs. The traumatophilia was a reaction to his mother's extreme hostility toward him even before he was born. The reason for this was simple: the physicians maintained that her unborn son very seriously endangered her life because of her heart condition. Her rejection of the child and her disregard at the same time of her doctor's advice were traced back to her reaction to the pregnancy of her own mother with her younger brother. When the war broke out she imagined seeing this brother "lying dead on a couch near the dining table." As this brother subsequently really perished in a German concentration camp, she believed she had experienced a sort of prophetic vision. In reality her hatred against her brother was displaced from her mother. The decision to carry through with her own pregnancy was due to an

unconscious suicidal fantasy in which she confused herself
with her (introjected) mother. (For further details see
"Genetic Scripts," p. 112.)

Social Codes and Individual Morality

A new element comes to complicate the problem of gratification versus restriction in preventive education, the fact that
parents have to teach children to recognize and adhere to
socially acceptable values. Such values are cleanliness, orderliness, punctuality, truthfulness, honesty, dependability, and
so on. We know by now that the psychic agency in which
these values are codified are the superego and the ego ideal.
Again the first attempts at inculcating values are made by
the child's mother, most specifically in the area of toilet-train-
ing. Ferenczi's expression of "sphincter morality" aims at
pointing up that the experiences of self-control at that age
create psychological grooves which will also be used later
for the consolidation of moral values. Many pathological
phenomena pursuant to moral conflicts draw their dynamic
strength from regression to this level. Sado-masochism, which
we know coincides usually, though not exclusively, with the
anal stage of development, often becomes rampant, though
well-concealed behind the façade of moral exigencies.

It is at this point that we must again shift our attention
to the etiopathogenetic influence of society which lends to
genetically determined behavioral norms and moral codes
their known character of cogency. Freud's concept of "social
anxiety" (fears of social ostracism) takes this factor into consideration. One receives the definite impression that the role
of society as an etiopathogenetic factor was rehabilitated as
a result of disappointment in psychoanalytically oriented
"mental prophylaxis." Hence the opinion of Fenichel that
"mental hygiene is limited by social conditions" (1945, p.
584). Still, as already indicated, it cannot be ignored that
striking differences are observable in the personality, symp-

tomatology and destiny of children living under identical social conditions.

The fact that parents mediate the social reality to the child does not explain completely or even basically the relationship between childhood experiences and pathological outcome. Thus, for example, *the psychological constellation and life style of each of the children of the same parents may show most remarkable disparities.* Also, successful therapy does not wait for changes in the social environment of the patient to free him from neurotic symptoms. If there is a growing tendency to excuse the failures of analytic therapy through reference to social and cultural restrictions it is a grave error: it supports intellectually the current noisy attempts which our youth, or at least a not negligible portion of them, are engaged in, to cast off social and cultural restrictions altogether.

Is Frustration Always Traumatic?

The fact has been overlooked that as a rule *consciously experienced frustration and suffering alone rarely if ever produce illness except in the earliest months of life,* or under most extreme conditions (for example in death camps), or else, most frequently, when the psychic resources are already impaired. It is only when the frustration becomes traumatic (1966, p. 235) and compels repression, i.e. relegation to the unconscious as a special *emergency measure,* that neurotic phenomena make their appearance.

As to the relationship between intensity of stress and psychic resources, the following clinically observable fact has been established: An individual's emotional resistance to traumas can be greatly reduced if his psychic resources have been impaired by *previous traumatizations,* especially in early childhood. Infants in their first year, deprived for several months of the presence of their mothers, were seen to develop severe depression (Spitz, 1945). Later in life, the distinction between frustration and trauma has to be kept consistently in mind, lest not only psychoanalytic education, but even psychoanalytic therapy go completely astray.[2] We repeat that an experience is traumatic only when the ego, incapable of coping with it, resorts to the self-protective measures which are known as *defenses*. Among these repression occupies the first place. The disintegrating influence that repression exerts on the individual, hand in hand with the drain on his psychic economy and the lability of the repressive mechanisms, ultimately gives rise to emotional disorders.

Society, Parents and Neurosis

But in view of the fact that there is an increasing tendency to shift the blame onto the socio-cultural conditions within which the individual is forced to live, it behooves us to take another look at the controversy about which really is more decisive, the occurrences within the family or the structure of society. Admittedly, external circumstances influence the vicissitudes within the family. Economic considerations are known to be of prime importance. For example, the desertion of the families by fathers, so frequent among the Negro population of the United States, has been found to a not irrelevant degree to be determined by concern about welfare support. Still, not all deprived families resort to the disappearance of the father as a means of coping with economic hardship. Nor can social factors such as laws, tradition, custom, and so on, be discounted as contributing determinants of neurosis. A marriage entered upon for neurotic reasons can be forcibly prolonged to the psychological detriment of husband, wife and

2. A distinguished reviewer of my volume on dual therapy fell victim to the almost traditional confusion between frustration and trauma. Thus he wrote that in my book I "disagree sharply with those who hold that frustration in therapy is of worth in promoting change in the patient." What I instead stated was that "therapy also must avoid as much as possible traumatizing the patient further," lest "regression during analytic therapy exceeds the degree which is indispensable for a favorable course of treatment." (1966, p. 235). There was never any doubt in my mind, and so it was conveyed to the reader, that every psychotherapeutic method including analysis has inherently frustrating aspects.

children when divorce is legally impossible or feasible only at a heavy cost of money and reputation. Still, it has not been proven even in countries where divorce laws are rigid, for example, in Italy, that this source of psychic stress on parents is of decisive importance in determining pathology in children.

Already Fenichel himself had to recognize that it is not the social environment which brings about neurosis, unlike tuberculosis the course of which can be decided by living conditions (Fenichel, p. 586). As to the "demands of civilization," the most popular view among analysts is that they are "inimical to instinctual gratification." The implication of this view, advanced by Freud as long ago as 1908 ("Civilized Sexual Morality and Modern Nervousness") and by Schilder (1942, "The Sociological Implication of Neurosis"), not to mention all others who shared the same opinion, are far-reaching. The opposition of culture to erotic enjoyment, reflected frequently in psychoanalytic literature, explains in my opinion why psychoanalysts, notwithstanding the many theoretically integrated and well documented rebuttals, beginning with those of Freud himself, are still believed to adhere to a most simplistic credo: sexual urges override all other needs in man.

Let us return to what has thus far been said to have a prophylactic value.

Fenichel made the suggestion that mental hygiene would have to be based on the prevention of conditions that mobilize old childhood conflicts. He added, however, that it would be more effective if we could prevent the pathogenetic conflicts themselves. To achieve this, he advised that when a parent has to interfere with the child's instinctual drives, one should not prevent him from *reacting to that interference*. This approach, he felt, would promote "more activity, reason, and independent decision. . . ." As a sign of the emotional shift of emphasis on the ego, Fenichel also stresses the necessity to develop "strong egos able reasonably to anticipate the consequences of their actions" (1945, p. 589).

More sophisticated insight into family interaction led, however, to the recognition of the limited effectiveness of suggestions for mental hygiene in cases of "chronic latent attitudes of the parents" toward the child's aspirations. Even the impact of a specific experience has been found to be either gratifying or threatening according to the psychological constellation of the child. This again we found to be determined by his previous experiences. Ultimately the following suggestions have been crystallized as conducive to proper mental health prophylaxis:

1. The child should be breast-fed if possible.
2. A rigid feeding schedule should be avoided.
3. Weaning should not be abrupt.
4. Toilet training should be gradual.
5. Training for cleanliness in general should be effected not too early, not too late, not too strictly and not too emotionally.
6. Special care should be taken in preparing the child for the birth of a sibling. His feelings should be explored and he should be reassured.
7. Whenever possible, the child should be prepared ahead of time for extraordinary occurrences like departure, illness and/or hospitalization of a parent or sibling.
8. When the educator has to interfere with the child's wishes, he (the child) should be allowed to express his frustration.

The implementation of these very sensible, though, as we shall see, very confined rules has its difficulties. It is endangered by the aforesaid influence of a "chronic latent attitude" of the parent.

To illustrate how a parent can produce effects opposite to those consciously aimed at, I shall take the admittedly extreme example of a mother who prepared her child for a tonsillectomy. Here is how she went about "reassuring" her son.

"Don't worry, everything will be all right. I hope that you are not worried that something else will be cut off by mistake. Some children think that blood will flow all over the place. That's ridiculous. There will only be a few drops. Are you afraid maybe that you will stay in the hospital for months? Don't be silly! And don't even think that I won't come to visit you. I will come as soon as I can." (For some reason she didn't mention her husband and she "prepared" her son in the former's absence.)

I leave it up to the reader to guess how much assurance the child drew from this type of communication. I shall also not go into the many reasons which compelled this mother to behave as she did, victimizing the child by projecting and then "objectivating"[3] in him her own anxieties about a man doing something to another's body. Suffice it to say that this same mother was in constant panic not only during intercourse but also when she was with her husband in a car he was driving. She exasperated her husband by shrieking whenever she thought they were going to collide with other cars and in general constantly criticizing him for his "reckless" driving. The boy had had plenty of opportunity to witness this. How could he then entrust himself to a stranger, the doctor, if his mother did not trust his father?

From the panel discussion on "Use and Abuse of Psychoanalytic Principles in Education" the views of Mary O'Neil Hawkins may be mentioned. According to her, misapplication of psychoanalytic concepts in education occur through "extreme indulgence, false use of reason, the use of interpretation as an educational device or correctional tool" (1952). In support of her first point, she reminds us that Freud had stressed the detrimental consequences of an educational approach which puts too much emphasis on the "fear of object

---

3. Objectivation is inducing a given state of mind or behavior in others. It differs from conscious suggestion only in that it is unconscious. About other unconscious processi of unconscious objectivation see Flescher, 1966, p. 79.

loss." "The undesirable result of 'spoiling' a small child is to
magnify the importance of the danger of losing the object (the
object being a protection against every situation of helplessness) in comparison with every other danger. It therefore
encourages the individual to remain in the state of childhood,
the period of life which is characterized by motor and psychi-
cal helplessness" (1925, p. 167).

Sophisticated Parents

Hawkins points out that the pleasure of being able to verify
childhood conflicts corresponding to psychoanalytic theory
(penis-envy, sibling rivalry, oedipal conflict and death wishes)
accounts for the fascination of parents and teachers in discussing these matters with their children. They end up by
encouraging these very phenomena through their own interest.
This view coincides with what we have elaborated when dealing with the impact of suggestive empathy of parents on their
children (1966, p. 36ff). Hawkins is also against the use of
arguments on the part of the parents because it leads to argu-
mentativeness in the children. She believes that the failure of
psychoanalytically oriented education results from neglecting
to consider the role of the ego strength, of sublimation and of
character development. According to her, it is mainly to these
deficiencies that we can ascribe the fact that *we do not yet
have an analytic method of education.*
Edward Liss for his part stressed that "parents, as part of
society, also have rights," and that "children must be helped
through education to self-discipline" (1952, p. 209). Of the
three types of mothers, the over-permissive, the rigid and the
middle of the road, according to certain investigators, the last
one safeguards best a stable development of the child.
The following example may show, however, how much
more complicated the psychological occurrences are in child-
rearing and how little guidance is provided by these and similar generalizations.

Why Was the Child Undisciplined?

Mrs. B., in her thirties, reached the decision that she and her husband must separate. They constantly clashed about how their four-year-old daughter Nancy should be raised. Mrs. B. lost her father very early and was spoiled by her mother who gave in to every whim of hers. She recalled especially the sharply critical comments of her aunt to this effect. She resolved, therefore, not to let the same thing happen to Nancy. Yet she found she could not prevent this because it was her husband who did the spoiling. Nancy didn't allow her mother to dress her, and would run around with her mother chasing her. Mr. B. on his part refused to catch the child because he had "great pleasure in seeing how cleverly Nancy avoided being caught by her mother." But the little daughter was also bedwetting. Usually it was the father who would pick up Nancy early in the morning, take her to the bathroom and then change her. The parents also tolerated, though with mixed feelings, the child's habit of crawling into their bed at any hour of the night. Significant is the following incident which occurred when all three were sleeping together in the double bed: The mother wanted to make sure that Nancy was properly covered and made a remark to this effect. Mr. B. misunderstood, saying; "No, I am too hot." Evidently he unconsciously identified with his daughter and we shall soon see why.

A similar tendency was discernible also in Nancy's mother. Indeed her identification with her daughter led to "objectivation" insofar as Nancy ended up by doing what her mother had done when she was a child. But as already indicated, Mrs. B. did not blame herself for this since she had tried her best to raise the child differently.

Both of Nancy's parents had been deprived of their fathers. Unknown to the other, each tried to correct this basic deficiency not only by over-permissiveness, but by acting out through their child certain specific fantasies. Thus Nancy's "cleverness" had a phallic meaning for her father. His own father had been most of the time away from the family. He had devoted himself to the medical profession to the degree that, through disregard of his own health, he died in the prime of life. After that, his son (Nancy's father) remained even more than before alone with his self-reliant and willful mother. Nancy's rebelliousness reminded him of this latter character trait of his mother. The closeness with and admiration for his mother became the most decisive cause for his problem around *sexual identity*. He was attracted to physically strong or otherwise resourceful and clever women, at the same time identifying with them. Hence his competition with his wife for the role of the all-permitting mother to Nancy, which resulted in her behavior difficulties. His wife wanted the daughter to have a father since she had lost her own when she was in the oedipal phase. Hence she allowed Nancy to come into the parental bed. Yet Nancy not only enacted her mother's unfulfilled (oedipal) wish, but also her childhood past: after her father died she slept with her mother. Mr. B. too revealed in the mentioned misunderstanding that Nancy's sleeping near her mother repeated for him his situation after the death of his father. He also shared the parental bed with his mother. Thus Nancy acted out for both her parents their infantile fixation on their own parents.

As I have already mentioned (p. 41ff.), if we were to revert to the old type of child-rearing, because of the failure of progressive education, much of what has been established beyond question as useful would have to be discarded. My feeling was that we should instead search for a new factor which might have been overlooked. Indeed one such factor could be gleaned from the study of those countertransference phenomena which escaped observation and correction in the traditional psychoanalytic setting. Opportunity for such study was specifically provided in the triadic setting of dual analysis. The same setting not only made possible the elimination of countertransference impediments to successful cure, but helped us to put the whole problem of prevention on a new and more reliable basis.

Gross Seduction of the Child

I know no better point of departure for presenting our findings than that of Freud's changing insight in the general etiology of neurosis. We recall that at the onset of his analytic investigation he was impressed by data furnished by patients about their traumatic childhood experiences. These were all, according to his patients, of a sexual nature: they all had been grossly seduced by adults (parents or parental substitues). These disclosures prompted Freud to confine the etiology of neuroses exclusively to these specific sexual-traumatic events in the history of his patients. However, when he came upon a few cases where the data were most patently contradicted by actual life situations, Freud began to wonder whether the majority of the so-called seductions had not been mere figments of the patient's imagination.

Freud's Concept of "Psychic Reality"

Freud did not simply discard the patient's allegations as consciously concocted stories; and he could not do otherwise. Psychoanalysis is a psychological method of investigation and therapy which rests firmly on the proposition of psychic determinism: the fantasies of his patients must correspond to some truth. The founder of psychoanalysis, therefore, quickly recognized that the distortions of his patients corresponded to their own specific wishes, though conflicting and repressed. He came to designate these wish-fulfilling products of imagination by the peculiar term "psychic reality." At first sight this term seems to bear the trace of Freud's frustrating experience as a researcher, because in fact the patient's revelations were quite removed from reality. Freud explained his choice of the term by his belief that these imagined experiences of seduction were rooted in the *reality* of the child's wishes and represented their fulfillment. I found this term to be peculiar because these fantasies actually violate grossly, one would be tempted to say almost delusionally, the test of reality. They indicate how much the child's psyche under the sway of the pleasure principle went astray or indeed regressed. Believing in the reality of what one wishes to the point of confusing image with perception is indeed identical with returning to that stage of infancy in which the distinction between what is real and what is imagined is still precarious.[4] Besides "psychic reality" seems a contradiction in terms because the separation between the psyche, moved by our wishes, and external reality is basic to the psychoanalytic theory.

Re-definition of "Psychic Reality"

The term "psychic reality" acquires, however, a new and most appropriate meaning if we consider the very factor which we are going to introduce into the field of our inquiry. This factor becomes evident if we simply expand the scope of observation to include not only the *behavior* of the child's parents or parent-substitutes but also their *psychic* (conscious and unconscious) constellation. In doing this in the triadic setting, we saw confirmed what we only hypothetically assumed, the almost *ubiquitous nature of unresolved oedipal and preoedipal positions in parents*. These may and actually must determine the real attitude of a parent towards his child, i.e. what the parent genuinely feels towards the child, which his action or words can only partially if at all nullify. The child therefore must not necessarily be grossly seduced, though this is by no means a rarity and certainly not as rare as Freud's embarrassing verification may lead one to think. But subtle seductions, no less deleterious than the gross ones because of their long duration, are incomparably more frequent.

A severely disturbed young woman in her twenties suffered from anxieties and guilt feelings rooted in the early break-up of her parents' marriage. The well-meaning and generous stepfather could think of no better way to bolster her self-confidence, about her desirability as a woman than to persist in his habit of asking her, "Can I make out with you?" Though it was evidently said in jest (the patient's mother was always present), some truth may have been behind that

---

4. Later on the inability to distinguish between imagination and reality characterizes the so-called "primary process," i.e. the mode of mental operation of the unconscious.

banter, as he disregarded his stepdaughter's rather vehement reaction: in evident panic, she would scream at him "You may not!" That she could not help comparing all her suitors with the seductive stepfather, and rebuffing them after such comparisons, was only one of the consequences of the "psychic reality" of her stepfather's attitude which interfered with the resolution of her oedipal fixation.

Not only the conscious but also the unconscious fantasies of parents are as a rule perceived *empathically* by the child. These fantasies represent the *reality core* of the child's allegations of having been sexually abused. We see now the term "psychic reality" to be most felicitously chosen if we make only one correction: the seduction fantasies most frequently reflect the reality of the parents' own conscious and unconscious inclinations.[5] With time we have discovered that this psychic reality, that is, that segment of genetic environment rooted in the parents' unconscious, is, in general, most decisive in determining the child's conception of others in relationship to himself. For example, a child may have a tendency to overvalue other people and underestimate himself if he perceives that his parents do not think very much of him. This is understandable in view of the fact that the stimuli and communications coming to the child from these quarters, especially from the mother, initially overshadow all the rest of the external reality. However, throughout the formative years parents retain the power of influencing the self-image of children because they are continuously mediating to the child the demands and restrictions of the external world.

The attitude of the parents revealed itself to be influential beyond the role of the child as a sexual object. An infinite

---

5. How much the parents' attitude can be influenced by a sort of feedback from the child's own wishes is a part of the complicated issue of empathic interaction, which is again best studied in the transference-countertransference interplay. The suggestive type of countertransference is especially pertinent here, though other countertransference types also allow for such feedback. Optimally all these phenomena can be observed and corrected in the triadic settings of genetic psychoanalysis.

variety of parental attitudes which do not emerge in action deserves the attention of the observer. These attitudes appear to account for certain urges and inclinations of the child. This, I find, is particularly true in the case of behavioral tendencies which are patently injurious and even calamitous to the individual himself, such as *addiction to food, alcohol and drugs.* But it is no less so with anti-social patterns like delinquency and gross criminality and those manifested in the sexual area like promiscuity, perversion, rape, etc. Ultimately, patterns not only detrimental but even dangerous to the community were traceable to the parent-child interaction.

"Valence" and Empathy

When grappling with the problem of unconscious influence of one individual on the other, I broached it on a much wider basis by developing the concept of valence (1951, p. 396). *Valence,* a term drawn from chemistry, was to indicate the total psycho-physiological influence of one individual on the other when both are engaged in a close interpersonal relationship. Phenomena of empathy, of "mutual induction" (in group situations) and even of telepathy form part of the valence but do not exhaust all the forms in which it can manifest itself. A distinction was made, furthermore, between *positive* and *negative* valences, depending on whether libidinal or aggressive impulses prevail in the relationship. The psycho-physiological influence was conceived as working in both directions, even if it is not reflected in overt behavior or consciously perceived either by the subject or by the object of a given valence. The effect of the parents' unconscious attitude on the child would correspond therefore to an unconscious valence operating in the direction parent-to-child. During analysis I discovered it to be an important source of "para-analytic" resistance to change. "Para-analytic" is a resistance of a patient to the therapeutic process when it is no longer determined by his own unconscious conflicts, but by the unconscious attitude of his close relatives.

An indirect confirmation of the validity of my view on the role of "valences" in interpersonal interaction is to be found in a recent paper "On the Physiologic Response: Active and Passive Participation in a Two Person Interaction." The researchers used the measurement of changes in plasma chemistry and heart rate in experimental couples to check the repercussions on the passive observer of a stressful stimulation of his partner. They found significant, equal and parallel rises of (these) physiologic variables. In conclusion the possibility is contemplated that "the similarity of autonomic nervous system response in this experimental setting might reflect a physiologic counterpart to the interpersonal transactional process of empathy." *Psychosomatic Medicine,* XXX, 1, 1968.

Antimaturational Valence

A widow may bring about, though not directly and openly, the son's unwillingness to separate from her after she has assigned to him the role of substituting for her husband. A father married to a frigid woman may oppose his daughter's resolution of her oedipal attachment to him. He does so because the latter has become an important source of gratification and compensation for what he has been deprived of by his wife. I have elsewhere (see note p. 21) enlarged on the almost ubiquitous interference of parents in the psycho-instinctual maturation of their children, simply because the parents assign to them a given function in their own (the parents') psychic homeostasis. Artificial and labile as the psychic equilibrium of these parents may be, they must oppose anything which creates an imbalance in them requiring a new effort of psycho-economic adjustment.

Obstructive valences are certainly not confined to parents and their children. They exist between marriage partners and in any other relationship of an intimate physical and emotional nature.

The wife of a man whom she has chosen because of his submissive and timid character, will oppose, without knowing it, any radical change in her husband's personality under the

influence of analysis, even though for certain contradictory
reasons she may be very critical of his "weakness." This is
because she acts under the influence of an unconscious anxiety
at the prospect of losing what she needs for her own psychic
economy, for example, the opportunity to play a dominant
and masculine role in relationship to a man.

Elsewhere (1951, p. 401) is described how I had to cope
with the influence of a valence which immobilized a patient
in his attachment to his mother, a widow for many years.
The patient suffered originally from work inhibitions and
inability to sustain a meaningful relationship with the opposite sex. While the former handicap disappeared progressively, the relationship with a girl who finally had met the
patient's expectations did not seem to go beyond an engagement into which he had entered despite a short but strong
initial resistance on the part of his mother. To my pleasant
surprise, however, with time she became even very helpful
in arranging the marriage. Yet for some obscure reasons the
patient's desire to marry weakened as the wedding date drew
near. I found out why when the patient's mother telephoned
me to help her with her deep concern: did I really believe that
her son had sufficiently improved to insure success in his
marriage? I did not hesitate to face the patient with this
worry on the part of his mother. He knew by this time
enough about human motivations to grasp the meaning of his
mother's "concern." However, I could obtain no more than
an intellectual agreement on his part that it was not impossible that the decrease in his eagerness to marry was linked
with his mother's apprehensions. The patient, nevertheless,
more out of obligation toward his fiancée than from a genuine
wish to do so, decided to proceed with the preparations for
the wedding. Shortly before the invitations for the ceremony
were to be sent out, the patient's mother fell ill with fever
and pains which the physicians were unable to diagnose or
treat effectively. Then one day the patient came to the session feeling, as he himself described it, both distressed and
relieved. He had just visited his mother and was shocked by
what he had noticed when he told her that he might postpone
the wedding because he was not sure about his feelings: she

seemed cured as if by a miracle! She left her bed within an hour, as if she had never been ill. This, more than my interpretation, made the patient aware of what was interfering with his emotional emancipation from his mother.

Such valences are rarely, if ever, entirely positive, i.e. based on libidinal attachment alone; usually they are highly ambivalent. In this case unconscious *envy* on the part of the mother was the most important basis for the hostile component of her ambivalence towards her son's marriage: her son was about to find a mother figure which she herself so badly needed. She had hitherto kept this need in abeyance by using the defense of proxy, i.e. mothering her son long after he needed it.

A Life-saving Valence

When studying the problem of suicide, I came to conclude that a prevailingly positive valence of only *one* person in the environment of an individual who contemplates suicide is sufficient to make the latter desist from his self-destructive intent, or at least from being effective in his intent. This and similar clinical observations pointed to the likelihood that the child, because the objective reality of the external world is screened for him by his parents, is especially attuned to the "extra-sensory reality," that is, to the influence of unconscious parental valence. The high rate of infant mortality is in my opinion due not only to the physical vulnerability of the child, but also to the combination of the inherent unfavorable *primary constellation*[6] in the child and the too frequent (unconscious) death wishes of the parent toward the infant.

To adequately appraise the extent of the influence of empathic communication, we have only to recall that even silence can be experienced as approving, favorable, hostile, impatient or discouraging, even if we do not see the silent person's facial expressions or gestures.

6. "Primary constellation" designates the quantitative relationship between libidinal and destructive energies in the conscious and unconscious psychological constellation of the individual (Flescher, 1953).

Thus many of the failures of progressive education can be attributed to the parents' negative unconscious valences, barely covered by what appears to be "parental liberalism or indulgence." A demand which was opposed by the child when coming from his parent, we have seen, is frequently accepted and adhered to when it is made by the therapist. The explanation lies in the child's aggressive response, again entirely unconscious, to the hostile valence of his parent.

Sexual and Self-preservative Drives

In order to illustrate the pleasure-seeking essence of Eros, Freud made the point that the most intense pleasure of man is that of sexual orgasm.[7] Nature bestows this premium on man in order to insure procreation. It was Freud who discovered that the quest for pleasure in general is ultimately sexual in origin and nature. It is the driving force behind many activities of the child, though not directly linked to the genital organs. To these belong sucking, rocking, touching, looking and all the derived (so-called "sublimated") activities in which the sensuous-erotic component is muted to the point of escaping superficial observation. Ultimately an erotic drive component was found in all activities, including those which have the aim of providing security, comfort and fulfillment of physiological needs of the *individual*, i.e. in all activities prompted by the *self-preservative drive*. Hence we have *two* sets of activities which betray the quest for erotic pleasure. In the first, the basic sexual drive asserts itself insofar as the direct and indirect participation of the opposite sex is normally necessary. This culminates in an intimate contact of male and female genitals which leads to orgastic discharge; the act of intercourse per se is clearly in the service of procrea-

---

7. It would be worth studying the actual repercussions of orgasm on our psychic economy as compared with the experience of joy. The same can be said about sexual pleasure and joy in terms of actual emotional experiences and of residual memory, that is of ultimate psychic enrichment. Nietzsche's statement that "joylessness is at the root of (sexual) excess" comes to mind here.

tion. In the second set of activities the individual's *self-preservative* strivings manifest themselves.

The advantage of sexual over asexual reproduction lies, according to the zoologists, in the recombination of inherited characteristics of each parent. The pooling of these genes creates the possibility that the offspring may be better adapted to survive than either parent was. Among these characteristics it may be assumed that the most important is the one which produces all the activities of the parent animals when they take care of and protect their young until the latter become self-sufficient. The overwhelming variety of functions and skills which animal organisms have developed for this purpose (habitually referred to as "instinctual behavior"), is well-known and does not require illustration here. It is an "instinct" which induces animals to engage in all the activities aimed at safeguarding their young ones, not only when they are already born or in incubation, but even before conception (*nesting* activities).

The equivalent in the human race of those instinctual functions is what I call the *parental* drive. Halfway between the two basic drives, it combines optimally the procreative, i.e. *species-preserving,* and the *self-preserving* drives. Indeed, underlying the parental drive is not only the general need to procreate, in which the primitive sexual urge expresses itself, but also the need to prolong and preserve something of the individual's existence and of his make-up. The simple fact that one "chooses a mate," a choice which reflects one's preferences, inclinations, taste, concern and values, reflects that component of the parental drive which corresponds, on a psychological level, to the genetic contribution which each parent offers to the biologically advantageous "recombination" of physical characteristics. The parental drive, one may finally assume, must normally interact, dovetail with and support the *maturational drive* of the offspring to make possible the attainment of physical and emotional maturity. Again, the parental drive also has to afford some premium to the individual to insure its proper realization.

CHAPTER FOUR

METAPSYCHOLOGY OF PARENTHOOD

In studying the problem of mental prophylaxis, I had occasion to point to the *psycho-economic gains* which parents draw from having children. Under the heading of "Psychological Advantages of Parenthood" (1951, p. 522), it was postulated that the parental drive, like every other instinctual drive, had to have a representative in the human psyche as a motivating force. This drive, I thought, was important enough to deserve our interest and scrutiny, both when it is normally active or when, for various reasons, it is failing in its function. Here in a nutshell is my reasoning on this topic.

Psychological Advantages of Parenthood

In the process of maturation many primitive phase-specific discharge patterns typical of infancy are doomed to disappear as such. They are either channeled into *sublimated activities* or buried deeply in the unconscious. Especially in the latter case (of repression), the primitive impulses are still dynamically active. This condition accounts in the first place for feelings of *tension* which are normally relieved at the sight of somebody else engaging in activities long given up by the adult. This effect I found to be not dissimilar to the pleasurable catharsis which comic situations in general offer. To enjoy, however, the pleasure from this source, two interdependent conditions have to be met: one, the parent's own infantile strivings must not be too strongly invested; two, he must have confidence that the child will sooner or later surrender these activities in favor of more mature ones. Such a confidence will naturally be missing as long as the parent is himself threatened by the temptation to revert to infantile discharge patterns. This concern will be proportionate precisely to the intensity of this investment (actually "fixation") still lingering in the parent. It is on this basis that the child comes to give a sort of *stage performance* in the mind of the parent: the infantile patterns of reaction and experience symbolize for the parent the pleasure principle itself, not yet tamed and restricted by the demands of reality.

Myth of Paradise

The fable of "paradise" from which man has been expelled, and significantly by the very act of procreation which nature has imposed on him, is thus constantly renewed in parenthood. The Biblical legend only omitted to say that though the parents were chased out of paradise, the fruit of their "sin" remained there, again going through years of "innocent" happiness: they are free from the obligation of caring for themselves and others before they in turn have to take on the burden of work and responsibility which parenthood realistically entails.[1] The Bible story also does not mention that the parents enjoy their children's paradise by proxy, as is shown by their dreams in which, in a more or less disguised manner, they always return to the dawn of their life, the paradise of carefree childhood. Parents are likely to exaggerate in fostering this proxy role in the child by protecting him from all the reality demands, while in their own behavior they may carry their sense of responsibility to the extreme. Closer observation may reveal, however, still another type of investment in the child's implementing a parental fantasy: the parent secretly and sometimes quite unconsciously enjoys vindictively the evidence of the price which his proxy pays for a life without obligations, tasks and commitments. The "care-

---

1. We recall the "punishment" decreed for Adam and Eve: they would henceforth "eat bread in sweat and tears" and "bring forth children in sorrow."

free" son or daughter loses then his self-respect and that of others and fails dismally in life.

(We shall see later how widespread in general is the parents' tendency to act out their own conflicts via their children and the influence it has on the latters' destinies.)

We have previously mentioned parents who are unable to enjoy through "regression by proxy" the children's behavior patterns. Such parents, in contrast to those who err by unduly prolonging their children's immaturity, are inclined to go to the other no less detrimental extreme: their anxiety about their own unconscious temptation to fall back on infantile sources of pleasure compels them to impose restrictions too early on the child's short and self-limited paradise.

The playful regression in which parents indulge while pleasurably observing their children and/or partaking in the play with them, are of considerable psycho-economic value. I have found them to be, as previously stated, at the root of the psychodynamics of humor and wit. Freud described in his well-known work (1905) how the comic element transiently is capable of relieving the (psycho-economic) burden of repression. It achieves this by allowing the conscious ego to indulge in a mechanism which is typical of the unconscious: the surrender of strict logic, order and reality principle in favor of playful juxtaposition of opposites. The same mechanism, I have found, underlies the joy parents experience at the antics of their children. The opportunity which parents have to laugh at what the children do and say is a pleasure of paramount mental-hygienic value. People smile or giggle at the mere sight of an infant, sleeping peacefully, because it represents their own wish for blissful peace removed from the harassing reality of tasks and commitments, of passions and aspirations. The infant's state is not seen by the adult as it actually is: a physiological condition of urgently needed prolonged restoration, needed because of the young organism's limited capacity to cope with external stimuli and unintegrated fragments of reality. To the grown-up mind the restful sleep of an infant seems, instead, to express careless imperturbability towards the worries of their adult world.

Reality Principle Suspended

More active ways with which children make adults laugh are those via "projective identification" (on the part of the latter). In learning to establish contacts with people and things, to understand the external world and coordinate himself with it, the child at first inevitably goes through experiences of bewilderment, confusion, helplessness, defeat and exasperation. The child's learning through trial and error, his ridiculous mishaps or crashing defeats, induce as much laughter in adults as a stage comedy. What—one may well ask—is so hilarious in the behavior of people whose faces are smeared with cream pie, whose hair and dress are messed up or who become drenched and soiled from having fallen into water or mud? Evidently the infantile feelings of not wanting to conform to the requirements of neatness, orderliness and even coordination are gratified vicariously.[2] The sudden release of repressive effort, containing the impulses of rebellion, appears as uncontrolled laughter. Thus we laugh at clowns sitting down on tacks or spikes, on hot or burning objects, crashing from chairs or stumbling over their own legs. What is it if not pleasure at seeing someone else passing through the same stage, when adults laugh at a child's bewildered and painful discovery that the world has its hard and cutting edges, its stringent requirements of equilibrium and its infinite potentials for suffering. This holds true even for our very first encounter with the world, when experiences of cold, wetness, constriction and pain put an end to the intrauterine bliss of a still earlier "paradise."

Laughter and Regression

Adults laugh when a child suddenly loses a garment, scrambles for the toilet or gets a hiccup because this reminds them

---

2. The pertinence of this pattern for the understanding of certain aspects of "hippie" culture is obvious.

of the human frailties and primitive needs which so often
threaten to spoil solemn occasions. We find it extremely funny
when comedians stammer during a passionate diatribe, bungle
an act of courtesy or insult instead of honoring. Do comedians
not magnify what parents so often observe in their children
struggling to preserve their spontaneity under the pressure of
the conforming, i.e. courteous and respectful behavior expected of them? "The child 'asleep' in the unconscious of
every adult" (Freud) rejoices at the sight of one who behaves
irresponsibly—that is, as the adult himself would behave if
he dared.

Maturational Influence of Parenthood

A certain amount of flexibility with the child's typical
pleasure-seeking patterns may, in my opinion, offer the parents something which they might not have had in their own
childhood. If parents are willing to observe their children's
behavior and play, and at the same time their own reactions,
they in their turn may achieve a belated spurt in genuine
maturation. They often need this, though they may not
realize it.

A specific example of the opportunity for maturation
offered by the existence of a child in the life of an adult is
the clarification of the parent's *sexual identity*. This maturational step in the parent is prompted by the corresponding
maturational need of the child, and most specifically by his
need to establish a biosyntonic sexual identity. To achieve
this we have learned that the availability of the same-sex
parent with whom to identify and of a heterosexually appealing love object provided by the other-sex parent is necessary.
This view can now be supported by the strikingly positive
repercussions of countertransference responses of therapists
who practice the method of dual therapy. I mean the required
countertransference attitude which deserves to be referred to
as "therapeutic countertransference." It comes closest to that
attitude which an integrated, vigorous and unobstructed *pa-*

rental drive fosters in any parent. The therapeutic counter-transference of an analyst could therefore also be called "parental," i.e. "maturational" in the same way in which a parent's empathy is "maturational" when it promotes the child's progress toward psycho-instinctual maturation.

The maturational countertransference is best expressed in the triangular transference situation of dual therapy where the therapist primarily plays a specific bio-syntonic role: the male therapist comes to stand psychologically for the father, the female therapist for the mother. This function, free of the ambiguities besetting the traditional analytic transference-countertransference interaction, has a *maturational influence on the therapist himself.* The fact that therapists, after having applied the dual method, often marry after many years of indecision, is only the most obvious sign of this influence.[3] Observation of this phenomenon within the therapeutic triad alerted my attention to similar developments within the genetic triad. And indeed, my anticipation was confirmed: a parent's sex-syntonic identification with his own parent can be belatedly completed and consolidated when parenthood affords him the opportunity to satisfy his child's need to identify with the parent of his own sex and to love the parent of the opposite sex. I naturally exclude those situations where neurotic elements in the parent are too entrenched to allow such a process of *reciprocal maturational interaction* to unfold between parent and child.

Love and Self-Love

An equally important psychodynamic advantage which parenthood offers the adult results from the fact that maturation consists basically of a progressive transformation of narcissistic (self-loving) libido into object (other-loving) libido.

---

3. A significant parallel to this observation is that of women who become pregnant after many years of sterility shortly after they have adopted a child. The psychosomatic impediment to conception was evidently eliminated by the reassuring experience of acting as a mother.

The polarization of libido from the self toward external objects which goes hand in hand with the deflation of the infantile magic belief in one's omnipotence and the lowering of
self-importance and egotism, is promoted and accelerated by
the existence of a child in one's life. By the simple fact of
being a product of the parent, both physical and psychic, the
child represents for him an object eminently suitable for the
process of shifting the emotional investment from the Self to
the object.[4] This process corresponds to the limitation of the
exclusive gratification of one's own needs, with a growing
capacity for considering the needs of others, the most decisive,
in my view, criterion of emotional maturity.

Biological and Psychological Heredity

In the psychological grooves of curtailment of the parents'
narcissism in favor of their children, patterns of drive discharge are developed and organized with much vaster scope.
They ultimately make self-abnegation possible, even to the
extreme sacrifice of one's life to protect others, in violation
of the basic principle of self-preservation.[5]

The parental drive has a wider scope than that of insuring
the physical survival of the "recombined" parental genes. It
goes beyond simple biology insofar as it transmits *psychologically* the residual memories of good and bad experiences
which the parents had in their own lives. These experiences
are superimposed upon those which they have in turn psychologically "inherited" from their own parents. All these ancestral precipitates are assimilated via complicated processi of
introjection and identification by successive generations. As
mentioned (in the introduction) parents represent for the

---

4. In the case of adoption, the child may play a similar role for the
adoptive parents, provided the "parental" drive has remained unobstructed
in them.

5. There is some point of contact here with an important though not
uncontroversial aspect of group psychology. (See volume on *Genetic
Prevention of Collective Irrationality*—in preparation.)

child the most influential link with this past. Thus the wish of adults to survive their own death finds not only a biological but also a psychological, that is, more individually qualified, materialization in the personality of their children.

Parents' Errors

If so many even biologically rooted gains beckon parents as rewards for the proper fulfillment of their task, the following questions become inescapable: Why is it that children so rarely reach emotional maturity? Why is it that so many children linger excessively in one developmental stage or revert to an earlier one with crippling effects on their personality? Why is it that educational requirements engender in so many children only unmanageable rebellion? Why do children so frequently fall prey to anxieties, to behavior or habit disorders at a very early age? Why do some children, after having amazed their parents, relatives and friends by their intelligence, school achievements, artistic abilities and strikingly conforming behavior, suddenly fall victim to severe breakdowns either at puberty or at the time of some change in their family constellation or life situation? Why do so many become depressed or withdrawn, or have manifest inclinations to addiction, criminal behavior or outbursts of violence against others and against themselves? Such behavior reactions may occur not necessarily at points of major crises but even at minor frustrations, thus betraying that long-standing accumulative inner tensions were only awaiting some triggering incident.

If we knew the right answers to these questions, we would also sooner or later succeed in preventing these problems. It is an appalling fact that a task force of psychiatrists recently reported that in the U.S.A. four million children under the age of eighteen were found to be in need of psychiatric treatment and among these at least 500,000 most urgently.

CHAPTER FIVE

LIMITATIONS OF TRADITIONAL ANALYSIS[1]

The contention is advanced here that the ways in which emotional immaturities of parents determine developmental disorders in their children could hitherto not be properly studied because the classical analytic technique suffers from a serious restriction of the observation field. The same factor also seriously limits the therapeutic efficacy of psychoanalysis.

The less pessimistic students of this problem thought that one possible way of improving the reputation of psycho-analysis was to develop more refined techniques of forecasting, for any given illness and personality type, whether and to what degree analytic therapy could be helpful: They hoped that a more dependable differential diagnosis, and perhaps also evaluation of the patient's past and current situation, might eliminate beforehand the cases in which psychoanalysis at its best could not achieve cure or might even aggravate the patient's condition.[2] The result of this approach has been a striking proliferation of restrictive norms for indication of psychoanalysis, without any visible improvement of its thera-peutic efficacy.

Scope of Psychoanalysis Undecided

Disappointment in psychoanalysis has not been lessened by some exceptional papers, like that of Stone (1961), which attempt to enlarge rather than restrict the scope of psycho-analysis. Ultimately, it has been suggested—and here again

---

1. A more detailed presentation of this issue is to be found in those sections of my previous work which deal with the history and ideology of genetic psychoanalysis (1966).

2. See note about psychotic breakdowns during analysis, p. 89.

Freud was the first to say it—that classical analysis showed its best results with simple neuroses. The most frustrating aspect of such an admission lies in the common knowledge that in the type of patients coming for help today, simple neurosis is relatively rare. Moreover a review of the cases which were considered and treated as neuroses by Freud himself, reveals them to be, in the light of our present knowledge, if not outright psychotic, at least severely borderline, which explains why more than a few proved with time to have achieved something less than a cure.

It was not recognized that the failure of analysis might be caused primarily by the difficulties deriving from the necessity that the analyst play the double role of father and mother. Yet the truth is that the most famous and best analyzed patient of Freud, the "Wolf Man," had repeated relapses which forced him (Freud) to resort to the help of a *female analyst*. I have commented elsewhere (1966, p. 4) on that remarkable historical fact and on the blindness of Freud's followers to its theoretical implications. This oversight lasted over half a century, indeed until I drew attention to it.

Dyadic Stricture of Psychoanalysis

The core of these implications is to be found in what we have already presented: We have learned that the most frequent handicap in comprehending the unconscious of the patient is traceable to blind spots in the analyst's understanding of himself. These blind spots stem from unrecognized countertransference responses of the analyst. However, the frequency of failures of psychoanalytic therapy made it appear likely that the source of error would be found in some inherent aspect of the analytic situation. This (technical) aspect would, I anticipated, favor the undisturbed operation of infantile fixations in the analyst which have *survived his own personal and didactic analyses*. Indeed, I assumed that the same technical aspect will probably also explain why, although the analyst's own analyses are intensive, extensive and repetitious (see p. 90), these unconscious conflicts had to remain unresolved. I don't think it is necessary to prove that the analyst's neurotic fixations are the very ones which provide the matrix for his *untherapeutic countertransference attitudes and responses*. I found this disturbing factor in the very nature of the analytic set-up, precisely in its *dyadic* design: it limits the therapeutic process to the one-to-one interaction between therapist and analysand. It is this basic feature which is responsible for the disruption of the maturational process at the basis of analytic therapy, and thus for its disappointing results.

And now a few more remarks about *how* the setting of classical analysis adversely affects the course of therapy. The analyst is expected to help the patient toward maturity, that is progressive substitution of the reality principle for the pleasure principle. This step corresponds to the surrender of infantile dependence and of the whole gamut of immature sexual and emotional patterns. The latter are directed towards each parent and consists of both tender and sensual aspirations for closeness and love. In both cases, the dependency on the nurturing and protective mother, as well as the oedipal aspiration toward one parent, goes hand in hand with the wish to eliminate any rival (parent or sibling) who stands in the way of exclusive possession of the object of one's investment. In fact, the resolution of the Oedipus complex consists most specifically in the child's acceptance of the parents as a *couple,* that is, in the surrender of the wish to separate them in order to have one parent (or each of them alternately) all for himself. As long as this is not achieved, the child and the adult with identical psychological constellations are inevitably prey to unconscious guilt and anxiety. We maintain that the classical analytic situation, instead of helping the analysand to surrender the oedipal strivings within the transference, by streamlining his transference needs towards the analyst, feeds his *illusion of having succeeded in breaking up the parental couple.* Gratifying as the illusory oedipal triumph may be to the unconscious of the patient, it *increases his anxieties and feelings of guilt.*

Pleasure Principle in Traditional Analysis

By confining the transference relationship to a one-to-one contact and interaction, the analytic situation has, through its very structure, remained a sort of reservation for the infantile unwillingness to share: indeed it *eliminates* most patently the *third member of the genetic triad.* The classical version of the analytic situation reveals itself to be burdened by an imbalance which, instead of correcting, duplicates and aggravates the "genetic disbalance" which I have found to be of decisive importance in the etiopathogenesis of emotional disorders. In short, I claim that the traditional setting allows the analyst to unknowingly participate in and abet the patient's infantile fantasies, to the degree to which his (the analyst's) own unresolved infantile strivings linger in him, unexposed to the maturational influence of the triadic principle.

We have long known that the analyst brings his share of psychological difficulties into the analytic situation. What we have not seen is that no protracted or repetitive analysis of the therapist himself can eliminate that type of countertransference described as "defensive," that is, rooted in his own unresolved infantile conflicts, if we continue to practice analysis in a setting which feeds these conflicts. I arrived at this conclusion only at the end of my rather extended inquiry into the metapsychology of countertransference. It was in the process of this that I came upon the problem of *communication and of understanding of the analytic patient* in general.

Contrary to the prevailing view, I concluded[3] that at the present stage of our knowledge we could *not depend on empathy* because the latter was greatly burdened and severely obstructed by the countertransference involvement of the analyst. Indeed I have pointed out the tendency to over-idealize empathic communication as a means of understanding, on the

---

3. "On Empathy, Intuition and Countertransference." (Paper delivered to the Kris Study Group; Chairman R. Loewenstein, New York Psychoanalytic Institute, April, 1962.)

basis of its traditionally accepted derivation from maternal empathy: it was supposed to safeguard the mother's understanding of the child before he is able to verbalize. I drew attention to how little "safeguarding" maternal empathy actually did, in view of the overwhelming variety of emotional disorders which find their inception precisely in this early stage of the mother-child relationship. I also pointed out how maternal empathy failed to contribute even modestly to the discovery of the emotional and intellectual world of the child, though mothers have incomparably closer physiological and emotional relationships with children than men do. I advocated and continue to advocate that one rely instead primarily on *intuition* validated by observation.

Empathy, Intuition and Understanding

Not only did I find that empathy was far too screened by the analyst's countertransference to allow him an undistorted vision of what was going on in the patient; I was also impressed by the discovery that empathy even *influenced* the psychological phenomenon observed. This is an interesting parallel to what occurs in the world of micro-physics: The observation of micro-electric phenomena was found to be rendered difficult if not impossible by the very act of observation, because it disturbs the course of the event observed.

An illustration may help to explain the parallel influence of empathy: The mother, being the most important part of the physical and emotional environment of the child, represents for him a constant source of psychic signals—supportive, discouraging, warning, and so forth. Let us take as a specific example the situation of her witnessing the child's first attempt at walking. If the mother genuinely wants the child to succeed in his attempts, the confidence emanating from her will represent that type of empathy which, while observing the child's efforts and "understanding" his intention, provides a substantial if not decisive impetus to the child's determination to succeed.

Suggestive Empathy and Parental Drive

The child, by partaking empathically in his mother's confidence, is likely to achieve quickly the mastery of the function he is in the process of learning. This type of empathy, evidently *suggestive* in nature, is constructive as it assists the maturational drive of the child. It is an example of the type of empathy fed by the *parental drive,* which dovetails with the child's maturational drive in the normal course of development. But if, instead, a parent is ambivalent about his child's learning any skill, the process of acquiring new capacities is greatly hampered. A parent's repressed hostility toward the child may typically be disguised as overprotectiveness. This usually is expressed in overanxious anticipation, to return to our example, that the child may fall and injure himself severely. These feelings of the mother will inevitably communicate themselves to him empathically, which in turn will engender in him an echo of her anxiety. In addition, it will activate all the child's own anxiety from his unexpressed *anger* because of his mother's original lack of confidence in his capabilities (Flescher, 1953). The weight of this anger-anxiety response to the frustration of the child's maturational drive increases with his age, hand in hand with his own aspirations to be capable and independent of parental help. As he grows older the success of these aspirations acquires an increasing influence in regulating his self-image.

Trauma of Neglect

It must, however, be stressed that even more detrimental—because to worry about the child's possibly hurting himself is at least a sign of *some* positive albeit ambivalent interest—is the attitude of a parent who does not care to assist, to encourage, or to show any interest in the learning process of the child. The lack of stimuli coming from the parent or his substitute has for some time been known to stifle and even to prevent maturation and most specifically the acquisition of ego skills. Even more important, lack of parental stimuli

prevents the development in the child of ego-syntonic discharge patterns for instinctual energies.

How does the classical approach in psychoanalysis fare in
this respect? In pursuing this question through closer study
of the metapsychology of countertransference, we found ourselves in a typical "feedback" situation. To the degree to
which we are able to isolate the irrational element in the
therapist's attitude toward the patient, we become alerted to
similar factors in parents.

Scope of Parental Empathy

We shall at this point resume our train of thought regarding the "screening" or "suggestive" influence of empathy. We
have seen that empathy is not simply confined to understanding or to communication, but that it has the capacity to
modify what is observed. We recall the effect of the mother's
attitude (in our illustration), on the outcome of the child's
attempt at learning to walk. It thus becomes necessary to
determine whether the empathy of the analyst who is committed to changing the psychological consequences of faulty
parental attitudes in the patient's childhood, is of a kind to
approximate a "parental," that is, a *growth-promoting empathy*. We have seen and are reiterating that analytic therapy
consists of furthering and carrying to its conclusion the very
process of maturation which the parents failed to encourage
in the patient when he was a child. Any other kind of help will
not do. Thus the therapist may be of great support and comfort to the patient and the latter may even surrender his
symptoms and complaints as a sort of "gift" or "bribe" to the
therapist (the so-called "transference cure"). Still the analyst
has not done what he optimally is supposed to do: to recapture the interruption of the process of the patient's maturation,
an interruption enforced by disturbing factors operating in
the patient's genetic past. If the therapist does not achieve
this at all or only incompletely, experience has shown, relapses
must occur. The same or substitutive symptoms or acting out

patterns do reappear. In cases of overextended "intensive analysis" a resentful disenchantment with the analyst often induces the patient to break off therapy.

Transference Neurosis and Psychosis

In other cases the analyst himself is unable to carry further the burden of a *transference-countertransference bind* and suggests, with more or less patent rationalizations, the discontinuation of analysis. Occasionally this type of transference ceases to be simply "neurotic" ("transference neurosis"): the patient suffers a serious aggravation of his condition to the point of becoming psychotic ("transference psychosis"). Freud explained such occurrences, in a letter to Edoardo Weiss, by ascribing them to a mishap: while removing a neurosis, the analyst has laid bare a psychosis.[4] A closer scrutiny on my part of what really was going on in the analytic situation of such patients revealed the remarkable fact that the analyst's countertransference responses merely duplicated and aggravated the traumatic influence to which the patient had been exposed as a child by his parents.

Optimal Analytic Attitude

Our conclusion, that what insures an optimal course in the analytic process is the *parental empathy* of the analyst, brings to mind the already mentioned (p. 15) definition of the analyst's function as one serving as a parental substitute, a

---

4. ". . . and through the cure of his neurosis you may have freed the way for a more serious sickness. That happens to each one of us occasionally and there is no protection against it." (The Psychoanalytic Forum, 1, 1966.) On the basis of the results of dual therapy I felt it to be my duty to disagree with this pessimistic view of Freud. Only in the traditional setting do such breakdowns occur. The triadic setting is the best preventative against such a mishap. It can even dramatically reverse a breakdown at its very inception in the traditional setting if the analyst is willing to include a colleague in the treatment situation; if otherwise impossible it may be even one of the same sex. For the theoretical justification of this compromise see 1966, p. 431.

teacher and educator. This statement of Freud has never been incorporated in the general philosophy of psychoanalytic therapy. Evidently the truth did not escape the discoverer of the unconscious and of its role in human psychopathology: *the requirement of "interpreting the unconscious" does not exhaust the function of the analyst.* But let us explore a little further the implications of Freud's view.

As analysts are supposed to operate under emotionally "aseptic" conditions—to use here a medical term, following Freud's comparison of the analytic process with a surgical operation—we must wonder to what degree they are capable of abiding by this. If there is any merit to the old Latin saying, "medice cura te ipsum" (Doctor, cure yourself), it is most certainly true for psychoanalysis. In no other specialty does the "personal equation" exert such a weight on performance. Actually, this was why Freud and his followers were convinced that a didactic analysis was an indispensable condition and qualification for the practice of analysis.

Indeed students of the problem of analytic training now admit to the fact that it is virtually impossible to find "normal" candidates. The only hope then remaining is that the personal and didactic analyses of candidates will eliminate their neurotic difficulties, at least to the point of preventing the repetition, in the analytic situation, of those parental influences at the root of the patient's problems. But have we not established that analysts are extremely vulnerable to a detrimental countertransference which duplicates parental attitudes injurious to the patient? Evidently the personal and didactic analyses did not accomplish what they were supposed to.

Quandary About Countertransference

The more courageous the analysts became in admitting the failures of their therapeutic endeavor, the more the task of controlling their countertransference involvement (Flescher, 1966, p. 54) became both urgent and staggering. Should Freud's suggestion of a periodic reanalysis of the analyst (every five years!) be implemented? Or should the analyst's didactic analysis become "interminable," as Freud maintained the analysis of certain types of patients has to be? Or should the analyst be supervised by a colleague for as long as he treats patients? The suggestion of perpetual supervision appears to be the most sensible, though the aspiration for "professional independence" makes it least likely to be implemented. But this same ambition should alert us to the following question: "To what degree is it safe that the one who analyzes, that is, exposes the patient to an intense emotional involvement with him, *should remain independent in his professional service?* Is the task of the analyst perhaps such as to make him basically different from any other medical specialty in which the aptitude, training and experience of one person alone suffice to insure optimal results?[5] But still other questions arose at this juncture of our inquiry.

If the parental drive, that is, a drive in *both* parents, is intended to safeguard the welfare of the young, is it not likely that such a drive cannot exert its best influence when the child's contact is confined to one parent alone? Why do courts insure visiting rights of a divorced parent? Why do adoption agencies traditionally assign children only to couples? Would it not be logical, and even charitable, since human errors and shortcomings are ubiquitous, to at least halve the child's chances of being vicitimized, by exposing him to the detrimental influence of only one parent or parent substitute, instead of two?[6] The answer is a definite "No!" Dis-

---

5. Actually there is one specialty in which the performance of the medical service requires the most direct and responsible collaboration of another physician: the surgeon needs the assistance of an anaesthetist. The pertinence of the parallel drawn by Freud between analysis and operation will become even more striking when it becomes evident that in dual therapy members of the analytic team (alternately) take over functions not dissimilar to those of the anaesthetist, in the sense of lessening emotionally painful reactions (anxiety, guilt, shame, etc.) to the interpretations and confrontations of the co-therapist.

6. The fallacy of this reasoning if applied to analysis has been exposed previously (1966, p. 225).

turbing countertransference patterns thrive in the analytic situation mainly because of its inherent dyadic disbalance, that is, automatic exclusion of the third member of the personality-shaping (here actually *reshaping*) triad.

The Analyst as Separator

As already mentioned, one of the most striking findings in my study of countertransference was the frequency with which the analyst excludes from the scope of his observation the patient's *extra-therapeutic involvements*. It is as though not only the patient develops a "transference neurosis" which ultimately ends by overshadowing in its emotional importance all other relationships, but the analyst himself unknowingly facilitates and even partakes in this process. If normally the child has *to grow up under the influence of his parents but also to grow away from them,* how can the one-to-one aspect of the analytic situation encourage such a course? It is precisely this dyadic feature of the analytic setting transmitted to us by Freud which I hold responsible for its failure to achieve that final psychological maturation of the patient to which analysis is committed. In spite of all the "parameters" introduced over the years in the analytic situation, like those in "functional" analysis (Rank), "non-directive" analysis (Rogers), "direct" analysis (Rosen), "deep" analysis (Bergen), "hypnotic" analysis (Wolberg), "narcoanalysis" and so forth, the original design of the analytic setting has remained basically unaltered: only the analyst and his patient.

To reinforce the dyadic core of the analytic process, there are many rules which in essence support the illusion in the mind of the patient that the analyst has no other involvements except the one with him. That the analyst has in his personal life consistent contacts with others is never mentioned to the patient even during periods of crises. The analyst's private life has to remain absolutely unknown to the analysand.[7] Such a restriction purportedly aims at facilitating the patient's use of the analyst as a "blank" or "neutral" screen (see p. 13) for his projections.

In reality this rule illustrates perfectly the tendency among analysts to thoughtless oversimplification. If the analyst has to be a (psychological) parent to the patient, as Freud maintained, how different must the analyst who adheres to the precept of anonymity then appear from a reasonably normal parent! Would a parent refrain completely from talking to his children about his worries, concerns and aspirations, and in the first place from giving evidence of his feelings toward the other parent and for his other children? Moreover, the analyst, in sharpest contrast to the parent, is supposed to judge or criticize the patient as little as possible, if at all, and to make minimal demands. He must, in short, according to the highly cherished precept, "forever refrain from being judgmental." In this event, how can the analyst fulfill the role of "educator" as advocated by Freud?

It is axiomatic—we do not mind reiterating—that success in analytic therapy is predicated upon the resolution of infantile dependence and oedipal love toward the parent, in both of which conflicts about *exclusive possession and rivalry* are rooted. The parents are supposed to provide warmth, acceptance of and physical care for the child. In the process they cannot avoid, and actually should not avoid, becoming the object also of the child's sensual love. Ultimately, however, the parents have to lose their overriding role in their offspring's investment. This normally should be accomplished without the child losing the capacity for trust and love, a

---

7. Here is an example of some second thought on this matter from an authority on the subject of analytic methodology, an example which will illustrate the absurdity to which this prohibition has been carried: "I doubt that the evolution of the transference neurosis is often seriously disturbed by the patient's knowing whether one takes one's vacation in Vermont or in Maine, or indeed (let me really be bold!) that one knows something more about sailing than about golf or bridge." Leo Stone, *The Psychoanalytic Situation* (New York, 1961), p. 48.

capacity which is tested by his willingness and success in developing new *extra-familiar* relationships. The child normally crosses the boundaries of the original genetic triad and enters into relationships with peers, teachers, persons in authority and members of the community in general. If this has not taken place in the life of a patient, however, how can such a developmental step be facilitated by a dyadic therapeutic relationship, which promotes infantile dependence and possessiveness instead of capacity to share? How can the tendency towards sexual (oedipal) monopolization of a parent be modified if the transferential parent-figure is not experienced, even most ephemerally, in the context of his or her relationship to the opposite sex? And in the first place, how can both infantile positions be relinquished if in transference the analyst offers himself as both an exclusive and sexually hybrid, that is, both maternal and paternal, object of involvement?

The application of genetic psychoanalysis for almost two decades by the staff of the Dual Therapy and Research Bureau and by myself proved how unfounded the concern was that the emotional intensity of the transference experience might be muted in the triadic setting. What we instead notice with each patient in dual analysis is how the elimination of the highly confusing ambiguity inherent in the overlapping transference investment actually *intensifies* the feelings toward the therapist. Not only, at the same time this very fact facilitates their spontaneous expression. Indeed, how can one express straightforwardly one's love and admiration toward one parental substitute, or one's need to be loved and admired by him, overcoming the concomitant anger and fear of the rival, if both are the same person? If a patient is prey to severe conflicts around dependency and suffers humiliating separation anxieties, how can he freely express his anger toward the disappointing therapist on the occasion of some transient separation (vacation), without fearing that he will appear too demanding and controlling and then lose him altogether?

Transference Neurosis and "Social Context"

As has been stressed, in transference neurosis the "social context" of the patient is typically disregarded to the detriment of the patient's extra-therapeutic relationships. Instead of becoming more meaningful, durable and gratifying, these frequently grow more and more shadowy. The relatives (husband, wife or parent) in such cases refer to the patient as "not being there" or being withdrawn, absent-minded, taciturn or else docile and compliant, in sharpest contrast to the analytic sessions which end up as a battlefield for all the contradictory expectations and conflicts of the patient. This stage in therapy is, in a sort of professional self-deception, seen by analysts as "precondition for successful cure." Unfortunately it often continues to be such a "precondition" for years and years, simply because a one-to-one relationship alone can hardly contain or reduce the intensity of the analysand's conflicts. Yet such a reduction is necessary to enable his ego to achieve that minimal distance from these conflicts that is indispensable for proper analytic inquiry and therapeutic insight.

Acting Out of the Analyst's Unconscious

The opposite pattern where the patient "acts out" in extra-therapeutic situations, prompted in this by the unconscious of the analyst, is well known. Phyllis Greenacre has found that the analyst's vicarious enjoyment of the patient's acting out "may be of greater frequency and importance than one might at first think. It occurs among analysts who display no overt acting out, but who react as some severely restrained adults who enjoy and tacitly applaud the impulsive behavior of their children who dare to do what they themselves have not been permitted" (1950, p. 467).

In this second constellation, we see the patient immobilized by something which comes quite close to a *negative dyadic bind* with his analyst similar to a negative dyad prevailing between a parent and a child (1966, p. 215). The analyst seems simply unable to put an end to the repetitive dramatic events in the patient's life outside of therapy. Behind the analyst's "tolerant" and "non-judgmental attitude" may thus be hidden the same active participation which, we shall see is disguised in the absenteism of the "excluded" parent in the negative dyadic position toward his child.

Psychotic Breaks During Analysis

An illustration in point is the patient who reacted to her (male) analyst's departure for the summer vacation, with a breakdown for which she had to be hospitalized (1966, p. 42). In describing how she became overdependent on him she explained, with a good degree of plausibility, that it grew out of his extreme tolerance and acceptance of her. Evidently, this colleague most rigorously applied the precept that the analyst should preserve a "non-judgmental" attitude. "I could have come and told him that *I had killed my mother*[8] and he would have understandingly nodded. . . . He was God for me."[9] The reference to the killing of the mother as an illustration of the degree of tolerance of her analyst has a decisive bearing on the philosophy of genetic psychoanalysis in general and dual therapy in particular. As the therapist was a male, his objective gender had its influence on her transference involvement with him.

To clarify a little better the dynamics of transference in this case, the following consideration is in order: Since clinical experience has shown that a separation trauma is most severe within the framework of one's dependency on the mother rather than on the father, there is no doubt that the breakdown occurred under the influence of the patient's ma-

---

8. Ferenczi long ago alerted us to the unconscious meaningfulness of seemingly random comparisons. The same is true, I have found, for *illustrations*. This explains why it is analytically rewarding if one develops the habit of asking for an example after a generalization of the patient like "we always quarrelled," or "they delighted in having secrets," or "she had the knack of tearing me down."

9. These words support strikingly the ill-repute of analysts of becoming "godlike" to their patients. (The truth of this reputation will be gone into a little later.)

ternal transference to the analyst. Unconsciously, however, she reacted to him also as a paternal, that is, an oedipal object. Thus she was constantly under the burden of oedipal guilt feelings because she had symbolically eliminated (killed) the third member of the genetic triad, since there was no female equivalent for her mother in the analytic situation.

In other words, in her analysis she was in a situation comparable to that of a daughter who after the divorce of the parents continues to live with her father. The analyst on his side had made short shrift of her husband by stating that she would never be cured if she continued to live with him. The colleague was not interested, however, in why this was so. Is it necessary to qualify what kind of countertransference was operative here? This patient constantly quarrelled with her husband, onto whom she had shifted much of her early frustration aggression, reactive to maternal deprivation. Throughout her life she had fought violently with her mother, which well corroborates Freud's observation that a woman's relationship with her husband often repeats the one with her mother rather than with her father. The analyst, perceiving empathically that the patient was potentially inclined to do the same with him in transference, protected himself by two measures: one, he was a most undemanding, understanding and all-forgiving God-father; and two, he supported her taking out on her husband what she felt against her mother. Thus when she said that he would have understood her even if she had "killed her mother," she was psychologically not very far from the truth: the analyst endorsed the constant emotional killing of her mother in the furious quarrels with her husband. But the burden of unconsciously mounting guilt feelings could not possibly be borne indefinitely, nor the bribing influence of the analyst's all-accepting attitude sustained forever.

The overloaded and ambivalent transference had to come to a head. The progression of her transference to this critical point of assuming features of a veritable transference psychosis is proven by the fact that the breakdown occurred not during the first but the *third* summer vacation of her analyst. The guilt feelings—which accounted for the patient's repeated attempts at suicide, one of which required an emergency tracheotomy—had to bring about a breakdown in the context of a frustration by the analyst. That this was so can be explained in terms of the interplay between maternal and paternal transference hopelessly enmeshed around the person of the analyst. (How inadequate, in view of all this, was the analyst's reaction when, exasperated by the patient's demandingness and dependency on him, he screamed at her: "I am not your father!") (Flescher, 1966, p. 57).[10]

As long as she could defensively put into the foreground the anaclitic, i.e. maternal, transference she kept in abeyance the oedipal transference toward her analyst as a male and the resulting guilt feelings. But when the analyst left at the height of her transference involvement, the separation trauma was too much for her to take. She broke down and was hospitalized. Her rages against the analyst and her violent accusations against his incompetence proved that the "tolerance" the analyst had shown towards his patient, to the point of favoring the killing of the third member of the genetic triad (a development typical of transference-countertransference binds), did not save him from being (emotionally) killed by the patient: her breakdown also had the purpose of exposing him to his colleagues as an inept therapist. In reality he was no more inept than the majority of analysts. Indeed he was

---

10. The emotional burden on the analyst's own unresolved countertransference involvements exacts, in my opinion, a stastically significant toll in psychosomatic complications, especially of a cardiovascular nature, and also in suicide. (". . . eight men closely associated with Freud . . . committed suicide." W. Freeman, 1967.) It is only a question of time until colleagues recognize that their burden, like that of parents, will be made much lighter by adherence to the triadic principle. It cannot be otherwise, because of the cathartic relief from tension provided by the ongoing intra-team communication. This the analyst will appreciate all the more as the neutralization of traumata suffered by patients and the ensuing frustration aggression inevitably complicate and exacerbate the transference-countertransference interaction.

While these lines were being edited, another well-known analyst committed suicide, a fact which I consider the most serious indictment of psychoanalysis as it is now practiced, especially in cases with a tendency to depression. It is my conviction that if this colleague had undergone dual therapy, or at least had had the opportunity as I have advised (1966, p. 271), to resolve his transference in a triadic setting, he would not have taken his life.

one of the major figures in the psychoanalytic movement in the United States. This, however, did not prevent him from falling victim to the basic shortcoming of traditional analysis.

What this and similar cases have taught us is that break-downs in analysis are both frequent and preventable. If Freud had paid more attention to the question of why his "Wolf Man" suffered relapses after being "cured" by him and why he improved during every analytic cycle with a female analyst (Ruth Mack Brunswick) (see E. Jones, 1955, p. 274), he would not have expressed the logically and metapsychologically untenable opinion that "through the cure of his (the patient's) neurosis you may have freed the way for a more serious sickness" and that "there is no protection against it" (see p. 89). It is the *aggravation* of the unconscious conflicts underlying a neurosis, and not its cure, that can lead to a psychosis. The danger of such an aggravation is present only in the dyadic situation of traditional analysis.[11]

The Overidealized Analyst

The tendency of the therapist to monopolize his patient's emotions, especially the positive ones, at the expense of other people in the latter's life—which I have found to be a most frequent occurrence—goes hand in hand with the decrease of

---

11. In a seminar on "Psychiatric Emergencies" at the New York Psychoanalytic Institute where cases of psychotic breaks during analysis were discussed, I expressed my disbelief that a more thorough diagnostic evaluation could prevent such occurrences. I saw instead these mishaps, on which the opponents of psychoanalysis so eagerly seize, as resulting from unmanageable transference-countertransference interaction typical of dyadic binds.

reality testing in the patient's evaluation of the analyst, as reflected in the known tendency of analysands to "overidealize"
their analysts. It is this tendency that Greenacre found to
account for the phenomenon of *addiction* to analysis. Our
patient after her breakdown resolved never again to have a
positive transference toward a psychiatrist: "Whenever I feel
that I start to like the therapist, off I go." Thus she ended up
by being treated for over two decades by a long series of
therapists, and only the dual setting finally succeeded in eliminating her misery. Evidently her rebellion against the need to
"idealize" her therapists had put an end only to her current
therapeutic relationship, but not to her continuing need to
fall back on therapy for help.

THE TRIADIC PRINCIPLE

Genetic Psychoanalysis and "Social Context"

As mentioned, dual therapy represents the prototype of methods based on the genetic-analytic principle. It dichotomizes the transference needs of the patient by offering him separate objects for the maternal and paternal transference. This alone prevents the overloading of the transference and also lessens the intensity of the various types of countertransference responses. At the same time the triadic setting, where the patient is shared with a co-therapist, conditions the analyst —actually *trains* him—most effectively to be interested in the analysand's *contact with another person*. In other words, the setting itself constantly revives the analyst's alertness to the patient's "social context." As such an alertness is incompatible with a too-deep entrenchment of fantasies of monopolization and exclusiveness, it is another preventative against the development of an overly intense transference and also countertransference, especially of a *reactive* and induced (suggestive) type.

We have recognized a source of error in the process of analyzing, in that the very act of observation changes what is observed. We have also commented that the suggestive influence of a parent and educator is modified by his empathy insofar as the latter is screened by his own defenses. This explains why the new (triadic) atmosphere must most decisively support the maturational goal of analytic psychotherapy: the psychological constellation which determines the degree and nature of the "personal equation" in the analyst is never the same in two therapists. It follows that what is

101

screened out ("scotomized") by the defenses of one member of the dual team is grasped by the other member. This is the more true since for any transference-countertransference entanglement of the patient there is always a relatively uninvolved observer available in the therapeutic triad. Each therapist has in turn the opportunity to observe from a distance the patient in interaction with his co-therapist of the dual team. This "observation from a distance" enables the dual analyst to grasp even things which are conflicted in him and his co-analyst and likely to be overlooked by both of them.[1]

The scope of error in the new approach is thus strikingly reduced by having two analysts, in *direct personal and repetitive* contact, observe the same patient and assist each other in the act of integration of the picture of the patient's genetic past. This enhances the opportunity for an optimal utilization of the known traditional criteria of validity in psychoanalysis: if a symptom is understood in its dynamic, economic and topical structure,[2] the patient is freed from his disturbance.

Indeed, psychoanalysis gained its worldwide reputation, in spite of the resistance of its detractors from many quarters, by accomplishing just this. Those shocked by Freud's discoveries about infantile sexuality, the Oedipus complex and the inherent limitation of our insight into what motivates us because of restriction of our psychological perception and scotomization within the field of self-observation, could not forever escape the evidence: patients afflicted by neurotic symptoms were freed from them simply by becoming aware of their unconscious meaning and resolving the underlying conflicts. This could not be achieved, however, without going into the patient's childhood history, his psycho-sexual organi-

---

1. This is the reason why, in addition to synoptic recording (1966, p. 132), we use in dual therapy "interaction" recording for intra-team communication.

2. I have added since 1950 (paper read at the "Psychiatric Forum") to the known metapsychologic criteria that of "dualistic": it defines the quantitative relationship between the libidinal and destructive energies of a psychic process, mechanism or formation (1953)a.

zation and his conflicts rooted in multifarious attachments to his parents. The correction of the detrimental influences to which the child had been exposed at the hands of his parents, became the most logical goal of a cause-oriented, that is, genetically founded, therapy. The many failures, however, of psychoanalytic therapy, the disaffection, dissension and dissidence of the "analyzed" followers of Freud which gave rise to the many splinter groups with their proclaimed theoretical and methodologic differences, exerted a sobering effect on those who expected analysis to provide the ultimate answer in the therapy of psychic disorders.

My supposition that the source of error in the approach to the study of mental prophylaxis lay in the very nature of the analytic situation, became a deep conviction: traditional analysis cannot possibly provide us with a true picture of the process through which faulty attitudes of parents have determined the child's developmental disorder, resulting in psychopathology.

Genetic Triad Reproduced

The triadic setting of dual analysis, instead, faithfully reproduces and clarifies basic dynamics in the genetic history of the analysand. It thus provides us with elements for a dependable theory of "genetic prevention." Here is an illustration:

According to the triadic principle, the child is as much a psychological product of *two* parents as he is their common biological product. In view of this simple premise the following question can be asked: If one parent has a faulty attitude towards a child and the other does not intervene on his behalf, is the parent's abstention actually due simply to his obliviousness, disinterest, ignorance or limited intelligence? Might it be that this is an *active,* i.e. intentional, albeit usually unconscious withdrawal from the situation? Dual therapy gave us in this respect a definite answer: the parent's unavailability is always

intentional.[3] Dual therapy can also correct parental errors by
default simply because the patient sees alternately a male and
female analyst, which does not allow for absenteeism of any
parental transference figure in the treatment process. It gives
us the unique opportunity to observe the results of the "corrective" substitution of the absent or abstaining parent, and
thus also to evaluate the contribution to the child's difficulties
of a parent's physical or emotional unavailability in general.

In the first place and most importantly, however, with the
dual approach it became possible to individuate the triadic
principle governing the process of maturation. Let us see to
what degree this holds true.

Triadic Principle of Maturation

The original biological unity which the yet unborn infant
forms with the mother is replaced by a stage of "dependency"
(anaclitic stage) in which all the infant's needs are attended
to by the mother. The infant therefore confines his perception
of the external world only to her.[4]

The mother is the first and most exclusive source of gratification of all the self-preservative needs as well as the need for
love. She is the one who provides the first and thus most intense and most lasting (in unconscious memory) experiences
of security, well-being and pleasure.

---

3. The seemingly completely irrational accusation of a child, that a
parent who died from illness or accident has forsaken and rejected him,
contains often an important kernel of truth: if the child had meant
enough to the parent, he would have known how to take better care of
himself.

4. A patient whose delusion consisted in the belief that he was the
object of an experiment in which the "whole world" was engaged, because
of the uniqueness of his personality, had regressed precisely to this level of
his development. The demarcation, in itself highly labile, of himself from
the image of his mother disappeared. Hence hand in hand with his megalomanic (ego-cosmic) overvaluation of himself, he grew convinced that he
was changing into a woman (his mother), that he had the same physical
symptoms as his mother, that he would die in the same month of the year
in which she died, and so on. (For further details on this case, see p. 175.)

The triadic principle of maturation, however, sooner or later compels the child to recognize that there are certain forces which may delay the gratification of these needs, forces which are beyond the mother's power to eliminate. Soon that disturbing influence in the external world is ascribed to another human being, usually the father, otherwise a sibling.[5] The capacity to adjust to this interference depends on its gradual nature and on the mother's consistent and relatively unambivalent attitude and ministrations to the infant. But ultimately the first adjustment to a triadic exigency has to be achieved and the child's *capacity to share* his first source of security and love has to be acquired.

In other words, emergence from the anaclitic stage is measured by the degree to which the existence of the third member of the genetic triad begins to be recognized and accepted. It is understandable that if such an object is not available, as is the case with children of unwed or divorced mothers, this developmental step is made very difficult, if not impossible.

In the next stage, sexual attraction becomes the predominant force in choosing the love object: the son loves his mother, the daughter her father, and both hate and fear the same-sex parent. (The opposite choice, we recall, also exists, though it is normally of lesser intensity, and reflects the bisexual constitution of every human being.)

Accepting Parents as a Couple

The successful transition from this stage is borne out by the child's capacity to accept the parents as a *couple* and to enlarge the recreated (in different terms) dyadic engagement with the preferred parent into a *triad*. An imaginary test sit-

---

5. The existence of a twin or another sibling close in age, with the same needs as the infant, or of a sick person (grandparent, the other parent, an older sibling), or any other external condition which interferes with the satisfaction of the infant's need to have a dependable source of security and love, prevents maturation and lays the foundation for serious clinical conditions appearing often at a much later age.

uation for another triad is represented by the fantasy of having a child by the preferred parent, independently if the normal or inverted oedipal variant is operating. The boy's wish to give mother a child and the girl's wish to receive a child from the father are replaced in the inverted oedipal complex by the opposite wish, displaced onto the parent of the same sex: the boy has unconscious fantasies of being impregnated by the father and the girl of impregnating the mother.[6]

Normally the oedipal position is abandoned following the acceptance of the oedipal defeat. This step actually is not entirely completed during the oedipal stage but continues throughout the *latency phase*. This phase is characterized by a physiological decrease in the pressure of instinctual demands on the ego. (It is most important that this respite be preserved; the child should be spared experiences of overstimulation, as these may bring the latency phase prematurely to an end.) The final psychosexual maturation is therefore, even under optimal conditions, actually not concluded until puberty is reached. It is then that interest in the opposite sex extends more decisively beyond the confines of the family and the *post-oedipal family triad* comes into operation.

What follows is a new dyadic experimentation of the pubertal and post-pubertal phase—the period of intense adolescent friendships and crushes towards members of *both* sexes— which again reflects the bi-sexual leanings of the young individual. Ultimately, however, the expectations become streamlined toward the *opposite* sex. The dyadic fantasies which reach their height as never before or after in life, in those longings for "union of body and soul," are again not final. Both the nature of a new family setting, the underlying instinctual needs (unconscious search for a new family milieu) and the demands of reality, enforce the extension of the dyadic bonds again into a triad: The new love object has to be and normally is experienced and accepted in the context of his

---

6. Nothing proves so cogently our bisexual predisposition as the ubiquitous presence of (unconscious) passive, receptive pregnancy fantasies in the male and active-phallic penetrating fantasies in the female.

(or her) past and current family ties. If there are unrelinquished infantile positions (so-called "fixations"), this triad is disturbed by a too-marked search for compensation for a defective genetic triad: the individual expects (unconsciously) from the mate's family, the *in-laws*, the fulfillment of needs which have not been met within the old family. Indeed, an individual's *ability to share*, which bears witness to his triadic maturity, is greatly tested by his capacity to adjust to the social context of the love object.

Parenthood—Test of Triadic Maturity

The triadic balance in the life of every man and woman, however, is most of all put to test by the *birth of a child,* which disrupts the dyadic constellation of the marriage. All the deposits of aggression in each parent, engendered by frustrations within the dyadic constellations of his own childhood (anaclitic dependency and oedipal involvement) are activated when the third member of the genetic triad appears, signaling the inception of the new family. The psychological burden of the past surviving in the unconscious of the parents prevents them from properly fulfilling the aims of the parental drive and thus also from meeting their child's maturational drive. As to the parental drive, experience with dual therapy has provided us with the answer to the question of when this drive can best assert itself. The parental drive reaches optimally its fulfillment if within the family triad there prevails a constellation which we call *genetic balance.* It presupposes the unequivocal involvement and participation of *each* parent in the raising and education of the child insofar as his adjustment to reality demands and his acceptance of behavior-regulating norms, instilled ideals and aspirations are concerned. Before we go into how the principle of *balance within the genetic triad*—this is what we mean by the term "triadic principle"—and the parental drive are brought to best fruition in preventive education, we shall study how infractions of the triadic principle determine pathology. From insights gained into the

consequences of these specific traumata, we shall draw inferences which may help us to establish guideposts for the
practice of mental prophylaxis through genetic education.

Genetic Disbalance

The most typical "genetic disbalance" is one where within a
genetic triad a "positive dyad" prevails between the child and
one parent concurrently with a "negative dyad" between the
child and the other parent. A positive dyad is one characterized by a parent's too intense and manifest involvement in a
child, to the exclusion of the other parent. Such an involvement cannot, in view of the above considerations, be based
psycho-economically on the parental drive. Indeed, the triadic
principle which has as its core the *difference between generations* (two parents and the child) is violated in any kind of
parent-child relationship which is dyadic. Insofar as *instinctual
aim* in the parent is concerned, a positive dyad can result from
a whole gamut of infantile fixations and conflicts in his unconscious.

> A mother who is overinvolved and seductive with her little
> daughter while cleaning her anal or genital region does not
> simply "overstimulate" the child, but may use her to enact
> some specific (unconscious) fantasies of her own. She may
> enact an all-giving mother, as she would have liked to have
> herself, that is, one who devotes herself totally to the child
> to the exclusion of husband and/or other children. She may
> repeat with the child the intense auto-erotic activities in
> which she has indulged in her own childhood. She may act
> on the compulsion of "cleaning away the dirt" in order to
> raise a "pure" child, untarnished by "dirty" impulses. (As
> is so frequently the case, in the very act of appeasing the
> demands of a hyper-moral superego, she unknowingly grati-
> fies, through proxy, the very pleasure-seeking needs which
> she deprecates and denies in herself.) She may also want
> through the cleansing procedures to humble herself as a

proof of her deep maternal love, when there exists the peril of a breakthrough of her hostility against the child.[7]

The father, in a negative dyad with his daughter, may in his turn disregard his wife's shutting him out because the daughter stands for himself on the level of his unfulfilled dependency needs or oedipal claims. On another level, he enacts his own father or a sibling to be excluded. He may through proxy gratify his own anal-erotic and passive fantasies. He may endow the observation of his wife's manipulations of the daughter's body with a "primal scene" significance, causing a rage reaction in him which he may repress or else express to his wife indirectly, i.e. for most irrelevant reasons. He is unaware that he does not dare to question his wife's pattern because it would in his unconscious be like interfering with his parents' sexual life.

The combinations of psychological constellations on which a positive or negative dyad can be based are infinite. What complicates matters even more is that dyadic alliances as a rule shift in the course of a child's life, either under the influence of biologically imposed or environmentally enforced changes in the child's instinctual constellation or ultimately following some change in the parents or in their marital relationship: the previously excluded parent becomes in turn a party to a positive dyad.

Scope of Genetic Psychoanalysis

In traditional analysis dyadic binds develop most typically, as repeatedly stressed, because of the very nature of its setting and the known rule aimed at "deepening" the transference.

What is of main concern here, however, is the disappointment in the psychoanalytic movement regarding the solution of the problem of prevention. We have elaborated already on the reasons why this was inevitable. But the same reasons have led us to the following conclusion: If genetic psycho-

---

7. The biblical ceremonies of washing somebody else's feet retained in some religions is probably based on this defense of denial.

analysis was to become a source of enlightenment regarding preventive education, it would first have to prove itself capable of bringing about definitely more favorable results than the traditional analytic method. And this indeed was the case. The many criteria—over twenty—for indication of dual therapy radically removed the restrictions and limitations which burdened the application of psychoanalysis as a therapeutic method (Flescher, 1966, p. 233). We shall not go into the theoretical and empirical data which support the contention that the dual method of analysis is more effective than traditional analysis in coping with cases which resist the usual approach. The volume, dedicated exclusively to the application of the triadic principle in genetic psychoanalysis in general and dual therapy in particular deals with this topic.

I hope that the reader will by now appreciate the reason why I have gone at such lengths into the drawbacks of traditional analysis. I did this not simply because of my conviction that the few thousand patients treated yearly by the members of the International Psychoanalytic Association often leave their analysts after many years[8] with less than desirable results, or because I felt they could fare better if they could have a dual analytic experience at least in the terminal stage of their therapy. The reason, instead, for giving so much room to the exploration of the dynamics of classical analysis was

---

8. A colleague had been analyzed for about 10 years, first by a male analyst and then by a female analyst. Still her depression remained unchanged. When talking about her analyses she volunteered that in her last analysis her (female) analyst "did not allow her" to express anger in transference. Only one who is familiar with the decisive role of self-directed aggression in the dynamics of a depressive condition will appreciate the fact that already in her fifth dual session she was able to say to her female analyst, "I am so angry that I feel like killing you." In traditional analysis she could not possibly have directly expressed such a wish to any of her (single) analysts: she had lost her father in the war before she was six, and two years later her mother was killed during a robbery. The guilt feelings stemming from the fact that life concretized her death wishes against her parents, especially her mother, made such a catharsis, within the transference to an analyst standing for both mother and father, as is the case in classical analysis, too threatening.

the concern for the millions of individuals who are constantly brought into this world of ours only to suffer because their parents don't know how to raise them to be healthy and to enjoy living. That this is by no means the most disastrous consequence of the failure of parents to meet their educational responsibility, we shall see when we come to the problem of collective irrationality.

CHAPTER SEVEN

GENETIC SCRIPTS

As to a dependable theory of mental prophlaxis, it stands to reason that the more thorough our knowledge about the causes of neuroses, the more secure we will be in preventing them. We know beyond the shadow of a doubt that the determinants of psychic disorders reach as far back as the patient's childhood history. This is true even if unusually severe traumas in adult life have unleashed a neurosis or psychosis. In these cases the choice of the symptoms depends on the genetic history of the patient.

Parents as Playwrights and Stage Directors

The assets of the triadic setting of genetic psychoanalysis consist precisely of this: it allows for a more exact, detailed, dependable and *doubly verified* reconstruction of the genetic history of the patient. Such a history is identical with the vicissitudes of the parents' handling of and attitude toward their children. Regarding how the psychological make-up of parents shapes the destiny of children, the following cardinal points of "genetic etiopathology" can at this stage of our understanding be made:

1. The biological need to procreate is supported in the human species by specific "genetic" fantasies reflecting the individual needs of each parent. These fantasies form the basis for the "genetic scripts" which parents enforce on the child during the years

112

of his development and for the genetic plays he enacts for the rest of his life.

2. If parents have reached emotional maturity themselves, their genetic script closely follows the triadic principle of maturation, i.e. *promotes an optimal display of the maturational drive in the child.*

3. There usually prevails a great discrepancy between a parent's genetic fantasy and his conscious reason for believing he wants to have a child.

4. The child is, via action or abstention and via the attitude of the parents, molded to fit a given role in the "genetic play," a role which determines his personality make-up and influences greatly the vicissitudes of his life.

5. The fantasies of parents which underlie their genetic scripts represent the direct bridge between the parents' own childhood experiences and their present psychological constellations.

6. Unresolved conflicts buried in the unconscious of apparently "normal" parents may still determine an antimaturational genetic script for their children. (This explains why psychic disorders often seem to skip a generation.)

7. The study of genetic scripts of parents and the genetic plays their children have been forced to engage in, reveals in which specific way the parental drive failed to meet the maturational needs of the offspring.

8. The genetic play imposed on the offspring has a most important frame of reference: the *genetic triad,* that is, the interaction between the two parents and between each parent and the child.

9. The child develops emotional disorders which correspond not only to the nature of each parent's genetic script but also to the synergetic and antagonistic aspects of the combination of both.

10. When the violation of the triadic principle is in essential aspects identical in the genetic scripts of both parents, the results are especially ominous for the child.

11. Antimaturational genetic scripts not only lay foundation for difficulties in the offspring, but continue to exert their influence decades later if the parents are still in contact with their children. They add substantially to a change-resisting immobilization of their offspring, long after the latter have reached biologic maturity.

12. If there is more than one child, the same parents usually assign to each child a different role in their genetic scripts.

13. The adjustment of the offspring to the role assigned in the genetic play can be modified effectively only through analytic therapy in a triadic setting.

14. Not only can genetic plays of the offspring be modified in triadic settings, but also genetic scripts of the parents. The latter changes strikingly abbreviate the therapy of their children even after they become adults.

We shall now bring examples of most typical violations of the triadic principle by parents, violations which give rise to developmental disturbances in their offspring. The maturational principle may be infringed by the parents either actively and manifestly, or subtly, or else through *omission* of intervention, identical with tacit consent. The material used for illustration is drawn from cases in which dual analysis or dual therapy has been most successfully applied. This is the more to be appreciated since, with very few exceptions, the patients had previously failed to benefit from long and very intensive traditional analysis.

Actually the causal connection between the ways in which

the parents in our samples failed to adhere to the triadic principle and the resulting psychic impairment in the offspring is so obvious as to make the corroborative proof of dual therapy superfluous. The absence of an unobstructed and vigorous parental drive in such parents accounts for their assigning the child a role in a life drama whose history has preceded his birth, sometimes by decades.

It is not by chance that psychoanalysis has introduced the term of "acting out" or "re-enactment" as an important though often unobtrusive way in which we recreate the past for purposes of emotional release. Plays, dramas and tragedies have offered mankind since time immemorial the comfort of cathartic purification for the mere price of admission. What my inquiry into genetic scripts has shown is the truth that a more dramatic "life theater" is staged by parents. The latters' emotional release is paid for, however, by their children-actors' pain, anxiety and guilt, and ultimately by their mental and physical illness. In the process of freeing themselves from their parents, the young ones sometimes "pay back" to some degree those who imposed their genetic script upon them, but rarely to a degree commensurate with their own suffering.

The tendency of parents to act as both script-writers and stage directors for their children's destiny is probably the most ominous—in its far-reaching consequences—example of unintentional destructiveness. The "genetic scripts" used for illustrations and the "practical rules" of prevention will hopefully show parents and all those who are committed to the physical, emotional and spiritual upbringing and education of children how, by adhering to the triadic principle of maturation, they can avoid transmitting unnecessary illness and suffering from generation to generation.

In illustrating the "plays" written and staged unconsciously by parents we are certainly not aspiring to exhaust the innumerable, or even the most common, variations of genetic scripts. The following have been chosen from among many others, no less striking, to exemplify the violation of the triadic principle.

FILIAL DEVOTION
or
"She is the center of my life"

This is what Leo would repeat when talking about his mother, Mrs. N. She herself had been both overconcerned and overindulgent with her son. "I learned that my mother was obsessed by fears that I might suddenly die. She would get up many times at night to see if I was still breathing. She would put my socks on and tie my shoes until—I was then ten—the superintendent saw us and bawled her out." This mother, further, did not intervene in the constant battles between Leo and his father, who was deeply religious. Leo, with his mother's knowledge and support, well knew how to evade observance of the prescribed rituals. He also made sure that father would catch him in his infractions. Underlying this pattern was the fantasy of being physically punished, which ultimately revealed itself to stand unconsciously for having bodily contact with his father. Yet this contact had to be such as not to betray Leo's wish to be loved physically by his father. This wish, imperiling the son's masculine identity, had the purpose of insuring Leo against a more dreaded danger: the punishment (emasculation, death) for his (oedipal) attachment to his mother. To be lifted by his angry father and shaken was unconsciously translated into being picked up and held lovingly and protectively in his arms. Actually the father was less ambivalent toward Leo than the mother. She minded neither Leo's flouting his father's injunctions nor his being berated and punished. There were sufficient elements to justify the assumption that the continuous aggravation of the father from this source alone was a most important, if not decisive, factor in his premature death.

Leo paid for his collusion with mother against father in the first place with a serious impairment of his sexual potency which he for a long time concealed from his analysts. As for Leo's mother, she was concerned not only about her son's general physical health but also about her own. She was a severe hypochondriac, as Leo also ultimately became. Indeed, the mutual recital of aches and complaints was for many years the core of communication between mother and son. Though claiming to be very irritated whenever she would bring up her physical woes, he still spent countless hours listening to them. The "wishful" element in all these fears about the other's health had its basis in the unconscious hostility which both harbored against each other. Sado-masochism had a different role here than in Leo's relationship with his father, where it mainly served, as mentioned, to cover up the son's need for closeness as well as his wish for and fear of punishment.

Mrs. N. had during her second pregnancy a vision of the head of her mother who died when Leo was one and a half years old. The hallucinatory experience which made Mrs. N. move to another apartment was the return of the "ghost of Banquo" because Mrs. N.'s unconscious death wishes against her mother had made her feel responsible for her parent's death. These death wishes had taken root in Mrs. N. when her mother was pregnant with her younger brother, and they became activated by her own (second) pregnancy. This brother had been, according to her, "preferred" and spoiled by her parents. He became an unmanageable delinquent and was for many years a source of anguish for the entire family because of his constant brushes with the law. When her own son Leo was born, it was inevitable that Mrs. N. displace her anger along the known unconscious equation (sibling=child), from her brother onto Leo. Her overprotectiveness resulted from her need to deny the wish to get rid of Leo. Even a slight cold threw her into a panic: she feared Leo's air passages might become clogged and cause his suffocation. In his turn, Leo developed (reactive) death wishes against his mother which compelled him to make sure that *she* was not sick and would not die. Thus he would for many years, even after he began traditional analysis, daily call her in order to get her "health bulletins." He would accompany her to doctors and frequently use the same doctor at the same time for a "thor-

ough check-up" of himself. His confusing himself with his
mother was also perfectly apparent in his tendency, through
physical complaints, to successfully manipulate his physicians
into exploration of his own body openings (the nasal passages,
the rectum and even urethra). Ultimately he found doctors who obliged him with genital and prostatic massages.

The violation of the triadic principle by his mother's dyadic
symbiosis with her son, and by her non-intervention in the
clashes between husband and son, was reversed through the
"corrective" influence of dual analysis: The patient's hypo-
chondriasis receded and he lost his need for constant medical
consultation. Hand in hand with his striking improvement in
the sexual area, he became more active and creative in his
professional activities and ultimately was rewarded with pro-
motions to positions of great responsibility and value for the
community.

THE PYGMALION MOTIF
or
"He wanted her to be a scientist"

What can be more understandable than the desire of a
father to see his daughter become what he himself had always
aspired to? He ardently wished that Fay would develop interest in scientific experiments and research. This was the only
way in which his daughter could also make up for his disappointment of not having a son. He unfortunately disregarded her own inclinations and preferences, such as her unusual gift for music. Though he himself enjoyed playing the
cello, and experts had predicted that Fay would become a

concert cellist, she became only an accomplished member of a chamber music quartet. This was, she claimed, only because her father was haunted by the dreadful vision of her becoming a bohemian artist and destroying what he felt was Fay's "real" vocation, that of scientist. It was not difficult to guess that for this father science stood for manliness. As, however, his daughter was musically more gifted than he, the motive of rivalry also partook in his opposition to her artistic bent. (This makes it more than likely that any son of this father would have fared no better than his daughter.)

Why did her mother not support Fay's own inclination and preference? Like her husband, she also invested in her daughter as a sort of clay to be molded according to her own aspirations. In itself this would not necessarily be destructive. The trouble was that these aspirations were fraught with ambivalence toward her daughter, as were those of her husband. Actually she too was disillusioned by the birth of a daughter, and scientific endeavor seemed to her also more masculine than the artistic. Evidently this mother had not outgrown her own masculine aspirations. On one occasion, in an apparent attempt to console herself and her daughter for being "only a woman," she commented admiringly on the latter's oversized clitoris. Was it surprising then that her daughter was in sharp competition with men? At one time, in striking contrast with her usual sensitivity and tact, she laughed uproariously at her own rather crude joke. She was describing one of the frequent clashes between her father and her husband (whom she later divorced): "I was watching and waiting for the moment their balls would come rolling toward me." Though basically frigid, the unusually attractive Fay was involved in an interminable sequence of affairs with men. But her insatiable interest in them was only narcissistic: they were what she herself wanted to be. But as she could not help hating men at the same time for their "undeserved" anatomical privilege, her ambivalence quickly put an end to each of

these involvements.[1] Initially, she appeared simply incapable
of denying herself to any man who desired her sexually. Later
it became apparent that underlying her sexual insatiability
was an unconscious castration fantasy of depriving her partners of their sexual vigor in the very act of satisfying their
desires: she equated a man's spent sexual desire with im-
potence. Only on rarest occasions was she capable of achieving orgastic fulfillment and, significantly, only with physically
handicapped men. With them, as in dual analysis it soon
became clear, she actually made love to herself, the "anatom-
ically handicapped" woman.

In transference, Fay appears first, in contrast to her attitude towards the female analyst, to disregard me completely.
I very rarely appeared even in disguised form in her verbalizations. Evidently she could not decide in which category of
men to include me. She made it clear at the outset that she
preferred to lie on the couch because, as she said, she had
become used to it from the many years of her previous analyses with two male and one female analysts. I instead decided
at a certain point that sitting up in front of me might make
her take more notice of my existence, at least visually. She
agreed to sit up, but in doing so she remarked, "I thought
that all men liked me more in the horizontal position." In
other words, the well-concealed fantasy on which her transference expectation centered was that for me too she was in
a "horizontal" position and that she would ultimately succeed
in depriving me also of my (professional) "potency" by making me into her lover.

Returning to this patient's genetic past, we find that the
wish for a son was the one and only point of confluence in
the irrational foundation of both parents' "suggestive" empathy. Otherwise there was a constant tug of war between
Fay's father and mother, a situation which is quite typical
for the constellation of "alternating dyadic binds." In Fay's

---

1. For the concept of "phallic conflict," see Flescher, 1951, pp. 106,
223.

life neither of the parents was markedly excluded, insofar as there was no *manifest* negative dyad with either of them. Characteristic of positive dyads is the fact that the investment in a dyadic object is multilevelled, that is, inserted in one's psychic economy with different motivations on different levels. Beside the narcissistic investment on the part of each parent in Fay, she had also become for each an object of oedipal attachment and therefore (alternately) also an oedipal rival to be jealous of and to hate.

As to which parent Fay herself sided most strongly with, an insight was provided by her admission following her father's recent death: "When father was away on a trip the home atmosphere changed. With mother I would have the most marvelous time. We had fun, laughed and enjoyed ourselves. It was a sort of happy vacation." Thus Fay reacted with evident relief to the passing of the father. I shall not go into this father's own genetic history, but his awareness of the closer tie prevailing between his wife and daughter was most likely a source of deep frustration and anger which sooner or later had to exact its psychosomatic toll. It was no major surprise for me to learn that he died while calling his wife with angry impatience to his sickbed: his heart gave out precisely at the moment she was going to the phone to congratulate their daughter who was having a birthday party.

Of the two parents, the father had been the one less able to adjust to the birth of Fay. His inability to stand the triadic test of maturity was reflected by his attempt to deny the intrusion of his daughter between him and his wife, by trying to see in her merely an idealized reflection of himself. That the Pygmalion-like investment led also to an oedipal involvement was inevitable.[2]

---

2. "My Fair Lady" owes its extraordinary success to the fantasy that everlasting love must crown the "educator's" commitment to his charge. Indeed Professor Higgins was not simply a "teacher" but a combination of both mother and father, because Eliza was taught by him not only to speak properly, but also to be clean and well-mannered.

COLLUSION TO FRAUDULENCE
or
"I always liked to listen to the conversation of bums"

Morton, a delinquent adolescent, adamantly refused psychotherapy. In view of this, his father, Mr. F., was persuaded to enter treatment himself in order to be helped in handling his son.[3] This father opened the first session with the following words, "I always was interested in the derelicts of society. I liked to go to bars, not to drink but to listen to the conversation of bums." This inclination was only one of the many signs of this man's need to find irresponsibility outside of himself. He himself was born after the death of his father. He excused his extreme permissiveness toward Morton by his, as he put it, "deep desire to be an especially good father. After all, I well knew what it meant not to have a father." Thus Mr. F. permitted his son to present his father's paintings to his peers as his own accomplishments. In connection with this, Mr. F. recalled with great delight the bewilderment of the owner of an art shop, when at the age of ten, he himself had ordered a whole array of painting utensils "for an affresco" while revealing at the same time that he had never before so much as touched a paint brush. Later in his life he actually painted highly idealized reproductions of his father's photographs.

Morton's father had another burning aspiration: he wanted to be a *writer*. "I was determined to write a book on adolescents. I wanted to know what makes those youngsters tick. I didn't tell Mort this. I only asked him to tell me all his thoughts." The son went along with this. It turned out, however, that Morton reciprocated his father's pretense by engaging in elaborate fiction in which he could apply his talents for lying. Morton also proved good at forgery, as he took to

---

3. Freud was the first to use, in the case of "Little Hans," contacts with a father to influence the mental condition of his son (Flescher, 1966, p. 94ff.).

the habit of signing his father's name—Morton's own version of being a writer—on sizeable checks. He needed the money primarily to impress his friends. He would buy them tickets for shows, invite them to expensive restaurants and so on. "What else could I do but pay his checks," his father commented. "At one point when I saw that he was ruining me, *I thought of killing myself.* Then one day I had a heart attack. Yes, I had one foot in the grave. This is how Morton paid me back for being a good father to him."

In dual therapy Mr. F. quickly came to recognize that he could not play such a role because he had had no father to model himself after. By being able only to "internalize" his mother he developed a "trans-sexual" (in his case) feminine identity.[4] For a model of how to behave with his son, Mr. F. could therefore draw only on his experience with his own mother. Indeed he slept with her in the same bed until the age of nine. This exacerbated further his oedipal attachment to his mother, entrenched initially by the total absence of his father. His "trans-sexual" confusion of himself with his mother coexisted with his incestuous involvement in her. "When my mother remarried (I was then nineteen), something strange happened. I actually don't recall the incident, but I was told that I disappeared for a whole day and nobody knew where I was." The context in which Mr. F. brought up this occurrence made him ultimately remember that on that occasion he for the first time had considered suicide. Later, as we know, he was again brought to the verge of suicide and death from a heart attack, by his son's irresponsibility. Why was he, even after this, incapable of controlling his son? "I was worried about Mort, day and night. I saw him running away and *killing himself,* especially when I tried to avoid paying his debts or after we had quarrelled. My wife felt that I was too weak with our son." By showing himself a more giving mother to

4. "Trans-sexual identity" is an identity not corresponding to one's actual biological and anatomical destiny, but resulting from identification with, or rather from introjection of, the parent or a sibling of the opposite sex (1966, p. 274).

Mort than his wife was inclined to be, Mr. F. also acted out his (inverted) oedipal inclinations, rooted in his trans-sexual identity. But there was no doubt that behind his trans-sexual identity, modeled after his mother, there was still his objective gender as a male. It was on this level that he was, as mentioned, oedipally attached to his mother. Mr. F. most typically defended himself against the guilt feelings about this attachment by delegating the oedipal crime to his son. He achieved this by eliminating himself as a father in the life of Morton: he played only the role of a boundlessly generous mother. Morton's fraudulence briefly had the purpose of covering up father's own violation of that most important of moral restrictions, the prohibition of incest.

When Mr. F. was living alone with his mother, the fantasies about his father and the stories which he made up about the latter's most adventurous life, as member of the Czar's personal guard (here lay the deepest root of his writing ambition), did not suffice to meet his need for a father. Hence he invested his mother with the dual role of mother and father. It was this double-barrelled investment (to be found frequently in *dyadic bonds*) which rendered the separation from his mother, when she remarried, so traumatic. Indeed, he had not been gradually prepared for such a separation by a balanced genetic constellation during his development. His act of "disappearance" at his mother's remarriage was based on the enactment of the introjected mother at the moment when she was about to become as unavailable to him as his father had always been.

As we are committed to consistent observation of the triadic principle, we inevitably have to ask the following question: *where was Morton's mother in all this?* The answer is that she also had a hand in the "play of fraudulence," by allowing the complicated dyadic tie between husband and son to dominate the family picture. *Her* stake in her husband's over-involvement in their son's delinquency was the following: in her childhood she had to contend with the existence of a younger brother, overindulged by her parents. This brother's *delinquent behavior* in the end brought about a heavy jail sentence. Her abstention in regard to her own son was therefore typically based on a "negative" dyad with him. By disappearing emotionally from her son's life and failing to discharge her duty as a parent-educator, she paid only lip service to her wish that her husband would stop spoiling Morton. For her the "moral play" she was staging was one of retribution which both her overindulgent husband (her parents) and her delinquent son (her brother) deserved.

As already indicated, Mr. F.'s experience with dual therapy very quickly brought about clarification of his identity. He desisted from the projection of his own suicidal impulses on his son, i.e. lost his fear that Morton would kill himself if Mr. F. did not bail him out. This gave him courage to face up and put an end to Morton's exploitative and destructive behavior. Such a development was markedly accelerated by Mrs. F.'s acceptance of a brief period of dual therapy, which soon made her aware of how much she had contributed to her son's delinquency by confusing him with her brother.

LIP SERVICE TO PROPRIETY
or
"Otherwise father might misunderstand"

"I have to buy a knife, I have to buy a knife." By repeating these words over and over, Paul, as his mother disclosed to her social worker, was driving his father crazy. Paul was diagnosed to be psychotic and barely escaped being hospitalized. Here are two fragments of his nightmarish dreams: "A devil appeared over my bed. The devil was all red and he put some kind of a bag over my mouth which I felt was filled with ether. Slowly the devil began to fade and change into a woman with an oriental look on her face. . . . A little man stood on the top of a tremendous tree with spreading branches. This little man reached down with very long hands and picked up people and ate them. Sometimes it seemed to me that it was not the long hand but the tongue of the man on the top of the tree which he used to pick up people." In dual therapy we learned about his background (1966, p. 259). Paul would constantly provoke his father, who would beat him mercilessly. At one time he almost smothered his son with a pillow. These incidents occurred mostly on weekends, as father was away during the whole week at work in a neighboring town. For this very reason Paul was practically raised only by his mother, a typical variation of the "genetic disbalance."

To have mother all for himself was, however, no blessing for Paul. When he was small, mother also would not spare the rod. She would beat him when he soiled (toilet training started at six months). She would also beat him later on when he started to masturbate. And, finally she would beat him to cure him from his tics. "I used the strap and, believe me, it helped. He stopped those twitches." Shortly thereafter, however, he began to suffer from nightmares. "Recently I saw a dirty butcher running after me with a knife in his hand." (The butcher probably had the very knife which Paul wanted to have and with which he indirectly threatened his father.) He always used vile language with his mother. This was to be expected, since she would frequently expose herself to her son in a state of advanced dishabille. Naturally he would ask her detailed questions pertaining to sexual matters, to which she would react by saying, "Go find yourself another woman," but only after she and her son had engaged for some time in mutual verbal exhibitionism. Hearing her husband return home, she would chase Paul out of the bedroom saying that "otherwise father might misunderstand." It never occurred to this mother that she could share the task of raising Paul with her husband, possibly without the beatings. She should also not have allowed Paul to "drive his father crazy" by his implicit threats. In the first place, however, she should not have had secrets with her son behind her husband's back, nor have been exhibitionistic and seductive with Paul. But the "excluded" father in this case was also typically one who, in *his* script, assigned his son the role of having the oedipal triumph. By maintaining a typical dyad of *negative* type with his son and removing himself from his role as a father, he condemned himself unconsciously to punishment for the brinkmanship of "incest via proxy." Hence he was incapable of firmly putting an end to his son's menaces. The issue of *buying a knife* was indeed the point of confluence of both his own and his son's *castration impulses and fears* (Flescher, 1955, p. 434).

PROXY–RIVALRY DEFENSE
or
"Your letter broke my heart"

With these words, a mother pleaded in a letter to her ten-year-old son Ronald that he should not write to her any more about his unhappiness and longing for home. Ronald, her second son, was away at camp for the first time. Her husband was frequently and for long stretches absent from home. This fitted in with her own childhood history. At the age of two, she had lost her father; consequently her tie to her mother became particularly strong, as the surviving parent usually plays the role of both mother and father. The attachment to her own emotionally overinvested mother and her own separation anxiety were at the root of her "suggestive" empathy which made it so difficult for Ronald to separate from her.

In classical analysis a patient most frequently develops a transference-countertransference bind with his analyst precisely because in this setting the latter plays, admittedly and inevitably, the role of both father and mother. Especially for those who never were able to master their separation anxiety because of their mother's identical fear, traditional analysis presents a veritable dead-end street.

Ronald's mother had the habit of writing *daily letters* to her own mother even after she herself was a mother of three. We do not know the contents of the letters but what prompted her to write them was very likely the same longing and anxiety which accounted for the emotional turmoil unleashed in her by the letters of her son. She should have told Ronald that she was confident that he would enjoy being in camp, as most boys do: instead, her "don't break my heart" reaction promoted in her son the same dependency (on a mother) which she herself had not outgrown. How much she contributed to her husband's long absences from home was not established, but her son somehow ended up by having as little of his father as she had had of hers.

Ronald's father, in his turn, was writing a "script" no less inspired by his own childhood than was that of Ronald's mother. He also had had no close relationship with his father and therefore did not give much thought to the fact that his sons rarely saw him. It did not occur to him to find out why Ronald was constantly attacked by his older brother. He was unaware that the constant clashes between the two sons tried, among other aims, to attract his attention to their need for him. Ronald recalled in dual therapy how frustrated he was when mother would ignore his pleading that she enlist father's help against his physically abusive older brother and the "cruel" nurse, ultimately hired to discipline the boys.

As this case, because of the intricate and also intertwining roles assigned to the patient by each of his parents, was the one from which I learned the most about the dynamics of the genetic triad, I shall go into somewhat greater detail about it.

The mother saw in Ronald's expressed need for the company of his father a rejection of herself as a woman. On this point she was very vulnerable because she had lost her father at the age of two, when her femininity could at best barely have started to bring rewards from a loving and admiring father. (We recall how the availability of an opposite-sex parent during the oedipal phase is essential for the clarification of the child's sexual identity.) The lack of this developmental stimulant accounted for a distorted oedipal constellation in Ronald's mother. Living with her mother alone, she was forced to draw mostly from an inverted oedipal complex. The wish to be a male, prevailing in the phallic stage of the girl's psychosexual development, became entrenched in her because there was no male for whom she would be willing to surrender her masculine aspirations. As is usually the case, along with her phallic aspiration she must also have harbored strong feelings of inadequacy because she was "only a woman." This must have added a new component to her fear of losing Ronald, lest he "prefer the male," his father. On yet another level, the separation from her son was dreaded because he was her "phallic extension," that is, used in order to (unconsciously) masculinize her body image.

To his mother's overriding fears of separating from her son, Ronald for his part reacted with marked castration anxiety; for him to separate from anybody (on the deepest level always his mother) was not only a re-experience of the anaclitic (dependency) separation trauma, but also like a separation from a part of his body, actually a very important one (penis). In addition, this mother assigned to him the role, through "projective identification," of herself. By not doing anything to bring Ronald closer to her husband, she succeeded in recreating in Ronald's life a situation almost identical to the one prevailing in her own childhood: she ended up, as we mentioned, by playing the role of both mother and father to her child, as her own mother had played to her.

In the letter to his mother, referred to earlier, Ronald complained about something else: the boys in the camp were "ganging up on him." This had a very important antecedent in his older brother's punitiveness towards him. Both parents were remarkably ineffective in putting an end to the constant fights between their two sons. In addition to the quest for father's attention, another motive has to be considered here: the patient's older brother resented Ronald, who was preferred by his mother because of his quiet and more tractable behavior. For the same reason (jealousy), the father did not mind his older son's violence toward Ronald. In other words, the older son had become the tool of punishment in the "moral play" (specifically the oedipal tragedy) which this father was making Ronald enact for him. In this the father was repeating an extremely frustrating constellation from his own early life: his father had been closer to his older brother than to himself; and now he was having a better relationship with Ronald's older brother than with Ronald. There was, however, an important correction in the situation repeated from childhood: this time *he was the frustrator, and not the frustrated.*

The older son, having been closer to the father when he was at home, modelled himself after him and ended up by entering his father's professional life. Ronald instead implemented the mother's artistic aspirations.

The negative dyad prevailing between the patient's father and the patient was determined and maintained, as is the rule, by the genetic past of *each* parent. The psychological burden of this constellation in Ronald was aggravated when a third child was born. Being a girl, she was used by the mother for the recreation of a mother-daughter relationship as a substitute gratification of her own dependency needs. As a result of this Ronald experienced the trauma of a sudden emotional loss of his mother. Moreover, the latter was depressed in coincidence with her own mother's sudden illness. The clashes between the brothers became more frequent and more violent. A governess (the "cruel" one) had to be hired as a disciplinarian to safeguard the mother's need for rest and quiet by putting an end to the boys' fighting. This governess became the (displaced) object of Ronald's preoedipal aggression against his mother. In addition, as her presence actually made mother more inaccessible, she became also the object of displacement for Ronald's oedipal hostility against his father. It was ultimately the figure of this both hated and feared governess which came to loom over every relationship of the patient with women. It was also she who was central to the patient's obsessional sadistic fantasies of subjugating and torturing women.

In therapy the patient again and again came back to the situation in which he pleadingly asked his mother to persuade father to protect him against his brother and the punitive nurse; not only was mother evasive, but—an omission to which the triadic principle constantly alerts the dual therapist—she also did not care to bring Ronald and his father together to discuss this matter. (We recall what accounted for her fears of losing Ronald to her husband.) The father equally did not mobilize himself to have contact with his son except on one occasion, which remained deeply impressed in Ronald's memory: his father in an effort to make him desist from fighting said, "You boys make too much noise. Don't you love your mother?" The patient did not recall what he answered, but only that in that moment he was prey to extreme anger and despair without knowing why. And indeed how could he possibly know that his father by his remark and question had failed him again? In that communication, Ronald's parent betrayed anew his total surrender of his role as a father, inherent in his negative dyadic tie with Ronald. Instead of appealing to Ronald's love for mother (fraught, as we know, with intense ambivalence) he should have said, "I expect you to show consideration for your mother's condition. I know that you miss her[5] and I intend to give you more of my time as I should have done in the past." But he could not say this,

---

5. We know by now that extreme dependency and separation anxiety are based on marked ambivalence rather than on love (Flescher, 1955, p. 430).

convinced as he was (from his own unrelinquished oedipal position and his lack of closeness with his own father) that a son loves only his mother and has no need for a father. Ronald therefore had to depend on his mother alone to fulfill his needs for both parents. In this situation, could any sense of independence and self-assurance develop in him? How could he adjust to any separation? The patient wanted later in his life to be a writer. Though he had on more than one occasion shown himself to be gifted, he could not realize his aspiration: whenever he started to write he would be overcome by a mood of utter loneliness and despondency. We discovered in therapy the reason for this. He could not enjoy and excel in something which was hateful to him because it had taken mother away from him when she was daily writing long letters to grandmother.

Now a few words about the patient's sexual identity. As mentioned, when his sister was born the patient was suddenly jarred out of the role which his mother had assigned to him, both as her masculine extension and as one who helped her to implement her fantasy of the always available mother. With the arrival of his sister the positive dyadic tie between Ronald and his mother was not given up, but went underground. As the mother was no longer available, Ronald absorbed (introjected) her into himself, acquiring a distorted sexual identity. Henceforth he perceived every male, beginning with his father, as a source of potential danger of sexual attack. In this anticipatory fantasy he equated himself with the (introjected) mother and at the same time projected on every male his oedipal wish (toward his mother) coached in sadistic terms, under the influence of intense frustration aggression. This was the overriding reason why he could not *by himself* go to his father and communicate with him. For such a step he needed mother's reassurance, and it was precisely of this that Ronald's mother was incapable. Thus her own anxiety about Ronald's separating from her and becoming close to his father only exacerbated her son's anxiety.

Regarding the question of why Ronald harbored sadistic

impulses directed against his mother, we simply have to recall that every positive dyad, by its restrictive nature, i.e. the
violation of the triadic principle, promotes mutual hatred in
both parties to the dyad. The opportunity Ronald had to project his sadism onto a woman, the "Prussian-type" governess,
was only ephemeral because she was dismissed a few months
after the birth of his sister. Not long afterwards, Ronald's
mother left home to assist her own mother in her illness. (She
had suffered an incapacitating stroke.) The depressive reaction of the daughter to this became chronic and was further
aggravated by her new pregnancy after she returned to her
family. Evidently her husband and children could not compensate for the emotional loss of her mother, who had stood
for both her parents, and the burden of a third pregnancy.
Indeed, after her mother died she herself suffered a stroke.
A second stroke, when Ronald was in his early teens crippled
her both physically and mentally. She died a few years later
from a cardiovascular complication.[6]

But in Ronald's unconscious introjection of his mother
determined still another change of direction of his hatred and
sadism against her, subsequently displaced onto the governess
and then in sadistic fantasies against women in general: he
ended up by deflecting it from objects of the external world
and turning it against himself. Actually we discovered in dual
therapy that the fights with his brother, in which he was always the loser, were often unmistakably caused by Ronald's
own provocation. The anticipatory anxieties about homosexual
and sadistic attack found their dynamic antecedents here.
Ultimately Ronald dispensed with using others in reality or
in fantasy to attack the introjected mother in himself. He instead implemented this impulse more directly in a suicidal at-

6. This and many similar cases studied in the setting of genetic psychoanalysis makes it appear likely that people often do not die prematurely
simply from one physical disease or another, but from bitterness, exasperation and *mortification*. (Does etymology teach us something here?) These
feelings are always traceable to the genetic scripts of those who die and
those who unknowingly help to cause their death. (See also note on
p. 154.)

tempt. The peculiar device he employed betrayed clearly that, as so often happens, the birth of the younger sister was the situation onto which his unconscious telescoped all his frustrations. It was this self-destructive act which brought him into contact with psychiatrists and later with analysts.

What did the triadic setting of dual analysis two decades later offer this patient? I shall mention only a few of the more outstanding "corrective" experiences. In the first place, within the transference he experienced the female therapist as a person who, contrary to his mother, was not threatened by his having contact with a male. At the same time, she helped him overcome the anxieties rooted in his "wishful" fears of homosexual attack. In addition, the availability of the male therapist in the analytic situation made amends for the physical and emotional separation from his father and promoted the identification with a masculine model. The evidence of the collaboration between the members of the dual team undid the repercussions of his awareness of the basic lack of communication between his parents. The signs of therapeutic progress were soon forthcoming: the violent outbursts of temper by which the patient attempted to disperse his anxiety attacks ("anxiety-relieving aggression"), and which appeared typically at the end of the traditional sessions (he had two overextended classical analyses before he came to me), disappeared very early in the dual setting. His relationship with women became more trusting and more meaningful. Ultimately he engaged in a deep emotional and physical relationship with a woman to whom he expressed—what he thought he would never be capable of—his love, and for the first time in his life he seriously entertained the thought of marriage. A psychosomatic (cardio-vascular) condition akin to the one which truncated the life of his mother and some years later also that of his father, and which might therefore be considered "inherited," ceased to be a cause for medical concern. He became most successful in his artistic pursuits when the influence of his mother on him in this direction was freed from the (oedipal) guilt feelings.

DEMONSTRATION LESSONS
or
"I would have protected my mother but. . . ."

Mr. T. had the habit, in the presence of his son Red, of putting his hand under his wife's skirt. Red would certainly have liked to "protect" his mother, or express his anger at his father's impropriety, but for one greatly disturbing detail: his mother, to whom he usually referred as the most "straitlaced" woman, laughed each time his father did this. At first it seemed that Mr. T. wanted to impress upon his son how "free" a man should be with his wife, or at least how "free" *he* was. But then Red recalled that his father was also free with other women. "My mother would cry but she could not do anything about it." However, Mrs. T. was more successful in handling her husband's involvement with male friends. "Dad had peculiar friends, drifters, bums and drunks. My mother did not tolerate this. One day she asked me to throw one out of our house. He was a drunkard whom father had hired to help around the house. I of course did what mother asked. I saw for myself that this friend of my father's was a no-good bum. I made him leave." Because Red had been put in such a position, almost as if he and not his father were the head of the household, one might have expected that he would grow up to be a most self-assured and manly adult. Instead Red grew up into a frightened youngster, with his fears centering on the conviction that his penis was too small.

> Any conspiracy of a mother with her son against the authority of the father exacts a most disastrous toll from the son. The participation of the latter in the act of emasculating his father lays foundation to unconquerable castration anxiety in the son, which accords with the dualistic view of anxiety in general (Flescher, 1955, p. 434).

Red's father carried his sexual license so far as to even have an affair with his wife's sister who was living with them.[7] Mrs. T.'s manifest distress on this account did not disturb the adulterer. However, for her own undisclosed reasons, Mrs. T., "straitlaced" and so effective in arranging with her son to get rid of father's friends, was peculiarly accommodating with her sister. She was not morally aroused enough to want to get rid of this sister, even after the latter in tears confessed to her that she could not effectively defend herself against her brother-in-law's amorous pursuits.

With all these "demonstrations" of the adults' "sexual freedom," Red grew up suffering, as hinted, from sexual preoccupations which after he reached adulthood gave way to a serious restriction of his sexual potency. He could only rarely avoid failure and then, significantly, only when certain peculiar conditions were met, one of which was that he make love in an extremely risky situation. He could feel manly enough only if there was a strong likelihood that others would catch him in the act. In other words, his intended exhibitionism mirrored the painful childhood experience of seeing how his mother enjoyed father's physical attentions in complete disregard for Red's presence and in sharp contrast with her vaunted sense of propriety.

We still have not answered the question of why Mr. T. allowed his wife to assign the function of the head of the family to Red in the above incident with father's friend. The most plausible answer, based on experience with a great number of "genetic" scripts, is that he used Red to deny his own oedipal defeat and to transgress the oedipal taboo: he assigned his son the role of Mr. T.'s own father. Thus the liberties which Mr. T. took with his wife in the presence of his son were based on the unconscious fantasy of his taking liberties with his own mother in the presence of his father. In this way Mr. T. probably reversed the situation to which he himself had been exposed when witnessing the "primal scene" in

---

7. I have seen too many exceptions to Freud's contention that whoever is bold in sexual matters is automatically bold in all others. Sexual "boldness" may very well be *anxiety-denying exhibitionism* as it is often present in people who are in other areas most insecure and fearful.

his own childhood. His affair with his sister-in-law was only another expression of his unwillingness to surrender the incestuous position. The inevitable guilt from such acting-out of the oedipal strivings was the reason why he did not demur when Red, though barely in his teens, deprived his father of the company of a friend. The same guilt feelings explain why Red's father could have as friends only derelicts of society. He identified with them and they could not possibly censure him.

MOTHER'S CURSE
or
"He lived only for his son"

Mr. K. would do anything for his son Edward who, as we soon shall see, badly needed this devotion. Edward, in his late thirties, was sent to me by a colleague for dual therapy because he was suffering from most rampant hallucinations. They began one day when he heard a neighbor calling him a "woman-hater." Edward found such an accusation unjustified because the only woman whom he admittedly hated was his mother. Mrs. K. had been throughout his childhood the strictest and most exacting tutor when she helped her son with his homework. She also, as Edward maintained, "distrusted and hated everybody." I later saw this description to be true. In this she was strikingly dissimilar from Edward's father, who liked people and was liked in return, helpful toward everybody and, as mentioned, especially toward his son. Mrs. K., on the other hand, did not conceal from anyone willing to listen that her son came as a sort of curse into her life. This was so from the very moment she conceived him. The doctors had cautioned her against carrying her pregnancy to its termination because it would endanger her life: she had a serious heart condition. She had, however, found other doctors who were less pessimistic, and she had refrained from having an abortion. Still, she bewailed the fact that she had paid dearly for this by being exposed to an endless sequence of illnesses and accidents of Edward's. Besides many children's diseases and complicating infections, he broke his legs and arms three times.

Her hostility toward her son is traceable, as it always is, to her own life history. At a very young age, she herself had lost her father. As her mother had to go to work, she was, when barely nine, put in charge of her "mischievous" younger brother and her sister. She recalled how she had to stand on a stool to *cook* for them. At the death of her brother during the Second World War, she recalled having had a vision at the beginning of the war in which she saw him "lying dead on a couch near the dining table." It was typical of her to constantly belabor how she hated *cooking* for both her husband and her son. Evidently, in her experiencing Edward as a calamity visited upon her, she was using the familiar mechanism of displacement of hostility from a sibling to her son. Edward on his side could not avoid responding with extreme hostility to this rejection by the first woman in his life. The accident-proneness as well as his psychosomatic vulnerability in childhood was most likely an expression of self-directed aggression from this source (attack against the maternal introject).

For acceptance and warmth, Edward had to fall back on the doting father, who seemingly was willing to substitute for his wife and to give his son all he needed. Was he then not an ideal father? Not if we consider the triadic principle of maturation. When Mrs. K. during one of Edward's convalescent phases showed a growing disinclination to visit him, and even refused to go to the phone when he called his parents, she seemed justified: Edward never showed her any respect.

He even openly berated his father for "living with that terrible woman" and ridiculed him for allowing himself to be dominated by her. His father, instead of talking it out with his son and bringing Edward and his mother together, only increased his devotion and helpfulness toward his son. For example, though already in his fifties, he did not mind changing the tire on Edward's car, and even found it entirely natural to mend his son's pants in spite of the fact that both parents were well off and Edward could easily have afforded to buy new pants. Evidently Mr. K. wanted his son to find in him the more loving parent. The motive for this was typical: an oedipally determined jealousy which made him dread facing the possibility that his wife might prefer Edward to him. This jealousy was exacerbated by what he had observed since he married: did not his wife place the infant's life before her own life, and therefore before her love for her husband? (That it was actually the guilt feelings over her death wishes against her mother and brother which compelled her to go through with her life-endangering pregnancy was naturally not known to him.)

By failing to mediate between his wife and son, and by offering himself to Edward as an exclusive love object, Mr. K. laid foundation to an unmanageable (inverted) oedipus complex in his son. Edward's persecutory psychosis therefore had two roots, one deriving from the open hostility of his mother, the other from the more hidden hostility of his father. The task of bringing such a mother and son together in therapy was not impossible.

Unconscious guilt feelings and anxieties of the parties to a dyad make them open to a conciliatory and pacifying intervention of a third person, the therapist. Such family constellations, although certainly less destructive than in this case, are extremely frequent. The promotion of the maturational influence of a triad through the mentioned type of intervention is the pre-eminent function of each member of the dual team.

The subsequent development of this case, which included dual therapy of both mother and son, has been presented previously (1966, p. 410ff.).

PROPRIETY BY PROXY
or
"I wanted her to grow up a lady"

This, Frances' father, an inveterate gambler and drinker, would reiterate when explaining why he beat his daughter, accusing her of promiscuity when she had barely reached the age of puberty. He did this on a sort of "preventive" basis: he wanted her to stay away from men. Initially it seemed that he was simply acting out oedipal possessiveness and jealousy. Yet when he himself revealed very early (to his female therapist) that his wife was "too lady-like," his make-up began to appear more complicated than it had seemed at first sight. Not only would he describe to Frances in detail just what he wanted her to avoid, but he would call on witnesses to prove to his daughter how horrible was the destiny of licentious girls. Thus he would take his adolescent daughter into bars and urge toothless old prostitutes to tell her what miserable lives they were leading. Somehow these forewarning demonstrations brought about results diametrically opposite to those at which this father was allegedly aiming. That his constant preaching on the dangers of vice was a cover-up for his own attraction to it appeared even more clearly when the earliest reason for his physical abuse of Frances became evident. He confused her unconsciously with his younger sister, whom he also frequently used to beat, once even after she was married.

The explanation for beating his sister emerged from a memory of the time when he hoboed across the country with a friend: he had been shocked at the sight of a white woman nursing a black child. Somehow this reaction was isolated from the rest of his very liberal attitude toward Negroes. He displayed a great sense of justice and fairmindedness and was vehemently critical of those who opposed racial equality. Actually he promoted the same attitude in Frances, only to discover that when she became promiscuous she went further than non-discrimination: she was strongly attracted to Negro men. This again severely taxed father's bent toward integration. Ultimately the deepest motive for his fear that Frances might become promiscuous was traced to his own latent homosexuality. While talking about his having been as a young man always compelled to outdrink Irish sailors, he mused about his so often having had to fight off propositions and physical advances from his drinking companions. In other words, the shock he suffered at seeing a black child being nursed by a white woman was a screen memory for his objection to his mother's nursing his younger sister. In that situation he introjected both his frustrating mother and the rival sister, acquiring a trans-sexual (female) identity. His beating his sister does not need to be explained, although his doing so even after her marriage was probably due to unconscious envy because she could be loved by a man without being a pervert. The "preventive" beating of his daughter had instead a defensive function, that of projecting onto her his own wish to be loved by a man. The fact that she became promiscuous showed that he finally managed to "objectivate" in her (see p. 61) his own wish to be loved by men: he conjured up the ghosts through the very act of exorcising them.

The history of the oral phase of this father determined his expectation that men should give him what his mother did not (see also illustration, p. 203). This accounted for the deep impression left on him (around puberty) by a young man's lending him some change and thus making it possible for him to win his first card game. It was following this that he developed the gambling and drinking habits through which he years later exposed his family to chronic economic hardship. The foremost consequence of this was that his wife had to work and therefore could not attend to their daughter's needs. But here Frances' father was more than willing to substitute for his wife. Indeed, during her absences he would take complete care of Frances, change her, bathe her and so forth. Evidently he preferred, as not a few fathers do (especially in the United States), to play the role of a mother, because he could not stand the sight of his wife doing something for Frances: it activated his anger against his own mother taking care of his younger sister. We shall not go into the many other elements of this man's genetic history which explain why his violation of the triadic principle had to take the form it did (1966, pp. 283, 526).

BELATED REVENGE
or
"He tortures and humiliates me. It kills me."

Herman, according to his mother Mrs. P., does not go to school, sometimes for weeks at a time. "Even when he does, he arrives at his classes hours late. At home, he always interferes with whatever I am doing. He orders me around, as if I were his servant. When I get angry and yell at him, he laughs in my face. It *kills* me. Coming home, instead of greeting me he throws his overcoat over my head." Herman, in short, makes this mother's life miserable, which always reminds her of her unhappy childhood. When she was barely five, she and her younger brother lost both parents. She was deeply *humiliated* then by relatives and strangers alike who had to take her in.

All these complaints she brought forth in her first interview with me. She did not so much as mention her husband. Evidently only she and Herman mattered. However, the superfluous third party, her husband, had somebody to fall back on. Mrs. P. continued thus her tale of woe: "Why does my daughter turn against me too and then pretend to be upset when I am in the hospital?" (Mrs. P. suffered from chronic colitis among many other physical ills.) Confronted with her failure to mention her husband, she said that they both (husband and daughter) understand each other better. "I seem not to exist for them." Apparently here *she* was the excluded third party.[8] Later it became clear that the daughter incited her brother against their mother. Evidently for the daughter the closeness with father was not a sufficient compensation for the involvement, sado-masochistic though it was, of her mother with her brother: she used the latter as a proxy to fight with her mother, thus contributing greatly to the persistence of the dyad prevailing between Mrs. P. and her son.

After Mrs. P. became an orphan, she had to share with her younger brother the little which the charity of relatives provided. He was the only one whom she could safely hate without fearing retaliation, because she was so utterly dependent on the adults in her life. The "abandonment" by the mother was the most painful loss she had suffered. To hurt, to attack and even to kill her mother was therefore her deepest (repressed) wish. Hence she could only complain, "Herman is *killing* me." Indeed, when asked why she did not seek the intervention of her husband, she typically answered: "He wanted to say something to Herman, but I told him to stay out of it because I knew things would only get worse." By preventing her husband's disciplinary action, she made sure that Herman could go on "killing her" as she had wanted to

---

8. This case could therefore be used for the illustration of the "play of divided camps," based on a quite frequent combination of two dyadic alliances within a family.

kill her own mother. The need to introject her mother for abandoning her (the unconscious, we recall, governed only by the pleasure principle, reacts even to a parent's death as wishful abandonment) provided the core motive of the sado-masochistic dyad with her son. In other words, she used her son for the "introject attacked by proxy" defense.

Actually, this patient had in the past attempted something similar with her older son who also "constantly defied and provoked" her. However, in contrast to Herman, who suffered from agoraphobic symptoms and almost never would leave her, the older son would frequently run away from home to escape fighting with his mother. (He probably could not take the hostility of his mother, aggravated by his conviction that she "preferred" Herman.) When the older son was killed while driving a car with "defective" brakes, Mrs. P. blamed herself for having caused his death by chasing him away from her: she was too stern and punitive with him. The guilt feelings about the loss of her older son played an important role in her masochism toward Herman, for whom she wanted to be an "always available mother." She feared (again "wishful fear") that he would end up by being killed like his brother if she did not watch him constantly. The sado-masochistic dyad of this mother was based on unconscious guilt feelings about her death wishes against her mother (herself) and brother (her sons). The price for her genetic script was the death of her first son and the schizophrenic condition of Herman. The latter was helped by providing him and his mother with dual therapy. Her daughter also benefitted from it greatly (1966, p. 369).

DIVIDE AND RULE THROUGH GENEROSITY
or
"He wanted me to have nice clothes"

Laura was father's pet, at least insofar as catering to her extravagant need for expensive dresses, hats, shoes and other accessories was concerned. By contrast, her mother would constantly curse her and whip her with a belt for squandering so much money on her wardrobe. What enraged this mother especially was that, against her expressed wish, her husband would behind her back give large sums to Laura, who, confusing generosity with real affection, adored her father. He even created a job for the "poor fellow" whom Laura finally married. The latter turned out to be a "good-for-nothing" who betrayed Laura with other women almost immediately after the wedding.

What became clear in dual therapy was that father's generosity had the unavowed purpose of maintaining the feud between wife and daughter. He himself had many brothers but only one sister, near in age, who had been the "apple of (his) mother's eye." For him any closeness between wife and daughter would activate memories of his childhood when he deeply resented his sister. After the birth of a daughter (three sons preceded her) he made sure that this time he would not be the excluded party. Moreover, in opposing his wife he punished his mother for preferring her daughter to her sons. It was no wonder that Laura could not answer when asked: "If life with your mother was such a hell and father knew about it, why did you not stop defying your mother and why did father continue to do exactly what mother so deeply resented?"

As is so often the case, Laura's mother also had a hand in this unfortunate state of affairs, created by the overlapping of two dyads with different dynamics, the sado-masochistic one between mother and daughter, and the one of "divide and rule" type between husband and daughter. She somehow failed to communicate directly with her husband, to try to show him how destructive his pattern was both to their marriage and to the upbringing of their daughter. The mother's genetic script was again the typical "oedipal triumph by proxy": the daughter was to succeed in separating father from mother and have him for herself. This, as we have seen always to be the case, allowed her then to hate her daughter for her collusion with her father, which she, the mother, actually promoted. In Laura, this mother could also hate her own mother for having come between her and her father. Indeed when her husband became involved with another woman, whom he ultimately married, the mother accused Laura of having brought him and this woman together.

Evidently the ghosts which this mother had conjured up from her own past had gotten out of hand. She spent the rest of her life at a clinic in a state of chronic mental confusion, while Laura developed, besides severe character difficulties, a tendency toward episodes of deep depression with suicidal impulses. In a conjoint session with Laura and her father, the latter's (until then well-hidden) ambivalence toward his daughter came through clearly: "All in all, I think that Laura exaggerates about her fights with her mother. To tell the truth, I was not even aware that the two were fighting." That his wife suffered recurrent breakdowns following terrible clashes with their daughter allegedly had escaped him completely.

Dual therapy succeeded in lessening Laura's guilt feelings toward her mother in bringing about a reconciliation during the latter's terminal illness. It achieved this simply because the setting and the cross-recorded communication prevented the creation of destructive dyadic alliances between Laura and her parental substitutes (1966, p. 121).

CONDONING UNDERSTANDING
or
"I told her that her brother is not her husband"

This is what the mother told her daughter Wanda after she and her brother had pushed their feet at each other under the table until an open fight broke out between them. It reminded her that she had said the same things on another occasion when she found her daughter and her son under one blanket. She must, however, have made that remark rather half-heartedly, because she commented to her therapist: "Actually they were lying foot to foot." When I observed that the couch must have been pretty long to accommodate two adolescents foot to foot, she acknowledged that there might have been some reciprocal touching of intimate parts with the feet. She then recalled that Wanda had had the habit of crawling into the crib of her younger brother, "but then she was only a child." Mother's "condoning understanding" of Wanda was grounded in her own childhood: she didn't feel entitled to prevent such a "habit" from taking root in her daughter because she herself had been seduced by her slightly older brother, a fact which she kept secret from her mother.

Wanda constantly defied her mother, who would retaliate with severe beatings which her daughter seemed on the surface to bear stoically. In reality, she also "punished" her mother, who preferred her *brother,* by turning her anger against herself. Her tendency to break legs, injure her kneecap, tear ligaments in her ankles and so on, however, not only was an attack against her (maternal) introject but also took care of her guilt feelings about her sexual play with her brother, in which pushing and kicking with her feet played a predominant role.

But the mother alone was not to blame. The "absenteeism" of the father, who could have observed what went on between Wanda and her brother on many other occasions, was traceable to his own genetic background. He himself had a very complicated relationship with his *sister,* the discussion of which in therapy elicited particularly strong emotional reactions on his part. Even as a father of two children, he was still smarting with resentment because of his mother's preference of his sister.

This father's non-intervention was (as in the case of Laura) his way of making sure that his frustrating childhood constellation did not repeat itself in his own marriage. Both parents made the point that at one time or another they *did* *tell* their children to stop their "nonsense" and "horsing around," but only in dual therapy did they recognize that they really had not meant it. After that things began to change for the better. Wanda improved in her school work, graduated from high school and responsibly fulfilled a demanding job. Her relationship with peers of both sexes changed radically for the better. Her accident-proneness, however, which became eroticized into self-destructive masochism was the most difficult therapeutic problem. It was solved but only after her mother was able to make progress in dual therapy.

DISCRIMINATORY MATERNAL LOVE
or
"I started to suffer because my mother could not take it"

Clara, a mother in her thirties and a survivor of genocidal persecution, was depressed. She accused herself of constantly quarrelling with her husband. She would have taken her life long ago if it were not for her only son whom she felt she could not abandon. She did not want another child because as she said, she had nothing to offer as a mother. Clara had lost her father through illness at the age of three. Her mother and her two sisters were killed by the Nazis. Clara felt particularly guilty about the death of her younger sister because she had advised her to run out of the room when she saw two German soldiers approaching the house. Her sister was shot to death as was the family in whose house she took refuge. She herself did not leave the room immediately because somehow she felt that nothing would happen to her. (In reality Clara did not care whether she was killed, because even at that time she was acting upon her conviction that her mother loved only her younger sister, Sophia.) "My mother had to have her near all the time, because my father had died when Sophia was only a few months old. She always slept with my mother, they were very close. . . . *I always took care of myself,* I was independent all my life. I was a mean and rebellious child. I always knew how to answer back to my mother. She would say that being too smart would be my undoing. . . . My mother used to tell me that she didn't want me in the first place."

Then Clara described the encounter with her mother, whom she had been trying to find while they were hiding from the Nazis. "My mother had walked and walked until she was seven kilometers from the little town. I didn't know where she was. . . . When I found her, the first thing she did was start to cry. She asked where Sophia was. I told mother that I hadn't taken her along as it was dangerous and Jews were not allowed to leave the town. Mother didn't believe me. She said 'I don't like what I see; *you are too strong* to look like this.' I was always the strongest in the family. I heard my mother talking to me, but at the same time, I heard those screams in my head. . . ." (She had witnessed the day before the pleading and the screaming of women and children who were being shot in the next house by German soldiers.) ". . . Mother was sick and weak but she walked because she insisted on seeing Sophia. . . . I was thinking, 'why should it not have been me, why could it not be me? I should have been dead, not her.' (Pause) I didn't think that my mother cared much for me. . . . Finally we came back to the house. It was horrible, when my mother saw that my sister wasn't there and saw the big holes in the cemetery (mass graves of the murdered Jews). *Then I started to suffer because my mother couldn't take it."*

The genetic disbalance in this case was created not only by the early disappearance of the father but by the mother's compensatory dyadic symbiosis with her younger daughter: after the loss of her husband she made Sophia (through projective identification) into herself, and herself into an "always available mother." The only way in which Clara could cope with the loss of father *and* mother was to introject first the mother and then the father. His passing away had been preceded by clashes between her and her mother, whom she had openly defied. At the same time the normal turning of a girl from her mother toward her father (in the oedipal phase) was made more radical not only by the birth of a sibling but by the mother's greater involvement with the second child during the (terminal) illness of the father. The latter, for his own (undisclosed) reasons, was seemingly also unable to adjust to the third pregnancy of his wife and instead of forming a compensatory dyad with his older daughter, as often occurs in such a situation, he surrendered to his malady and let himself die (see pp. 150, 151).

Our patient's not wanting a second child in her own marriage was an attempt to correct the trauma of her sister's birth, aggravated by the loss of her father and rejection by her mother. Her guilt feelings about the violent death of her sisters, especially of the younger, followed by that of her mother underlay her depression with serious probability of suicide. Paradoxically, such an impulse was contained by the admitted concern over abandoning her son, whom she must have identified with her sister. In other words, the guilt feelings about Sophia's death made it difficult (though not impossible) to abandon her own son, whom she identified, as parents frequently do, with her younger sibling. The genetic disbalance in Clara's history could be corrected only by providing her with a clear-cut maternal figure in transference. Dual therapy brought about a striking improvement in her condition and, in the first place, the elimination of the danger of suicide (1966, p. 379).

PARENT REINCARNATED
or
"My father knew very important people"

Mrs. E.'s husband wanted everything on the dot. "He would get upset and honk the horn of the car if I was only a few minutes late." When Jack, their son, touched things in his father's laboratory, Mr. E. would completely lose control. He once almost choked Jack. Mr. E. was a typical victim of the mother's and the son's assigning him the role of cruel disciplinarian, constantly challenged by them. One day Jack came home from a ball game with father. His face was all swollen and he was crying: his ears had been boxed. Mr. E. had lost patience with his son's seemingly deliberate tardiness and uncooperative ways. This father's perception that Jack was acting upon an empathic "message" of his mother enraged him because the dyadic conspiracy between wife and son reopened most painfully in him old oedipal wounds. The occasional physical violence toward his son did not offer sufficient relief to his anger, constantly refueled by the evidence of Jack's defying him, with his mother condoning and supporting this. Death wishes against his son, displaced from an unresolved Oedipus complex, aggravated if not determined, Mr. E.'s heart condition. During a quarrel Jack told his father to drop dead; the father suffered a heart attack and died within a few hours.

Even before this occurred, Jack developed into a schizo-

phrenic youngster with many symptoms and character peculi-
arities. The most outstanding among the latter was his habit
of writing or telephoning prominent people in public life,
posing as an important person. He advanced his career in this
to the point of attracting the attention of the White House
Secret Service.

This pattern of Jack's was also shown to result from his
mother's "role assignment." When talking about her father,
she would always admiringly mention that he took pride in his
great influence in their home town because he was rubbing
elbows with local politicians. Her son was simply a reincarnated caricature of her father. It was this caricature, more
than her manifest admiration, which betrayed what she really
thought of her father, the braggart. How little this mother
wanted to put a stop to Jack's game of impostor is well illustrated by the following incident: One day it was discovered
that Jack, with a most serious demeanor, had sold to com-
muters some worthless pamphlets which had been freely dis-
tributed at the City Museum. On hearing this, the mother
berated the people for their stupidity in buying them. It did
not occur to her to censure her son for his deception.

PREFERRED GENDER
or
"My son simply was not a fighter"

Lenny was markedly retarded. "We gave him all the love
and attention besides the medical care which he needed. Betty
(his sister, three years older) could take care of herself. She
was normal. But then she began to imitate Lenny in the way he

walked and talked. She became sloppy and behaved and talked like a moron." Evidently Betty hoped in this way to divert the attention and care of her parents from Lenny. Though not only professional people but even close relatives saw through Betty's act, her mother, Mrs. R., continued to be very protective of her. Mr. R. complained: "I cannot open my mouth. If I want to tell Betty that she should at least wash her dirty hands or comb her hair, my wife shushes me up. How can Betty change if she sees that her mother does not allow me to teach her proper manners?" Admittedly the mother was overprotective of her daughter out of guilt feelings for having neglected her. There was, however, also on Mr. R.'s side some "half-heartedness" in his educational efforts. His inability to be firmer and more effective with his daughter was not entirely explained by his wife's overprotection of Betty. Some time ago Mr. R. had been hospitalized for ulcerative colitis, which he was told by the treating staff physician was aggravated by what went on at home. Indeed, he was cautioned that if he continued to allow himself to be upset by his family troubles, he would be running a serious physical risk.

In dual therapy it ultimately became evident that Mr. R. as a child was neglected by his parents, especially his mother, in favor of his two sisters. Their whims were indulged, while he and his brother had to go to work before they were ten. At one point a conjoint interview was arranged with Mr. R.'s mother, a widow who lost her husband and her older son from an identical illness: a heart attack. She was in general strikingly reluctant to go into her younger son's background and simply reiterated that she had the "best" family in the world and there was "nothing wrong with her children." Ultimately the following came to light: While the older son had been breast-fed for three months, the second son (Mr. R.), born a year after the first, was raised on a bottle because for unexplained reasons her milk was both "little and not good." Exploring the reason for such close pregnancies, this mother admitted that she had badly wanted a girl. After she was again disappointed, she tried once more for a daughter and became pregnant fourteen months later. This time it was indeed a daughter. "After this," she said, "I took it easy." After six years she had another daughter. She breastfed both daughters without any difficulty. "But as to my son," she volunteered, "believe me, Doctor, there was absolutely nothing wrong with him. *He simply was not a fighter.* When his sisters wanted something which he had, they simply took it from him. He had the habit of sort of giving in." That her preference for daughters had something to do with her son's constantly losing his battles with his sisters does not need proof. It was, therefore, not surprising that he had a total amnesia concerning the first ten years of his life.

It is more than likely that Mr. R. very early responded with frustration-aggression to his mother's rejection because his gender did not meet her expectations. His anger was aggravated by the trauma of the too close birth of a sister. He then turned the aggression against himself, as his father and brother must also have done, since they both died prematurely from a psychosomatic disorder involving an organ pre-eminently affected by emotions (the heart). The old saying about daughters living longer with their mothers assumed in this family a new meaning because of the pronounced physical vulnerability of the males.[9]

In a conjoint session, Mrs. R. accused her husband of preferring Lenny to Betty. "At least Lenny asks me how my day was on the job," was Mr. R.'s retort. The high degree of

---

9. It cannot be ruled out that Mr. R.'s ulcerative colitis may have had a more specific origin, as it affects the digestive system: his mother's nurturing propensities were certainly not deployed with him. The shorter life span of men in general as compared with that of women, is traditionally explained by some biological inferiority of the former, of undisclosed nature. On the basis of therapeutic experience with genetic psychoanalysis, this fact finds a much simpler explanation in the frequency of dyadic ties between mothers and daughters or mothers and sons, with ambivalence clearance toward males (fathers, brothers). In other words, the males in the family more frequently than not bear the brunt of the hostility prevailing in disbalanced genetic triads.

Lenny's mental retardation and his limited capacity to feel a deeper interest in anything points up the pathetic significance of this father's remark. He evidently married, as so frequently happens, a facsimile of his mother who did not care very much for males.

We understand now why Mr. R. was also "weak" with his wife and did not insist on his right to have a say in raising Betty. His professed wish to change his daughter and to make her more appealing was merely lip service. As long as his daughter was unacceptable to his wife, he was protected against the repetition of a most painful condition in his childhood: mother's discrimination against him and his brother. (We notice the frequency with which this constellation is repeated in our examples.)

His wife's contribution to Betty's refusal to give up being sloppy and copying her retarded brother in speech and manner was also too transparent to be overlooked: in sharpest contrast to her daughter, Mrs. R. was most carefully groomed and tastefully dressed, graceful in demeanor and highly articulate in speech. Evidently she did not wish to risk being outshone by Betty in the hidden but ever-present competition between mother and daughter. We refrain from going into the mother's childhood history which explains why she had to be particularly insecure in this area.

SON AS FATHER
or
"He was about to throw the toaster at my head"

Harold had left his home town to continue his studies else-where because he had rebelled against his teachers and con-stantly fought with his siblings and peers. After a short period of respite, the same pattern continued at his new college. He began to clash with his roommate in the dorm and with his counsellors. Ultimately he was expelled and had to return home. Hand in hand with this, he developed a psychosomatic condition suspected to be an ulcerative colitis, for which he had to undergo proctoscopy. He objected violently, insisting that it entailed indescribable pain. In view of this his psychia-trist felt that he could for the time being do without these examinations. Harold's mother was supposed to tell him of this reassuring decision, but somehow she was unable to do so: "I cannot understand why Harold blew his top when I tried to tell him that he does not have to go to the doctor to be examined. He screamed and carried on like a madman, saying that I should stay out of his therapy. Every time I opened my mouth," she continued, "to tell him that he did not have to worry about the test, he did not let me. At one point he lifted the toaster to throw it at my head. But this *didn't frighten me.*" Suddenly she broke into tears. A memory had come to her mind of how her irascible father used to chase her around the block, beating her. "Yet," she added, after she had stopped crying, "I somehow *didn't fear him.*" I then learned that her husband did not enter in all this because he did not get home until after midnight. Allegedly he never could finish his work in his office and had to do overtime. It turned out that she was unaware that her sado-masochistic relationship with her son was a faithful copy of the one with her father. The absence of her husband was a convenient (and self-abetted) condition of her life: it reproduced the non-intervention of her mother in the dyadic bind with her father. I shall forego the details of the background of her husband's negative dyad not only with Harold but with all the numerous children he sired, and the reasons why he preferred the appreciation of his bosses for his willingness to work late in his office to the "constant hell" at home.

Harold's conflict was rooted in regressive fantasies about his father of whose presence he was deprived. The fantasies were of enacting his (introjected) mother in the act of passive submission to the loving father. His enraged insistence on her not interfering in his contacts with doctors was a reflection of his unconscious accusation that his mother deprived him of the company of his father by keeping the latter away from home. Dual therapy helped him to separate from his family (he enrolled at a university abroad) but under psychic conditions entirely different from those in the past.

UNWILLING MOTHERHOOD
or
"Father would beat me daily"

Selma's mother was a talented musician who frequently gave concerts in schools and for charities. At home she was not very involved with her daughters. She left all their physical care to her husband, who was willing even to bathe them, "but not beyond puberty." Selma was bitter about the way he had discontinued bathing her when she began to menstruate. As he was deeply religious, she became "untouchable" to him.[10] "He cut himself off from me as if I were a leper or something," she said, lifting both hands in a gesture of repulsion. She succeeded, however, as we shall see, in forcing him to touch her after all. Selma became an irrepressible tomboy in accordance with the unconscious of her mother, who was admittedly deeply disappointed at not having had a boy. Her disappointment became more acute when after a few years still another daughter was born. Selma was put in charge of her younger sister, of whom she took devoted care, to the point of lying down with her every night at seven-thirty until she fell asleep. (Many years later when she was already married and a mother herself, at *exactly the same hour* she would disregard the presence of her husband and her daughter and give in to an apparently uncontrollable impulse to sleep. In her dreams she was sleeping with her mother, as she did when she played the role of mother toward her younger sister.)

The frequent absences of the mother from home and the seduction by the father resulted in the introjection of him: Selma became the "bully on the block," physically, sometimes even seriously, attacking other girls. She knew that her mother would dutifully report on her behavior to her father, who would without fail beat her mercilessly on the buttocks. This was how she still managed to make her father use his hands on her. This type of physical contact must also have been gratifying for him, because Selma did not recall that he had ever suggested they sit down with her mother and jointly discuss her misdemeanor. It seems almost unbelievable that neither parent wanted to understand why she accepted again

---

10. Orthodox Jews are not supposed to even so much as touch their wives for the two weeks encompassing their menstruation. In our case the menstrual taboo appears intimately linked with the incestuous taboo. The ritualized prohibition was most likely inspired by the ubiquitous *fear of menstruation* which also underlies not a few allegedly medical hygienic rules pertinent to this aspect of female physiology. The fear is rooted in the *castration complex* which we know acts as an incest barrier: the element "bleeding genital organs" accounts for the frequent (unconscious) confusion by both men and women of menstrual bleeding with castration.

and again the severe beatings of father, rather than change her behavior.

The genetic disbalance in this case was found principally in the dyadic tie which mother promoted between father and daughter, by her absence from home and by allowing Selma to be bathed by him. Stimulation through exposure to and being touched by father thus continued throughout the oedipal stage and the latency phase up to puberty. Then her mother made sure that this tie between husband and daughter would continue, albeit under the form of a sado-masochistic interaction, when she actively supported her husband's way of disciplining her daughter.

Selma's mother's self-elimination, rooted in the usual unconscious wish that a daughter should get rid of her rival and remain alone with father (oedipal triumph by proxy), was combined with strong masculine strivings. These, displayed in her behavior (leaving home while her husband attended the children) as well as in her writing of the "tomboy" script for her daughter, laid the earliest foundation to Selma's masochism. Its core was imbedded in (unconscious) fantasies of sadistic attack against women, especially of the bosomy type, who reminded Selma of her ungiving mother. Thus provoking her father into physically punishing her was also determined by the defense mechanism of "introject attacked by proxy." As an adult, when an operation on an enlarged thyroid and on ovarian cysts seemed to be necessary, Selma was panic-stricken at the thought of being examined by the gynecologist. She refused adamantly to go to him for a check-up. In analysis it emerged that she was projecting onto the doctor all her own sadistic fantasies. There was an antecedent to it: At the time when she was the "bully on the block," she had once, playing doctor with a girl, actually injured the "patient" by pushing a twig ("thermometer") into her rectum.[11]

11. All the interpretations given Selma in classical analysis did not succeed in freeing her from the terror of the doctor. As soon as the dual setup was introduced, she accepted not only the medical examination but also the necessary surgical intervention. This case was presented by me in a Study Group of the New York Psychoanalytic Institute (1966, p. 327).

The agoraphobia from which Selma suffered (among other phobias) was rooted in the original fear of separation from her mother. This is why, as already mentioned, she was such a devoted mother to her younger sister with whom she (projectively) identified herself. Selma's repressed anger of sibling rivalry against this very sister, was taken out on her peers (ambivalence clearance) in the manner described. In addition, after she became a mother, by sleeping early in the evening, Selma removed herself from her daughter. She did this also by sleeping late in the morning so that her daughter had to make herself breakfast before going to school.

The violation of the triadic principle by Selma's mother centered, as we have shown, on the oedipal complex which succeeded in asserting itself in the way described. But it was stated most directly in the reaction of this mother to her daughter's complaints about her unhappy marriage. She simply asked: "Why don't you leave your husband?" For obvious reasons such a suggestion from a mother can be very effective, and it was so in this case.

> Oedipal guilt, like so many paradoxical consequences of one and the same psychic conflict, can force a young couple in one case to comply with their parents' wish to separate them and in another to resist it successfully. However, in neither case is the outcome satisfactory. Similarly, the oral trauma can lead to unconquerable and life-endangering anorexia or to extreme obesity. The explanation lies in the fact that another contributory factor on a different psychic level may tip the scale on one side rather than on the other.

SACRIFICIAL MOTHER LOVE
or
"I would have cut off my fingers for my son"

This is how far Daniel's mother, Mrs. P., assured me she would have gone to make her son happy. She described him as a "sweet child" and said how incomprehensible it was to her that he had turned out to be a most seriously disturbed adolescent.

She was relating the accident her husband had suffered when Daniel was about eleven. "We were planning to go to a neighborhood movie. But my husband first had to go to the store to take care of something. When he didn't return I became angry. I thought he had changed his mind. So I went to the movies by myself. I know I should first have made sure why he did not come home. He was found hours later lying on the floor, bleeding heavily and unconscious. He had tried to fix something and had fallen from the chair, injuring his head on the radiator."

Mrs. P. described her husband as a cold person but sexually demanding. "As for myself," she added, "I could do very well without sex." He had high blood pressure, and not long after that accident suffered a serious stroke. "Daniel was very upset when my husband fell ill. I assured my son that we always would have something to live on. We had adequate insurance even if the worst were to happen. I don't understand it but this didn't seem to help, because Daniel became more and more morose and impatient with me. He moved away from me completely and spent hours with his father." She conceded that her husband was very hard-working and efficient. "What made me especially angry was that my husband would come home after work and bury himself behind the newspaper. He left the disciplining of the children who were constantly fighting, entirely to me. (– – –?) No, it would not have done any good to ask him to help me with the children. Anyway, he would not know how. (– – –?) No, I don't know why I didn't try him out."

The situation is a typical concomitant of dyadic constellations: the very mothers who resent their husbands' non-par-
ticipation in the raising of children actually never enlist their
help and quite frequently even *oppose such intervention* (see
p. 153). This paradox can be explained by all the factors
which bring about and maintain dyadic ties.

How external appearance may be misleading in this regard is shown by her amending her information: actually her
husband was not completely excluded from raising the children. "I would always tell them to ask their father also for
permission to go to a movie, but" she added with a twinkle
in her eyes, "I knew that he would say what I wanted."

She had told also her son that *for him she would cut her
fingers off*. His reaction to this token of maternal love was
reflected in his pathology and in his (regressed) associations.
Here is a sampling of his verbalizations revealing the aggravation by a mother of the oedipal conflict and of the castration
anxiety in her son. "The petting of my lips comes to my
mind, I mean touching them with my *fingers,* actually with
only one of my fingers. The first finger." Daniel feared very
much for the life of his parakeet. He said: "The last time
she (mother) told me she wished to scare the parakeet out
of its cage, I yelled at her. . . . Then she told me that she
would not take care of the bird any more." He would fight
against masturbation with the help of his "system." He would
think of five girls whom he knew and then "select one to have
the (sexual) fantasies about." He would do this by assigning
a girl to each *finger* on the left hand. Then he would count
fingers and knock out a finger with the corresponding girl
until only one remained. . . . He once cut his *thumb* while
having an argument with his mother. She didn't want to help
him. . . . "You remember I told you about the Goddess-
mother without a blemish. My mother used to be very good-
looking." He read an article about suicide and the importance
of feelings of rejection. "I don't think that I am schizophrenic;
perhaps I only want the unattainable. . . ." Pretty girls re-
mind him of his strolls with his Goddess-mother. When father

became sick, Daniel turned against his mother "because mother took over the role of father and this confused in my mind the identity of my mother." (!) When his mother told him that his father had died, his first thought was, "I am glad that there is one person less who knows about my masturbation. . . ." Daniel had the thought of dipping his *hand* into the blood of a frog, thinking, "that means I established dominance over my father by dipping my *hand* into the blood!" He felt elated when he dipped his *hand* into the frog's blood. . . . When he touched meat with his *finger*, he licked it. He was proud that he finally was able to do this. . . . "I told you about the time my mother mentioned menstruation to me and since then I could not stand blood."

Daniel in dual therapy had the opportunity in a conjoint session with his mother to hear from her again that she would sacrifice her fingers for him. By then he had recovered from his serious illness. In the next session he expressed his bewilderment about his mother's willingness to be a woman for him rather than for his father. (By now we know that such a bias is fatal to the development of a son.)

> In such a case what ultimately defeats the "oedipal triumph" of the son is the recognition that mother's statement was not necessarily a sure sign that she was irresistibly attracted to him. She simply, as is usually the case with seducers of children, felt more sure of herself with a son because with him she could always be in control. With children the adult seducer is less threatened because he can always put an end to the exciting situation; with an adult partner his pleasure depends on the degree of trust with which he is capable of surrendering himself to the shared experience.

Mother's stressing that Daniel was "sweet" probably had something to do with her having had no brother but only several sisters. This points to another layer of her son's fear for his masculine identity, in addition to his empathically perceiving her objection against father's maleness. Daniel's drastic removal of himself from his mother after his father's stroke was therefore as much due to guilt feelings about his oedipal dyad with his mother as to fear of his mother's hostility towards males in general.

I shall close this illustration with a reference to the response of both mother and son to my suggestion for a conjoint session. Both expressed in almost identical words their objection on the ground that they "would not feel comfortable." In the conviction that the dynamics of a dyadic bond quickly become comprehensible if both parties are exposed to a triadic setting, I overcame their opposition. That I was justified in doing so was proven by the deeper insight I received into the patient's genetic background. Daniel ultimately became a very successful member of his profession and a responsible father to his two children (Flescher, 1966, p. 286).

FEIGNED DISINTEREST
or
"Why don't you talk with me?"

A positive dyad between a parent and a child of oedipal nature is quite commonly concealed by a paradoxical incapacity to communicate. This was true with Ida and her father. "My mother's constant fighting with Herman (her younger brother) made it impossible for me to talk with my father. I always felt that father would be able to understand me better than mother. But whenever I felt like approaching him, he would wave me away. It was as if he feared me. I could not understand." That it was not disinterest but the opposite which accounted for this frustrating pattern, could not be grasped by the daughter, even when the father reproached her for entering therapy: "Why do you need this? Why don't you talk with me instead of that lady (the previous therapist in the traditional setting)?" Ida's misunderstanding of her father's attitude and the ease with which he succeeded in brushing her off were not unrelated to her own inhibition. This was ultimately traceable to her mother's feeling threatened by the possibility of closeness between her husband and her daughter. To make sure that father and daughter would stay apart, this mother constantly berated her husband and quarrelled with him. To Ida she presented her father as a "weakling" and a "Milquetoast." She would say again and again that she must have been blind when she married him. At other times she would explain her choice by saying that he was the only man available when she wanted to free herself from her family. The first sign of the positive influence of the female therapist's encouraging Ida to seek me out for inclusion in her therapy appeared in the first dream she had, while in this new setting. "A mouse suddenly jumped on my bed. Usually," she remarked, "such dreams frighten me but this time, I don't know why, I found that mouse cute." Ultimately the corrective effect of the triadic setting (the mother figure in transference was not threatened by Ida's involvement with the transferential father) allowed the patient in a surprisingly short time to make up her mind regarding whom to marry. Clearly, the unconscious fear of making the same error as her mother claimed to have made had been eliminated (Flescher, 1966, "Indication for Short-term Therapy," p. 369).

HONESTY AND FRANKNESS
or
"I had to confront my daughter with reality"

The "reality" which this father felt he ought to make his daughter face was that his wife would often lose her temper when nearing the menstrual period. On that occasion he would say to Tess, "You just have to take it, mother is out of sorts from time to time." It is evident that such an "honest and frank" communication put the daughter on the level of her parents and created the typical genetic imbalance which we have seen to be incompatible with the child's maturation.

Here I shall only mention the repercussions of this communication on the mother, who overheard what was conveyed to Tess. (Her husband did not conceal it from her.) Her reaction to the husband's allying himself with their daughter against her—it was not the only sign of such an inclination in him—could not have any other meaning than the following: For the second time in her life, she was losing out in a triadic constellation, the first time being the oedipal defeat, when she had had to surrender her father to her mother. Hence the oedipal rivalry lingering in her from her own childhood had to reach a climax in the death wish against her daughter. The tension ultimately had to be discharged in a symptom of phobic avoidance: she did not allow Tess to chew gum out of fear that she might choke on it. The unconscious death wish hidden behind this fear was the outgrowth of her reactivated death wish against her own mother.

FATHER'S CHIVALRY
or
"I didn't dare to look at my mother"

Actually *both* of Isabelle's parents were loyal to each other to the point of never so much as slightly criticizing the other in front of their children. This very popular educational principle fails to consider the fact that what one "shows" to one's children can hardly reverse the influence of clues the children obtain empathically of what actually is occurring between the parents.[12] In our case it was the father especially who always behaved "like a perfect gentleman" toward the mother. Their daughter Isabelle, unusually attractive and intelligent, was involved, in surprising contrast with her great sense of propriety, in a chain of affairs with men who either were married or had serious sexual difficulties. In consequence there seemed to be an inherent self-limiting factor in each of these involvements, with the patient unable to realize why she chose relationships which anybody with a modicum of good sense would have considered beforehand as doomed to failure. An incident in her family threw some light on this question. Isabelle's mother "never let anyone forget that she was suffering physical pain," which she almost always was. Recently it was a most persistent backache. During a game of charades Isabelle and her sister decided that each would choose, of all things, the name of an illness which the other had to guess. "Naturally mother was the only one unwilling to participate," the patient said, implying that her mother probably had grasped what they were up to. When the patient chose the word "backache," her father laughed more heartily than she had ever seen him do. *"I didn't dare to look at my mother* for fear that she would

---

12. In a recent case of a child who developed a tendency to lie, there was no doubt that the parents themselves never told a lie either to the child or to each other. They overlooked only one detail: they would conceal most carefully from the child that they often fought furiously when they were alone. The child somehow perceived the controlled anger and the sham of the parents' manifest behavior.

stop the game." The patient obtained on that occasion the direct confirmation of what she had already sensed was hidden behind father's "chivalrous" attitude toward mother. The guilt feelings about the oedipal triumph over mother—am simplifying here by eliminating this mother's own contributions to the genetic script which the patient had to live by—made Isabelle *"stop the game"* with every man. For that matter, she arranged (unconsciously) her affairs in such a way that they were inevitably discovered by her mother, so that Isabelle had to face the wrath of the "damaged third party," the oedipal rival, who then put an end to the affair.

The main task of dual therapy with this patient was for both therapists to be on guard against the patient's need to put the woman therapist in a role identical to that of her interfering mother. They refused to go along with Isabelle's need to repeat in transference or in extra-analytic acting out both the oedipal triumph and the atonement for it. In dual therapy such patients have a strong need to separate the co-therapists, who if they are mature in a triadic sense succeed easily in preventing this.

REIGNING BUT NOT *DIVIDING*
or
"My husband and I loved our daughter very dearly"

This is what Beverly's mother told the staff psychiatrist of a residential treatment center, where their daughter had been placed because she was diagnosed as schizophrenic.[13] At first sight, it seemed that she equated her husband's buying Beverly black lace panties and perfumes ("My Sin") with paternal love. This mother did not mind this habit of his even after both parents had been enlightened by the child's therapist about its impropriety. It had been pointed out to them how upsetting such a pattern must be for a daughter in a precarious mental condition and in the throes of a puberal crisis. But the therapist's cautioning fell on deaf ears. Indeed, after Beverly returned home, her mother continued unconcernedly to be the "providential" playwright and stage director for her daughter: she forced her husband out of her apartment (allegedly because "he was getting on her nerves") and arranged for their daughter to live with her father which both naturally preferred. The meaning of this arrangement became clear when mother's therapist learned that thereafter she allowed her husband to visit her, with one change: while before she had denied herself sexually to him, now she was amenable to relations with him and even enjoyed it. She had, however, the peculiar habit of cursing him during intercourse.[14]

Evidently this mother gratified her oedipal wish in two different ways: one "through proxy" when she tolerated her husband's seductiveness and maneuvered him and Beverly into

13. Results of dual therapy have convinced me that, contrary to the popular constitutional theories about the pathogenesis of schizophrenia, an overwhelming number of cases thus labeled represent an environmentally-induced psychic "decompensation" and therefore are reversible. In other words, the failures in therapy of schizophrenia are in my opinion not due to the incurability of this frequent clinical syndrome, but to the inadequacy of the therapeutic setting.

14. This illustrates the mechanism of "ambivalence clearance *within* the relationship" described in *Anxiety, Guilt and Aggression* (*op. cit.* p. 21).

enacting the fantasy of the oedipal triumph of a daughter over her mother, the other by making her husband and daughter into a parental couple. While having intercourse with her husband she triumphed over her mother, whose role she assigned to her daughter. She knew, however, that her husband would not go so far as to have intercourse with the daughter. (Occasionally such mothers take even this in their stride.) The anger she expressed against her husband in the very act of love-making was directed against her father. In other words, the "play" she staged with her husband and daughter did not influence her (oedipal) frustration anger. She knew very well (unconsciously) that father and mother still belonged to each other in a sense which was denied to her.

Why did father go along with the genetic play his wife had concocted for their daughter in which, instead of separating them, she manipulated husband and daughter to live together away from her? What was in it for him? A very important motive must have swayed this father for him to blithely disregard the therapist's objection to his seductiveness towards his daughter. Was he simply criminally callous? Again, it accords with my experience with genetic psychoanalysis that except for the most regressed psychotics, if immoral behavior is too openly displayed, and without apparent conflict, it serves a defensive function: it covers another impulse about which the patient feels more guilty. In this case the blatant seductiveness disguised his deep-seated hostility. This father, who harbored unconscious death wishes against his daughter, did not mind being accused of lusting for her. For him she was the psychological reincarnation of his sister, to whom he had very early lost (emotionally) his mother. Anything which would spare him the sight of his wife caring for his daughter was agreeable to him, including living away from his home. This was all the more so because his cooperation with her "arrangement" was rewarded by his wife's sexual compliance.

SHARED GUILT
or
"My father always competed with me"

This is what Marvin steadfastly maintained. At first sight it seemed that he simply ascribed to his father his own inclination to compete with him for his mother. Did Mr. W. (Marvin's father), a self-made man, not also have the right to want a certain professional diploma and to work towards it? Was it not to this parent's credit that, though advanced in age, he finally succeeded in achieving what he wanted? Could it not be simply coincidence that the field he chose was the same one in which his son was excelling? Yet the fact was that no possible advantage could accrue to the father from having the diploma except for the satisfaction of proving himself capable of obtaining it.

There were other signs that Marvin was right, his own (oedipal) rivalry with his father notwithstanding. The signs of Mr. W.'s rivalry unfolded slowly when the reasons were pursued for his peculiar hesitation about putting his son in his place as any normal father would have done. Marvin revealed one day in a dual therapy session that years ago while talking with his father he had made direct reference to his sexual desires for his mother. "Father was then sort of passive and uncertain, actually rather embarrassed." The reason for this began to take shape when the son read a short story to me. In it he triumphed over his father who had asked him to write a test paper. Indeed, the story reported a true fact. It was that paper which made it possible for Mr. W. to pass his test, the last and most decisive one which he needed for his diploma. Though this father was more dishonest than the one who allowed his son to present his paintings as his own (p. 122), in both cases there is no doubt on whose shoulders the moral responsibility lay and what the driving motive was: the "oedipal triumph by proxy"—a son should win over his father in his sexual quest for mother. This explains why Marvin was arguing in the session that his incestuous desires were only an expression of the "insane integrity" of which Kafka was an exponent as one of those "dependent artists" who, instead of adjusting to the reality of having to give up their mothers, are "waiting for their luck to change," and that just these "artists" are the ones who have "the power to overwhelm generations," all references apparently taken from a book on Kafka.

It ultimately became clear that Marvin had been assigned the role of recreating his father's relationship with his own grandfather. Throughout Mr. W.'s whole youth his (paternal) grandfather had acted as a substitute after his own father emigrated to this country, leaving Mr. W. with his mother. Marvin had actually been named after his great-grandfather. In doing so, his father facilitated the process whereby Marvin came to play in his (Mr. W.'s) unconscious the role of the grandfather. This accounted for the fact that Mr. W. surrendered his capacity or, to be more precise, his moral right to play effectively the role of a father.[15] By reversing the sequence of generations, he specifically lost the right to face his son Marvin with the irrationality of his desires for his mother: Mr. W. was very likely himself (unconsciously) guilty for the incestuous fantasies which he must have kept in abeyance after his own father left the country. Mr. W. was "passive" as well as "uncertain" and "embarrassed" simply because he shared with his son the same infantile (oedipal) position. That there was truth in Marvin's complaint about his father's always competing with him now became clear. (I have for the sake of illustrating the main point, left out other dynamic complications deriving from the fact that the patient had a younger sister.)

---

15. The prohibition in the Jewish religion against naming a son after his father when he is still living must have been inspired by the hope of avoiding the oedipal rivalry between sons and fathers at least during the latters' lives.

PATERNAL COMPASSION
or
"I love my father more than anyone else"

These words could hardly describe the depth of the feeling Norman, in his middle twenties, harbored for his father. He appeared to him as the epitome of wisdom and human kindness. Indeed, for women Norman felt mostly contempt. But in an apparent paradox, he was most successful in making them his mistresses, and changing them with remarkable speed. Not that they did not count at all for him; on the contrary, their company seemed indispensable. "I could never fall asleep without having one of the girls with me. Alone I get the blues, become restless and anxious. But during the day, I find them boring even if they are Phi Beta Kappas." Actually he had needed a woman in his room in order to fall asleep since the age of five. Then, however, it was his mother who objected to spending hours in his room before she could leave him sleeping. Only father, the patient felt, had real compassion for him: at that time Norman had uncontrollable fears of ghosts and in general displayed verbally and in behavior great insecurity.

"The atmosphere at my home was always tragic ever since father lost money in that idiotic business deal. I was then four or five. He had to work seven days a week in his store and I and my brother, then about twelve, practically didn't see him because he came home very late at night. For that matter, mother was not around either. She had to help father in the store." Thus Norman repeated, in his being unrelated to girls during the day and using them only as soporifics at night, what he had experienced with his mother. But it turned out that father's compassion for his son was inspired less by love than by guilt feelings. This discovery, however, was made only after a great detour in our scrutiny of the patient's genetic script. The "deep love" which the patient felt toward his father somehow coexisted with a compulsive need to prove his parent wrong and, surprisingly, also to demean him. "What I mostly

resent in my father is the "tragic" atmosphere he created for
the entire family. Would he or would he not succeed in making
up for the loss of that damned money? My whole childhood,
for that matter my whole youth, was spent breathing in this
atmosphere of worry and apprehension, of fear and uncer-
tainty. Yesterday I again lost patience with him, calling him
stupid, dim-witted, etc."

The patient's own anxieties centered on the separation
from mother, for which father's financial crisis was undoubtedly responsible. We already know that she had to help her
husband, and therefore spent most of her time away from
home. When the circumstances of the crisis were discussed,
it became evident that this was not only avoidable but that
father must have acted under the influence of some obscure
need to make himself and his wife unavailable to his children.
The ultimate link in the understanding of this baffling event,
which threw such a dark shadow on Norman's childhood,
was obtained when, in describing his father's own background,
he remarked, "My grandparents were so poor that my father
had to go to work as soon as he was twelve." This was also
the age of Norman's brother when the father suffered that
financial setback. Evidently, he was compelled to repeat the
separation from his home through proxy by inflicting it on
the older son. Paradoxically, the older brother whose age
triggered father's re-enactment of the past[16] suffered less from
it than our patient. The former turned out to be a most pros-
perous businessman, as was father's ideal, while his younger
brother still floundered in various undertakings. A likely explanation could be that the trauma of separation (from the
mother) struck the older of the two sons at puberty while
the younger one was still in the throes of the incomparably
more vulnerable oedipal stage. Later an additional factor was
uncovered, i.e. the mother's exacerbated wish that the second
child be a girl, which accounted for much of her unconscious

16. See "anniversary hypothesis" or "traumatophoric number or date"
in *Anxiety, Guilt and Aggression* (*op. cit.* p. 21).

rejection of her younger son. The negative attitude of this mother explains why the patient's father had to insist that she help her son cope with his fears of ghosts and nightmares by staying with him until he fell asleep.

A CANDID MOTHER
or
"Robert, don't look!"

The following habit developed within Robert's family: Around the time that father's brother died when Robert was about twelve, he was "allowed" to come into his parents' bedroom during the middle of the night. When he would get into bed between his parents, not only did neither object, but his father even accepted mother's request that he leave and go to sleep in Robert's bed.

Robert, in his late twenties, was sent for emergency dual therapy on account of his psychotic break. He presented his past sex life as "very normal." There was, however, one peculiarity in this area: He could only have sex with a woman with whom he was not involved emotionally. As soon as he began to "really like a girl" he felt he ought "not to touch her," though he did not know why. This pattern naturally led to a succession of complicated involvements until he found a girl who had a similar pattern. With Jane, whose beautiful features reminded him of his very attractive mother, things reached a dramatic impasse because he "really fell in love with her," though nothing prevented him from still looking for other girls to satisfy himself sexually. The difficulties arose when, contrary to his custom, he began to feel that he could have a "complete" relationship with Jane. He was so convinced that he proposed to her. Unfortunately, Jane insisted that she had only friendly feelings towards him and nothing else. One day Robert had begun to feel that he was the center of a fantastic plot, "a sort of experiment" in which the entire city of New York was participating. Sometimes people "tried to give him confidence and then good things would happen." When he rode in a Jaguar and the driver of another Jaguar honked at him, he had a sudden feeling of happiness because it was "a sign that people were planning good things for him." At other times, however, he felt that he was responsible for ruining the careers of many people whose trust he had betrayed. He had recently been demoted, but felt that he was expected to achieve "something of national significance" in order to advance in his career.

The female therapist noticed that from time to time he would open his eyes wide for a second or two as if struck by a sudden vision. Exploring this further, the patient recalled how mother would frequently show herself to him in the nude but at the same time would exhort him, *"Robert, don't look!"* To the male therapist, who noticed that a naso-labial tic occasionally distorted his face, the patient revealed that his mother had the same tic. Hand in hand with this he became convinced that both male and female therapists were the parents of Jane, whom he so desperately wanted to marry. As he identified himself with his mother and therefore also with Jane (see above), we, his therapists, and (transferential) parents became also Jane's parents. (Incidentally, as soon as Robert was made aware of this unconscious equation he lost his delusional belief.) Robert's self-image, in general, easily blended with that of any girl with whom he became emotionally involved, because the image of his own self still merged with that of the first woman in his life, his mother, as normally occurs only in earliest infancy. The megalomanic delusion of being the object of a "citywide experiment" was ultimately traced back to the fact that Robert's mother, by allowing him to share the same bed, played into his (oedipal) fantasy of being her lover and husband. In reality, however, his mother only "played" with him, "experimented" with him, because he literally "only slept" with her, that is, was neither her lover nor her husband.

Robert's father on his part was of no help in restraining his wife's seductiveness. He was chronically sick, which most likely was not unrelated to the fact that he allowed himself to be shunted out from the family triad, and to his helpless rage over his wife's licentious behavior. "My father knew about my mother's running around with other men. Not that he didn't protest: he would rant and rave when this came up but could do very little about it. My mother was the stronger one." (The details of the extremely enlightening and successful therapy of the psychotic decompensation in this young man have to be postponed for another occasion.)

REVERSED GENERATIONS
or
"I am everybody's wife and mother"

Dorothy (suffering from a borderline condition) seemed to be just bragging when she told her dual therapists that both her parents and her brother considered her either a spouse or a parent. There was a lot of truth to her statement, but in this illustration we shall concentrate mostly on her father. "Father would praise me to the skies, telling me how intelligent and attractive I was, how I was really his type and so on. My mother instead would ask me for advice on practically everything. I had to tell her how to furnish the house. She could not even decide between two kinds of drapes!"

Indeed, the overriding aspect of this patient's constellation seemed to be that she dominated the family picture. Here is an excerpt from a (dual) session:

"Father and mother are always fighting and I am the big instigator (laughs). I have fallen (after the previous session) and hurt my knee. I think I wanted to punish myself (sounds almost triumphant). Dr. X.[17] did not achieve anything with me. (Brightly) I see already that you will tell me, 'You are too much for me to handle.'" (I knew that Dorothy was exposed to erotic overstimulation by her father's caresses and kisses.) At this point she displayed the eye tic from which she occasionally suffered. When I drew her attention to it she made a face, saying that she could not control it. I mentioned that it looked like winking and wondered if she had her father in mind. She smiled flirtatiously, "Oh, go away." Dorothy's tic disappeared and she resumed her associations: "I like father more than mother. He is really warmer than she. . . . Mother makes me responsible for her unhappiness. . . . Father kisses me too much. Perhaps he doesn't kiss me too much, but he kisses only me and nobody else (giggles). I cannot stand to have you mention all this (in synoptic cross-recording) so that she (the female therapist) will hear it." Her laugh, however, at this point betrayed that the "psychological presence" of the female therapist was actually of great relief and assurance to her. "Father would say that he should have married somebody more like me." She distorted her face in an ugly grimace. I drew her attention to it. She tossed her head and her face brightened up in a most attractive and seductive smile. "My mother always makes me feel guilty." "How?" She disregarded my question.

In this case, father's oedipal seductiveness with Dorothy repeated the genetic triad of his own childhood. His mother was seductive with him, preferring him openly to his older brother. The ensuing guilt feelings forced him after the death

---

17. She had been for six years in analysis with an experienced male analyst. Following this she had two years with a female therapist, who then included me in the dual analysis of the patient.

of the father to work in a subservient position for this brother. The latter often humiliated him, exploiting his guilt-induced masochism which he constantly refueled in his attitude towards Dorothy. His daughter thus correctly perceived that also for her father she stood as a wife and mother.

RELAXED STANDARDS
or
"I did not mind that he was a little sloppy"

Barry's father had been raised rather strictly, especially by his mother, who taught him to keep an immaculate appearance. Paradoxically, he did not mind his son's more than careless dress and manner. It therefore seemed plausible that he wanted Barry to be raised differently than he himself had been. However, this father significantly had not revised his own standards in the least. His own aspect and demeanor were impeccable so that his mother who lived nearby could not possibly criticize *him* for transgressing her standards. He related an interesting dream which dealt with the issue of dirt: He appeared to be angry when he found a heap of refuse in front of his house. He had some difficulties in parking his car, though he tried again and again from different angles and in the process became increasingly angry. Ultimately he aroused the suspicion of certain people, especially *three*[18]

18. Three stands, as is known, in the symbolism of the unconscious for the phallus, though I have found it occasionally also representing the genetic and, in transference, the therapeutic triad. In this context the latter is alluded to as a setting which makes possible the *observation* of what is really going on in analytic therapy though its usual meaning (of a phallic symbol) was also with our patient the more important.

"observers." He felt that he had to excuse himself to them for his impatience and also for the fact that his *finger was bleeding*. In commenting on the dream, the patient with striking unconcern spoke about Barry's having fallen from his bicycle and injuring himself so that his *finger bled profusely*.

The unconcern betrayed that beneath this father's "permissiveness" regarding Barry's appearance there was hidden the wish that his son displease both his mother and his grandmother. The central motive of this father's attitude toward his son, his own oedipal rivalry, was not difficult to grasp. At a deeper level of the dynamics responsible for this father's unemotional report on his son's injury was the *castration anxiety* rooted in this parent's oedipal position.

According to the dualistic view on anxiety (Flescher, 1955), the fear of castration is proportionate to the son's wish to castrate the father. This constellation explains more plausibly the ubiquitous nature of the castration complex in the human race than does Freud's speculation about the memory traces of actual instances of fathers castrating their sons in primordial times. Fathers often (projectively) identify with their sons because of oedipal rivalry with their own fathers. Castration anxiety is therefore most frequently the crucial point of contact and conflict between the oedipal constellation in both generations.

If there were any doubts that Barry's father was writing a genetic script for him based on the oedipal rivalry between a son and a father for the third member of the genetic triad (the mother), they were dispelled by the following dream of the patient: "I had this dream in connection with the death of Dr. X. (his previous analyst). I dreamed that I was praising God for the wisdom of His acts. To express this praise most fittingly I gave a concert for the glory of the Creator. I was the conductor and succeeded in giving with my orchestra a most stunning musical performance." In reality the patient was not in the least musical, but the widow of his ex-analyst, a physician (notice the pun-like overlapping of "doctor" and "conductor"), was an accomplished pianist and impassioned musician.

SEPARATION ANXIETY
or
"I am neither productive nor creative"

Claudia, in her early twenties and still a severe nailbiter, had a quarrel with her fiancé. It occurred Saturday morning as usual: she cannot help clashing with him over weekends. She herself recognized that it had to do with her incapacity to enjoy her days off from work. She constantly labored under intense guilt feelings about not being sufficiently productive and creative. In reality she was a hard worker who tried very much to please her boss, a woman, even though the requirements of the job turned out to be completely different from those presented to patient when she was hired. In the clashes with her fiancé, much older than she, Claudia would display extreme demandingness for both affection and love and accuse him of being unsure of himself.

In their last quarrel she again harped on his indecisiveness when he told her of his concern about an impending crisis in his job: The head of the department, to whom he referred as a "father figure," was about to leave, causing great worry in all the employees. In the conjoint session Claudia confessed that she could not understand why the allusion to the "disappearance of the father figure" upset her so much. I picked this element up in the following (dual) session, reminding her that she had in the preceding one (her first with the female therapist), discussed a crisis which occurred in her own life when she was five. Her mother had given birth to a sister but could not return home after delivery because of an inter-current illness. It was at that time that Claudia developed attacks of severe separation anxiety. She would not allow her father to go to work, clinging to him frantically and holding on to his hands while she was lying in bed (as her mother was bedridden in the hospital and later also at home).

In Claudia's panic at the prospect of father's leaving (the "disappearance of the father figure") the separation anxiety from her mother played a decisive role. Indeed after mother returned and Claudia had to go to kindergarten, she developed the habit of throwing up and her nailbiting started. The quarrel with her fiancé, following the mechanism of "trau-matophoric date" (her mother returned Saturday morning thus putting an end to the closeness with father), had the function of releasing the unconsciously activated aggression against her mother and her father, who both in succession exposed her to object loss. Though it is pertinent to our main thesis, what interests us here is not her double investment in her fiancé (standing for both her mother and father) which accounted for her demandingness and insatiability. Instead at this juncture, we find the fact that she accused herself of lack of productivity and creativity, which has all the conno-tations of a superego-imposed criticism, to be directly linked with the oedipal position: rather than become aware that she was inclined to criticize and hate her mother for having left to deliver a child, the patient accused herself (unconsciously) of not being able to *create* and *produce* her own child and to bestow it on her father.

> The turning of the aggression against the Self is typical of the dynamics of the superego in the context of frustration.
>
> From Freud we have learned that in cases of frustration the provoked aggression can be absorbed into the structure of the superego, which then becomes exacting and critical to the point of cruelty (1930). From Ferenczi we know the component which the superego formation draws from ex-periences involving bodily openings. Especially the anal com-

ponent is pronounced ("Sphincter morality") (see p. 56) which explains why morally objectionable impulses are often referred to as "dirty" while the opposite are "clean" and "pure." But a no lesser contribution to the dynamics of the superego as carrier of the moral requirements comes from the *oral* level. The German "Gewissensbisse" (literally "bites of conscience") and the English "remorse" (from the Latin and Italian "mordere"—biting) indicate how self-directed oral aggression burdens the relationship between ego and superego often with an oral sado-masochistic quality. I mention the last factor, because of the patients' severe nailbiting.

As is seen from the inception of her oral symptoms at the kindergarten age (vomiting and nailbiting after her mother's return), the oedipal conflict has added a decisive quota to the patient's problem of separation anxiety.

This case therefore illustrates strikingly how much the resolution of the Oedipus complex is at the core of the problem of morality and of the operation of the superego: The superego is actually molded from the oedipal complex on the basis of the child's experiences with the parents, especially the parent of the same sex, experiences which are exacerbated by the inevitable frustrations incumbent on the oedipal position. Indeed, as I have shown elsewhere, the main dynamic accent, for the very development of the superego is the introjection of the aggressor. In other words, the superego, as a deposit of the aggressive impulses directed against the same-sex parent in his role of oedipal rival, is the avenger of the incestuous impulses of the child. (This fundamental aspect of the dynamics of morality will be enlarged upon in the next volume (see note p. 80).

Though it was not for this that Claudia, at least consciously, had originally decided to enter dual therapy, yet she became aware that her fiancé, older by 25 years, was indeed for her a father figure in whom she was disappointed from the two above-mentioned sources. She broke off her engagement and, shortly after returning to her hometown, married somebody closer to her age.

BELATED INTERVENTION
or
"You have a father complex"

This is what mother told Irene when she finally found out
that her daughter had become infatuated with a married man,
father of three children. "She always has phone calls and
refuses to tell me who it is," complained her mother. Irene
had succeeded in concealing all her affairs from her "nosy"
mother, except this one. "She doesn't have a right to control
my life, to tell me whom I should love or who is good for
me and who is not," was Irene's exasperated retort to her
mother. Thus it was apparent that this mother was right: her
daughter indeed had a "father complex." Yet I soon learned
that Irene's mother had a big hand in this. When their daughter was barely three, her father had resolved to make her into
a swimming champion. He gave her daily lessons and personally supervised her practicing for hours. Later on Irene had to
follow him to the pool immediately after school. "When I
asked my husband why he didn't allow her to come home first,
he would invariably answer that Irene didn't feel like spending any time with me." No, she could not talk directly with
her daughter and ask her how she felt about these lessons
and whether she didn't miss her mother, because "as soon as
she got home she would fall dead tired on her bed and sleep
like a log." Unbelievable as it may seem, there was no other
opportunity for this mother to have a talk with Irene about
the fact that she (the mother) was so thoroughly shut out
from any contact with her daughter.

"Now since Irene has divorced her husband and become
involved with *that* man, she lives only for her three cats.
What does she need them for? Are they her babies or something?" The chagrined mother was not far wrong in her assumption. These pets were very likely her daughter's babies,
as the wife of the man of whom Irene was enamored had three
children. The fights between Irene and her mother were often
dramatic, with mother threatening suicide and each accusing

the other of both rejection and a wish to dominate. In reality, now that Irene's father had died and her divorced husband no longer counted, both mother and daughter expected from each other an impossible feat of impersonation: to substitute for the missing man and at the same time to submit to (phallic) domination and penetration. The latter wish was due to each having introjected the lost male. (One of the most furious battles, with the mother threatening to jump from the speeding car, took place when—as she related with great bitterness—Irene refused to allow her mother to put something in her (Irene's) suitcase.) Mother's present "nosiness" about which Irene complained, evidently was intended to make up for her previous non-intervention in the dyadic bond between husband and daughter. Similarly, Irene's goading her mother with the "secret" phone calls, which she claimed to be unable to keep hidden from her mother, was a way of trying to make up for her past involvement with her father: this time Irene (albeit unconsciously) wanted mother to interfere in her tryst with a married man.

THE SUPREME PRICE
or
"Father wanted me to trick my stepmother"

Albert's father asked him to write a check, which he (father) would then show to his (second) wife as a proof that he was very badly off financially. He hoped to show her in this way that he had borrowed money. The pretense had the purpose of dissuading his wife from wanting to go south for a vacation. In reality Albert's father had a sizeable bank account. He would also allow Albert, when barely ten, to bring mother gifts more expensive than his own. Indeed for mother's birthday only Albert would give her presents. The father disregarded completely his son's lying and even stealing in order to buy them. (The son helped himself generously to the family kitty.) When Albert got his first job, his parents "allowed" him to purchase expensive furniture for their home (on installments) which the father could very well have paid cash for himself. It was on that occasion that Albert went into debt for the first time. From then on, he was perpetually in financial troubles, to the point of being unable, after he himself became a father of two children, to pay even the grocer or the milkman. This was only one of the many consequences of the genetic script his father wrote for Albert. It centered on his father's wish to make him into a successful rival for the favors of his mother. At least it seemed so at first glance. With time, however, the motivation of Albert's father revealed itself to be more complicated. He himself had lost his mother through divorce (by her default) when he was in his early teens. Following this he had lived with his father, who completely dominated his son emotionally. Evidently, he also would have liked to keep his son attached to him, as he himself had been tied to his own father. Hence he used Albert's oedipal strivings toward his mother, and later also his stepmother, and the ensuing guilt feelings to keep him emotionally bound to himself.

> I have found this pattern (one parent promoting the oedipal closeness to the other parent and then exploiting the inevitable guilt feelings to prevent the child's emotional emancipation) to be surprisingly frequent.

In response to this subthreshold (homosexual) seduction by his father, Albert developed a corresponding highly *ambivalent* attachment to him. This accounted for a most marked and characteristic biphasic pattern in the patient's relationship with males in general and with his clients in particular: he was very energetic and creative in order to "help them" with most constructive ideas and projects, only to glaringly neglect his obligations when it came to their implementation. The ultimate result was a constant turnover of his clientele and a severe curtailment of his earning capacities. Thus the second reason for his being constantly in financial straits became evident and accessible to analytic help.

A GENEROUS MOTHER
or
"You can have him"

The father of Cora, an attractive but obese young woman, was in the hospital for minor surgery. She had just been complaining about having to visit him every day. Cora was again on a diet. "He is bored with my mother because she reads the newspaper. He only talks with me." From father's therapist it was known that he had been "very affectionate" with Cora when she was much younger: he allowed her endlessly to jump up and down on his lap. He admitted years later to his therapist that he could not help being aroused by this. Somehow the mother seemed not to care about what was going on between husband and daughter. On the contrary, she would reward her greatly overweight daughter with delicacies whenever she kept father company. When talking about this Cora casually mentioned that her mother generally had a tendency to entice her into breaking her diet by baking special cakes which Cora could not resist. She also constantly made derogatory remarks about Cora's father ("hypochondriac," "fanatic," "crazy in the head," and so on), often concluding with the words, "Believe me, any moment you want him, you can have him."

It was then not surprising that, with the seduction coming from both parents, Cora as a child had spells of violent rages, displayed impudent behavior and used obscene language. Later on she adopted a most characteristic pattern of relationship with the opposite sex: she had first to flirt with and captivate her suitors, then to deride and demean them and finally to drop them one after the other. This was not the only consequence of the genetic formula prescribed for Cora by her parents. The empathic perception of the hostility concealed behind her parents' "generosity," together with the inevitable guilt feelings from oedipal overstimulation, ultimately took a heavy toll in Cora. As her "wildness" subsided, her obesity became intractable and she plunged into a severe depression. Both were interrelated, and dynamically rooted in the oral phase.

Illustrative of her oral fixation and regression was an incident which occurred after she had finally lost weight while in dual therapy. She witnessed a friend of hers berating her husband. Her reaction of compassion traceable to her own mother's demeaning her father, did not escape her friend's husband. The very next day he asked if he could visit her. She was honest enough to admit that she "knew what he was up to." But she assured me that she did not allow him to do anything more then touch and kiss her breasts and "nibble a little." All through this man's attempts to arouse her, she was without any response. After he left, however, she was overcome by such an urge to eat that she gorged herself with food as she had not done for a long time. (While reporting on this incident she was busily nibbling at the top of her pen. At one point she was pretending to bite her closed fist, at another she tapped her fist against her teeth. Thus the unconscious fantasies of attack against the maternal breast and the paternal phallus, as a retaliatory reaction to parental seduction and inevitably ensuing frustration, revealed themselves to be at the root of Cora's problem.

However, the *choice of the form* this retaliation has assumed has been influenced by the early maternal and, as is usually the case, *oral* frustration.

> This clinical sample well illustrates the fact that we have to distinguish between fixation of the form (of gratification) and that of the object. In the *fixation of the form,* the instinctual need of a given infantile stage persists beyond its corresponding age level, e.g. in the above case the oral needs of the patient. In the *fixation of the object* a given instinctual demand (or aim) clings to an object beyond the corresponding phase. A girl may, for example, cling to her mother when she actually should have already passed into the stage of intense involvement with her father. Usually there is a combination of fixation of both the form and the object.

In our patient, traces of the oral need for the maternal breast were easily observable with all the displacements from one object to another. I had on several occasions drawn her attention to the fact that when lying on the couch (she was wearing a sleeveless dress) she would draw her left shoulder toward her face so that her mouth came to rest on something which by its soft roundness could well stand (unconsciously) for the maternal breast. As to the displacement of a fixated (oral) need from one object to another, we notice the shift onto the Self (the man touched, kissed and nibbled at her breasts, she herself was biting her fist) and onto inanimate objects (food, pencil). The voraciousness (devouring), the nibbling and the biting betray the role of frustration aggression; the symptomatic act of hitting at her teeth reveals the wish to punish them for the impulse to bite and devour. The last element underlay the core dynamics of her depression: the turning of aggression against the Self.

AN "UNDERPROTECTIVE" MOTHER
or
"I didn't think that it could happen"

During one session, Mrs. D. told me in an empty tone, "I was reaching over to get something from the windowsill. He (her son, Larry) was standing on his high chair. Suddenly I saw him falling and I couldn't catch him in time. His head struck the leg of the table and he passed out for a short time. Then within a few days he progressively lost his speech, and stopped eating. I had to call the doctor. I tried everything. To feed him, I was told that I should hold his nose and shove food in as soon as he opened his mouth. It seemed to help, because after a few weeks, he was all right. . . . I was surprised when he fell. I didn't think that it could happen."

Twenty years later, Larry, who had always been extremely lean, had as a (platonic) girlfriend an unmarried mother. He was playing with her little son, throwing him up and catching him until the child hit his head against the arch of the doorway. While in dual therapy he became intimate with a girl for the first time. The night before, she had enraged him, pretending to prefer another young man to him. Ultimately, however, they spent the night together. "In the morning everything was hunky-dory. She made breakfast, and then out of the blue, while I was lying in bed, she bit my arm. I had to defend myself, didn't I? So I hit her in the temple, I mean on the head." His act of self-defense was quite effective because he sent her reeling to the floor. Whereupon she broke with him.

The second time Mrs. D. was "surprised" was when she learned that her son's "friend" had killed his father. The victim, an alcoholic, had told her about the gun he had bought his son as a gift and showed it to her, before taking it home. "I asked him if he thought it was such a good idea. Who could guess that his son would use it against him? (– – –?) Yes, I knew from Larry that Fred had threatened one day to kill his father because he was constantly beating up his mother." Mrs. D. was unaware of the sexual perversion the two youngsters were indulging in. Mrs. D.'s lack of foresight and her co-responsibility (by omission) in the patricide were rooted in her own bond of friendship with Fred's mother. Indeed, it was she who was Mrs. D.'s closest confidante and adviser in her fights with her husband, who was trying to evade the financial obligations that divorce would entail. She had separated from him because he was not working.

With time it became clear (both Mrs. D. and Larry were undergoing dual therapy) why Larry too did not lift a finger to prevent his friend Fred from carrying out his threat. How could each of these adolescents better deny the frustrated need and love for a father, which in turn exacerbated the usual filial (oedipal) hostility toward the father, than to commit patricide, one directly and the other by proxy? (Traditional analytic therapy could not possibly have coped with the problem of still another bond of guilt, this one prevailing between our patient and his mother, which made Larry feel he did not deserve to have a father, as his mother, by not remarrying, showed she did not deserve to have a husband.)

Admittedly it was one of the most protracted dual therapies (on a once-a-week basis), yet the patient acquired a new emotional and physical interest in the opposite sex and ultimately learned to hold a job, instead of running from one occupation to another as he had been forced to do by his overwhelming need to insure punishment through provocation (guilt-relieving aggression).

The central theme of our therapeutic effort was to analyze, in dual sessions and in conjoint sessions with his mother, why Larry persistently "forgot" the sessions with the female therapist, without even calling her to explain why he had not come: he finally became aware that in order to be able to trust any woman, he had to work through his fear of and anger against his mother's homicidal and defensive (oedipal) hostility towards men.

In order to explain her deep-seated hostility, we would have to go into her own mother's genetic script and especially into the latter's rejecting attitude toward Mrs. D.'s own father and how much it contributed to his premature death (when Mrs. D. was only twelve). Actually her own divorce was to a substantial degree "willed" by her unconscious need to relive (repetition compulsion) the trauma of separation, this time from her husband. Now, however, she had the comfort of being the initiator in the re-enactment of an experience which she as a child had had no control over.

THE WAGES OF GENEROSITY
or
"Why did she not say a word?"

The patient was very depressed yesterday. This mood of his became especially acute when he went to visit his parents (in a nearby town). He has again spent the night with his girl-friend. He didn't sleep a wink because he made love the whole night. He tries to limit his contact with girls and he has only three other girls besides Kay. (– – –?) "You mean because Kay assured me that she has only three boyfriends with whom she goes steady? (– – –?) I don't know why I stick to Kay. After all if I would marry her I would never trust her. Yet it is she who turns me on more than anybody else. It is crazy because when I think that she goes to bed with other men between one date and another, it drives me nuts. . . . And then, why am I always boiling with anger? I get everybody's goat. Especially my father's. When a girl at a cocktail party told me she liked her boss, I suddenly got so angry that I walked away. Whenever I see nice-looking girls I start boiling inside. (– – –?) Yes, why do I get so mad? I feel as if they were teasing me.

"It began to come over me when I was about *thirteen*. The girls in the class all seemed to tease me. I mean those who were attractive. . . . I know they had their eyes on older boys but I felt that they sort of made fun of me. It was just like with the friend of my mother's who was my babysitter. (– – –) I was then *thirteen* or was I younger? She didn't really babysit. She sort of kept me company. The way in which she looked at me and moved around I felt that she was telling me, 'You'd like it, wouldn't you? But you cannot have it. You are only a little boy.' (– – –?) Yes, I also can't understand why I don't have enough of Kay. The whole night . . . and yet I am not any happier. (– – –?) Why I became depressed on the way to my parents? I was thinking how different their life was. They really have a family life. They really care about each other and love each other. Yet by the way I live it is almost as if I would want to show them up as squares. It all started when my buddies initiated me to sex by bringing me when I was *thirteen* to a prostitute. . . . Girls from good families with good background and good character turn me off. I don't understand why. This is why I can't bring home any of my girls. My parents would be shocked. I wonder what they are thinking about my sex-life.

"With X. (female therapist) we tried last time to find out why I am so mad with everybody. She spoke about my attachment to my mother, I don't see any of this. Yes, I recall having told you that the thought of others enjoying themselves drives me crazy. I always have the impression that I am losing out. When I am alone I always think that the whole world is having sex and I am leading a miserable life. (– – –?) Yes it sounds like a joke with all the sex I have. (– – –?) You mean to say that when I am with Kay I cannot stop making love for fear that she might leave me and go to other men?"

Why this patient's erotic memories centered around the age of *thirteen* was explained only in the seventh month of dual therapy by an incident of "confession through enactment." During a visit with his parents he did not find any more suitable place for having his (dual) telephone session with the female therapist than his parents' bedroom. After listening to the tape recording of the session, I asked why he spoke with an anxious and whispering voice. This conjured up a memory of a seemingly self-induced trauma, but one the parents, if they had really wanted to, could have avoided. One afternoon, at the age of *thirteen*, he entered the bedroom of his parents and found them both naked and about to have intercourse. His emotional reaction to this "primal scene" experience was quickly repressed but revealed itself to be the dynamic source of his obsessive envy of "the whole world enjoying itself," of his need to sexually "over-satiate" the woman, of his sexual responsiveness only to girls who would "shock" his parents as he was shocked by them and finally of his irascibility with everybody and especially of his need to berate his father.

In a conjoint interview with the patient's parents (Mr. and Mrs. U.) two most significant facts came to the fore and should be mentioned here. First of all, the father excused his financial generosity and over-all helpfulness toward his son, as well as his constant giving in to him, to which his wife objected, by his fear that his son might "suddenly lose control and commit violence more against himself than against others." (See similarity with case p. 122.) By this Mr. U. tried also to explain why he allowed his son to blow his top with him. Secondly, the triadic constellation within this family became clear when I asked what was Mrs. U.'s reaction to her son's behavior towards her husband. Before she could answer, Mr. U., evidently encouraged by my question to confront his wife perhaps for the first time, exclaimed, "That's it! I always was furious, asking myself: 'Why doesn't she say a word?'" Mrs. U. remained silent at this and I didn't press for an explanation. I found here the first root of this father's hidden hostility against his son. How could he not resent his wife's condoning of their son's disrespect for him? That she did not intervene because she felt her husband to be too permissive and too sacrificial with their son goes without saying.

Actually I obtained an inkling of Mr. U.'s real attitude

towards the patient from the question he raised as soon as he entered my office: Was it my idea to make him come or his son's? The reason why he asked became clear to me when I learned that both son and father "agreed" that the latter should pay for the son's therapy. (The son could afford to pay by himself.) The "helpfulness" of this father was a violation of the triadic principle insofar as it was motivated, albeit unconsciously, by the wish to show up his son to his wife as immature and dependent on his father. Through his "generosity" Mr. U. acted out his oedipal rivalry, which in turn was unconsciously understood by the son, and therefore resented. I have to renounce elaborating here on those determinants of mother's "non-intervention" between husband and son, which were rooted in her own genetic history.

GRANDSON FOR A DAUGHTER
or
"What a beautiful girl he would make!"

Benny's grandmother said this, after she had tied a colorful kerchief around his face, when he was about seven years old. This I learned from Mrs. P., his mother. Ultimately, Benny complied with grandmother's (father's mother) enthusiasm: after a few abortive attempts to develop some kind of relationship with the opposite sex, he joined with another homosexual in a marriage-like menage. The "male" role, in terms of being responsible for their upkeep, paying the taxes, etc., was played by his friend. Shortly after, I found out that Benny's father, Mr. P., must also have conformed to his mother's expectation of having a daughter instead of a son, because he became her most willing helper. He would enthusiastically do all the chores around the house, would assist her in cooking, dishwashing and ironing. Mr. P. in general would spend many hours in his mother's company because of the father's chronic illness which required repeated and prolonged hospitalization. Mr. P. recalled with embarrassment that his mother had gone through with him the same "beautiful girl" routine.

Later on, Mr. P. grew up to be a rebel who fought authority and constantly changed jobs because he could not stand being "humiliated" by his bosses. These "humiliations" revealed themselves to be reactions to his wish to be loved by father substitutes, a wish imbedded in unconscious fantasies in which he was the irresistably "beautiful" girl his mother wanted him to be, long before his own son Benny approximated the realization of this wish in manifest homosexual perversion.

For other details on this very instructive case see Flescher, 1968 in J. H. Masserman, *Current Psychiatric Therapies,* Vol. 6, p. 38.

THE SACRIFICIAL LAMB
or
"We had to knock father"

Mr. S. explained why he spent so much time in his older brother's company: he hated to go home to his family. At first the therapist thought that he seemed to rationalize his need for a protective father figure. Yet it soon became clear that his bitterness against his wife and daughter was the cause of his staying at home as little as possible and that he was justified in doing so. At a certain point, both his wife and his daughter joined him in dual therapy.

Mrs. S. was strikingly underweight. She had been obese as a young woman, and her "starvation complex" manifested itself first in her eating quickly and in great quantities. She (unconsciously) feared that others would otherwise eat up everything so that nothing would remain for her. Besides, by filling herself up she hoped she would never be hungry again.[19] Later on Mrs. S. developed instead the fear that if she ate as much as she wanted there would not be enough left for her and her children. She began to deny herself food and became extremely thin. Her daughter, however, did not pass into this second stage and remained for a long time overweight, actually until dual therapy helped her to diet successfully. Mrs. S. became more and more stingy with food, though significantly only for herself. In order to make her eat a piece of cake, the children would mash it up and then pretend they were going to throw it out. Only then would she hurriedly eat it. Mrs. S.'s pattern pointed toward the root of her life-long suffering from depressive bouts: her own mother was too involved in the collecting of antiques to have time to care for her daughter.

Mrs. S. ended up by making her own daughter into her mother: she was unable to decide on anything without her daughter, who would either come along when she went shopping or at least assist her with advice on the phone. But what happened to Mrs. S.'s anger against her depriving mother? As is most frequently the case, it was turned against herself, which accounted for her depression. That this was so became apparent when her daughter disclosed that in order to lift her mother out of her depressive moods and angry silences they (she and her brothers) simply had to knock father. "As soon as *we would start to knock father,* she would begin to smile and talk with animation." To shift onto her husband the anger directed against her mother was the most natural thing for

19. The hoarding of food in one's own body out of concern for the future most likely follows the psychosomatic groove of that instinct which makes animals gorge themselves prior to hibernation.

Mrs. S. After all, he was supposed to secure food and shelter for her as mother once did, or at least should have done, when she was a child.

Freud's opinion that the relationship of a woman with her husband often mirrors faithfully the one with her mother, has to be modified in the sense that the husband most frequently becomes the target of the wife's repressed (and certainly unexpressed) feelings of frustrated dependency on and rage against her mother.

Indeed Mrs. S. never dared in the least to show her anger against her mother. She also had to substitute food for the lack of adequate mothering. Hence in this case it was not possible to establish with certainty "who started first." Did the husband deprive her of his company by preferring to be with his brother, thus forcing the patient to fall back on her daughter for her unfulfilled dependency needs? Or was *she* the first to force her husband to fall back on his brother, by making Mr. S.'s life miserable at home where he was "knocked" by his children to cheer up his wife? This example also illustrates the transmission of a neurotic pattern from one generation to another. The weight problem which manifested itself so differently in mother and daughter had in both the same earliest root: maternal deprivation.

SEXUAL FREEDOM
or
"How can I trust you?"

The patient was suspicious of everybody. He felt that people on television imitated him. "The actors on TV move their lips the same way I do. I had to move them only because they were dry. My mother had dry lips when she had high fever. . . . I fear that I may become sick. . . . Nothing special, just sick. I fear also that I may suddenly become a homosexual. . . . If a man would grab me and take me for some kind of a fag I would kill him. . . . I don't like that you and X (the female therapist) don't level with me. I don't trust you, that is sometimes. But Mr. B. (chiropractor) I always trust. In any case I trust him more than you. He did me a lot of good. So what if I didn't understand what he was doing? He would push his thumb at the end of my spine, somewhere there (points to the back), and with the other hand he would push and twist my head. He called it cock-something (coccyx-bone). I asked him: 'How this could help my asthma?' And yet he did me a lot of good. Sometimes he would press so hard that I would groan with pain. . . . I went to him several times a week, all in all for about six years. Sometimes I feel that even now an 'adjustment' by him could do much more than all this talk about my unconscious. . . . I always asked my friends to come with me to help me buy a suit or shoes. . . . I always needed some sort of mother. They were good friends but I somehow felt they controlled me. I did everything they asked me to do (– – –?) Yes, let's go back to my fear that I may become a homosexual. (– – –) How could I think that I am my mother? Only because I have dry lips and am afraid of becoming a homosexual? . . . It occurred to me yesterday that when I want to excite myself I think about women being tortured, groaning and moaning. (– – –) I knew that you would say that. Yeah, just as I did with the chiropractor. You know I started with him right after mother died! And that damn doctor who did her in! She went to him for

years. My father objected; he thought she was having an affair
with that doctor. But my mother did not care. She trusted this
doctor and nobody else. (– – –) You mean as I trusted the
chiropractor?"[20] . . .

Pertinent here are some comments concerning the mush-
rooming new modifications of "group process" approaches
("Feeling Therapy," "Sensitivity Training," "Nude Therapy,"
"Marathon Therapy," "the Esalen Group," "Encounter," and
so forth). They all seem to me to have in common, though to
a variable degree, a) frequent body and eye contact and b) the
quick removal of defenses through the emotional pressure of
group interaction.

While reserving my comments for a more appropriate context on the likelihood that permanent personality changes can
be obtained in this way, I consider it to be my duty to convey
already here the following: I agree with S. R. Slavson, the
founder of the American Group Psychotherapy Association,
on the basis of extensive experience with the dynamics of
therapy-groups when he draws attention to the danger which
patients with vulnerable egos are courting through these
methods. I can also believe, though I have not had direct
evidence of it, that borderline conditions and latent psychoses
may be aggravated, under the impact of sudden group-psychological removal of defenses. As these methods seem, however,
to provide something which in my view was lacking in the
earliest mother-child relationship, I would, on the basis of
a few patients' experience while in dual therapy, suggest
the following compromise: Experimentation with these group

---

20. Chiropractice is of great help to its devotees, not only through physio-
therapeutic measures and suggestion but also—and this particularly interests
the genetically oriented analyst—by providing a "corrective experience":
those who as infants have not had enough early maternal care respond
favorably to tactile and kinetic manipulation as well as to the acceptance
and warmth from somebody who comes to be identified with the earliest
helper and soother in life, the mother. Unfortunately, as in the above
case, by overstimulating certain erotogenic zones (see also case on p. 116)
chiropractic manipulation can also aggravate seriously unconscious conflicts, especially those about homosexuality and incest.

approaches should be undertaken while the patient continues in individual psychotherapy—preferably in a dual setting, for its anxiety- and guilt-reducing effect—so that he has the opportunity to ventilate and integrate his reactions to the group experience.

A more ideologically integrated group-analytic approach has been recently introduced by Martin Grotjahn (1969, p. 1) as a method to help a group of experienced colleagues in the analysis of their neurotic residues. These have survived—as I had already suggested (1966, pp. 228, 396)—the analyst's personal and didactic analyses because they could not be completely analyzed in the "one-to-one" setting of classical analysis. Grotjahn's approach which gives more direct evidence of his being familiar with my work and especially with the triadic principle, deserves a careful evaluation. I must, however, postpone also this to a later occasion.

LIKE PARENTS, LIKE CHILDREN
or
"Never mind that she drinks like a fish"

Mr. B. addicted to alcohol, had squandered the estate his father left him. He would promise his wife to come home as soon as he had left the office. Instead he would spend many hours in different bars. When he finally came home he was drunk and displayed violent temper with his wife in front of the children. Ultimately he deserted his family after having for years shown himself incapable of providing for them.

Both parents had been given to alcoholic excesses, especially his mother. She would neglect him and his younger brother, and father would frequently send his sons to look for her in the neighborhood bars.

"I know that I should not drink. I am ruining myself, my job. . . . Yes, and my family. (Silence) My wife constantly gripes and gripes. Who cares? Sometimes she seems to talk to somebody else. (– – –) To my parents? They both drank. Who tells her to wait up for me? She is up until I come home. (– – –) What has this to do with my waiting for mother? I cannot stand it that she sort of manipulates the children to be up when I come home. . . . So what if I drink in the company of men. (– – –?) Was my mother with other men? Silly. I am not a fag. I don't sport lavender handkerchiefs and lace cuffs and such. (– – –) I know you didn't say it. As for my mother's drinking, father is to blame. I just drink for the fun of it. . . . He was some boozer! I never get stoned. Greta (his new paramour) is a good woman. Never mind that she drinks like a fish (chuckles). She is one who doesn't like to gripe. She is not like my wife. No sir. . . ."

A few weeks later: "Yesterday Greta let me have it. For the first time. She blew her top, saying that I am starting with her what I did with my wife. But yesterday was a special occasion. Rob (a friend) had a son. So we had to celebrate it, didn't we? What is wrong with that? I suggested going to some bar and that was all there was to it. So I came home late to Greta. So what?"

How little Mr. B. was inclined to celebrate the birth of anybody's son and how much, on the contrary, such an occasion left an indelible mark on his personality became clear when the patient recalled a crucial incident in his childhood: When Mr. B.'s younger brother was born, a nurse was hired. The nurse's son John, a few years older than the patient, kept him company. One night John induced him to perform fellatio. "While I was doing this, John's mother suddenly appeared. She threw herself on him, beat him viciously and dragged him out of the room." Thus the first situation in which a male played the role of a nurturing mother substitute found a sudden end through the intervention of a mother figure whom he hated anyway because she was taking care of his younger brother.

(Appears drunk for the session.) . . . "Don't worry about my driving, Doc. I can hold my liquor. Stop griping, nothing can happen. . . . Besides I don't care. (Long silence) Some friend Rob is! He wallows in money, has a lot of people working for him, but for me, he can't find a job (cries). To hell with him! Some friend! How can I pay you and all the others who are after me? I have no money-making machine. I have to leave. . . . I am going to tell Rob what kind of a friend he is."

His older companion, by offering him oral gratification when he lost his mother to the younger sibling, laid foundation to his expectation that other males would give him things for nothing, as an infant is entitled to get from his nursing mother (see p. 141). The compensatory, and at the same time vindictive, component in this pattern appeared first in his dissipation of his father's sizeable holdings, and later in his incurring debts which he was unwilling to pay. He was constantly pursued by people whom he owed money.

I have found that being chased by many creditors who are interested in his whereabouts, trying to get in contact with him, soliciting him, and so forth, is translated in the unconscious of an inveterate debtor, among others, as not being "left alone," like a woman pursued by her ardent admirers. This mechanism is not unrelated to the dynamics of paranoid ideation which, as we know, is an outgrowth of a latent homosexual conflict in the "persecuted." The relevance of orality in the interaction between the (financially) frustrated creditor and the emotionally frustrated debtor comes through in the expression, "to take one for a sucker," which alludes to the unconscious wish of the frustrated to frustrate somebody else by making promises with no intention of keeping them.

It is my impression, subject to further verification, that with alcoholics a "corrective" oral experience, i.e. feeding with no strings attached, is necessary. By this I mean that at least for a certain period the patient should be treated free

of charge, in order to compensate for the severe oral deprivation suffered by the alcoholic. Such an experience seems to be
indispensable before the patient can become mature enough
to be able to display a behavior-regulating sense of responsibility, instead of ineffectual guilt feelings and self-reproaches
or, as in this case, a self-righteous attitude on one side and
need for self-punishment on the other. The triadic setting
seemed to speed up this process on the strength of its effectiveness against the homosexual impasse (in the unconscious) on
which alcoholic addiction of both sexes is based, as this case
most tangibly illustrates.[21]

THE DANGEROUS SLAVE
or
"She was too powerful for me"

Mr. M. repeated during the session, while constantly rubbing his right eye, ". . . She practically made the bed heave
when we made love. I don't know why I have to think of her
just now. . . . Still, she was not as powerful as my wife (divorced) who practically immobilized me in a sort of vise. You
know how many women there are, especially in this country,
who like to dominate men. They like nothing more than to
show how strong they are and how they can ride men. Certainly I would like to remarry, but who wants one of those?

21. On the issue of payment for genetic-analytic therapy of addiction
in particular and psychic disorders in general, there will be another occasion (in the second volume) to advance some suggestions. They will be
based on the relevance of the triadic principle to the overall methodology
of mental health programs.

. . . I know that I make good money and B. herself earns almost as much as I do. But what if she suddenly became sick and unable to work? Who would want such a financial responsibility? You recall my father's sickness and the many years the whole family had to nurse him? What a life my mother had! He could do what he wanted with her. She was his slave. (– – –?) Isn't it strange, I always forget that. Yes, she was not a weak woman herself. I will never forgive her for forcing food down my throat. She did it with everybody. Relative or guest, whoever came to visit, off she went pushing food into everybody. . . . And then the enemas and the nose douches! The slightest cold and immediately she would run for the bag to unstop my nose! . . . Why did she have to tell me that father no longer slept with her? After all, he was then in his sixties." (Attention was drawn to his again rubbing his eye.) Mr. M. suddenly sat up and turned around: "Now I know why I fear women! One day father was helping mother to put up curtains. She stepped on a rod which swung around toward father. His glasses were shattered and splinters got into his right eye. The oculist said that a fraction of an inch deeper and father's eye would have been lost." But the "danger" presented by this mother-slave came through no less clearly in the way in which she presented father to his son. Not only did she castrate her husband through her disclosure about their sex life, but she demolished his authority as a father by giving their son money behind his back. The guilt feelings about this variation of oedipal collusion with his mother, as well as her almost causing his father to lose an eye, made Mr. M. experience women as exposing him to physical and financial risks. Moreover, these guilt feelings accounted for his lifelong pattern of (psychologically overdetermined) inability to achieve economic security, until he obtained insight into its unconscious origin.

HUNGER AND ENVY
or
"I feel all puffed up"

"I joked to my daughter that I was pregnant. Ruth (daughter) and Bob (husband) were 'lovey-dovey' yesterday. They teased me by holding hands and by pretending that they were going to marry. Ruth lies down on our bed and pretends she is going to sleep there the whole night. I am down in the dumps again. I hope that this time I will not have to scream and scratch myself as I have done before. Now when Bob is in his office I only get depressed. I can control myself. Now when I think about his being with his secretary, I get less upset. You may be right: I was clinging to him as I did with my mother. . . . *I never had enough food*. I was plump. . . . Yesterday I thought there was something wrong with my gall bladder. I felt nauseous and had pains. I went to my doctor. First I thought I was pregnant. But how could I be? I am on the pill. Perhaps this is what makes me feel *puffy*. The doctor found, however, that I have a new ulcer. I told him about the ulcer I had when Marty (the first child) was born. It reminded me of the time when Bernard (her younger brother) was born. I was constantly crying, and everybody poked fun at me. When my older brother and I had ice cream, I would quickly eat mine first and then trade something for his. . . . All my aunts *kissed* and kissed me. *They never had enough of kissing me.* One of them even now reminds me of it, saying, I would kiss you so-mmm—almost take chunks out of you!' . . . When I breastfed Marty he would *bite my nipples* so that I could not stand the pain. Sometimes I thought there was something wrong with my milk, but I could not bring myself to taste a drop of my own milk to find out. (Grimace of disgust.) By the way, yesterday Marty pretended to *bite* Ruth's arm. . . . I don't know why they are all teasing me. Do you think that Marty resents Ruth because he saw me nursing her? With Ruth I was more relaxed and it was easier. My mother also preferred my younger brother. You are right about this jealousy thing. I am jealous and envious of everything and everybody. . . . What makes me really mad is that I cannot stop eating. On leaving I said to X. (female therapist), 'I notice that you have thinned out' (after her pregnancy). . . . Now I can start dieting. . . . When Bob touches or *kisses* my breasts something in me winces. *I am afraid he might hurt them,* perhaps *bite* into them or something, and I might get cancer. . . . When Ruth was looking at TV I was fuming, and I screamed and cursed that I had to work and she was not doing anything. (Her daughter was recovering from the flu.) Ruth did not hear it because my vacuum cleaner was going. When I am with people I often feel like screaming but something closes up in my throat. Now you know why my voice drops and people can't hear what I say. In the end *I eat myself up.* Tuesday I have to go and see my doctor who will tell me what the x-rays show about my ulcer."

It was evident that oral envy and frustration played an important role in this mother's overeating, as well as in her inclination to develop ulcers at real and imaginary pregnancies. They probably provided the central motive for the genetic script she had prepared for her son. He suffered from a most serious disturbance of sexual identity, a condition to which his father contributed to a no lesser degree.

MOTHER'S DISGUST WITH SEX
or
"She would rather sit with me and watch TV"

"We both knew father was waiting for her to make love. I would nudge her and say, 'Why don't you go to him and get it over with?' But she would have a bored expression on her face and would not budge. Then finally she would go and return after a few minutes and say 'ech' as if she wanted to vomit, and go on looking at TV, sitting sort of too close to me." It was evident that Myrna's mother, in implying that she was disgusted with her husband's sexual needs, used her daughter as a mother substitute to re-enact the oedipal triangle of her own childhood. This alibiing pattern, as is usually the case, was enforced by unconscious guilt feelings rooted in the identification of her husband with her father. Preferring to be with her daughter rather than with her husband, this mother also compounded lesbian seduction in her alibi.

As is common, Myrna's own oedipal aspirations were only aggravated by her mother's rejection of her husband. The usual unconscious conviction of a daughter that she could make the father happier than mother ever did was only deepened by the evidence of mother's deprecating father. On the other side, this mother through her pantomime implicitly forbade her daughter to accept her father, the first male in her life, while offering herself as a love object. Myrna ultimately and typically "defended" herself against heterosexual or homosexual incest by running away from home and becoming intimately involved "with the first man who came along." A pregnancy out of wedlock was the result of *her* need to prove that she was not sexually interested in either parent. As is the case with all "defenses," the underlying wishes succeeded in asserting themselves in the very act of the denial of their existence. In the first place, as soon as Myrna became pregnant, she broke with her boyfriend and returned to her parents, thus acting out the typical fantasy of the little girl who wanted to bear her father a child. Secondly, by leaving her boyfriend because, as she said, "she could not stand him" and "there was nothing in common between him and me, he only needed me for sex," she duplicated her mother's rejection of her father.[22]

LONGING FOR FATHER
or
"We almost killed each other"

The patient and her husband had had one of their most terrible physical fights. She had married a man who would repeat for her what she had witnessed with terror as a child: father's physical abuse of mother. She recalled that whenever she tried to protect mother by clinging to her legs, mother unexplicably would beat her on the head, telling her to stay away. As an adult she now was capable of protecting herself and fighting back against her husband. For that matter she

22. This and similar clinical illustrations bear out that impending or existent unmarried motherhood is an urgent indication for dual therapy, not only for the unmarried mothers, but, because the latter are so frequently recidivant, also for their parents, interlaced with the so-called "intergenerational confrontation" (W. Haas, 1969). I have used this approach with good results since 1950 mostly within the framework of dual therapy, in "conjoint sessions" with parents and their offspring (1966, pp. 512, 519, 526, 535). In this encounter between the two generations the young one, even after he has become a parent himself, is given the opportunity to express his feelings spontaneously in the assuring and mediating presence of the therapist. The cathartic and integrating effect observed with this type of *parent-child confrontation* is most impressive. It shows how the release of feelings deeply buried, sometimes even for decades, brings about very dramatic changes in the psychological situation not only of the offspring but, surprisingly, also of their elders.

would often be the first to attack, when she felt provoked, as on the occasion when she ran into the other room, grabbed a heavy fireside iron and swung it at her husband's head. She could not stand his spending hours in bars, and especially in a bar where her father was referred to as the "best customer." In reality she herself greatly benefited from dual therapy after she had recognized that her pattern of going to bars "independently," i.e. paying for her drinks herself, was a way both of enacting father and of (unconsciously) looking for him. She ultimately gave up visiting bars and improved so much that she lost her disgust for men. She divorced her first husband, who was as unreliable a provider as her father had been, and remarried. This time, however, she had to contend with a husband who in another respect reminded her of her father, but this was "discovered" only after marriage: he also liked to drink, first only "for business" then also "for company."

The frequency with which people with similar genetic scripts become intimate is striking. This naturally only aggravates their basic problems and moreover provides each of them with plausible reasons for blaming the other. This is well illustrated by the fact that the "warmest" father figure her husband had was a much older brother, who was a chronic alcoholic. In other words, both husband and wife frequented bars in an unconscious search for a father or father substitute, with this longing regressively expressed in terms of the (oral) dependency on the mother.

BLESSINGS OF PARENTHOOD
or
"Believe me, Doc, it is only excess energy"

He suffered from a rather excessive jerking tic of neck and shoulders. First he asserted that he had had it all his life. "You know, it is simply because of too much energy in me." Later on, he recalled that it had appeared shortly after the birth of a sister when he was twelve years old. "But believe me, Doc, I loved this sister and still love her! It is only that they (parents) controlled me every moment, screamed at me, 'Don't slam the door! Don't bang on the table! Don't scratch the floor!' I practically could not breathe. Where else could my energies go?" Somehow both his mother and father were themselves irritated at the time. "They were blowing their tops every moment. Devil knows why! . . . Those jerks practically disappeared, I mean they were much less when I grew up, began to work and moved away from home. Only about *two years ago* they came back a little stronger. (– – –?) You mean feelings behind my tics, which I fear to see in myself? (– – –) You mean everybody? (– – –) Yes, but what if those feelings are bad? . . . You know there are people going around who would like to smash things, bash everybody's heads in. (– – –) Have I ever felt like this myself? Never! . . . But who knows? I could go nuts. I guess I am all right. I prefer not to pay attention to it. My wife doesn't mind it (the tic) and I love my daughter. She is *two* and is the apple of my eye."

A "MATERNAL" FATHER
or
"How exciting to let oneself go and to swoon"

These her words led to the emergence of a childhood memory: She had lost her balance and fainted and then was carried in the arms of her father. This came back to Mrs. Z. when her marital difficulties were being discussed. She felt frustrated because her husband was not affectionate or "motherly" enough. But at the same time she was sarcastic about "his need to constantly prove his virility." She recalled having played with her younger sister the game of limp abandonment and of being carried. But then she was the one to carry her sister in her arms. It emerged (in her father's dual therapy) that he was more than only willing to play the role of mother to his two daughters. As is usually the case, he did this not from any deep parental affection but simply because he could not stand the sight of his wife taking care of the daughters. It reminded him of his mother's taking care of his younger sister, with whom he fought furiously throughout his childhood and adolescence. Hence, while his wife went to work, he remained at home and took care of the girls, bathed them, fed them, dressed them and so forth. "Daddy would play with me a game which he never wanted to play with Irma (her sister) though she begged him to do so. He would walk, letting his pants slide down at every step. I would run after him trying to catch them but could not make it. I recall how we all shrieked with laughter." The patient retained a lifelong compulsion to look at people undressing—except for her husband. With him, she could not explain why, she always had to look away. She would even be overcome by a feeling of utter contempt, because it seemed to her that he was exhibiting himself "in a sort of bragging way."

In his "pants falling down" game the father satisfied his exhibitionistic needs, towards which Mrs. Z. seemed extremely sensitized in her marriage. Evidently she confused her husband with her father. In addition, by always excluding Irma from the game with Mrs. Z., this father evidently inflicted upon the former his own experience of being excluded after the birth of his sister: he had identified one daughter (Mrs. Z.) with himself and the other (Irma) with his sister.

The disbalance created in the genetic history of these two daughters by their father's playing a mother role, and at the same time being exhibitionistic and seductive, resulted in a serious disturbance of gender identity of the Self and of the object in both women (i.e. a trans-sexual identity, 1966, p. 274). The contribution which the mother of these two daughters made to insure such an outcome see *ibid.*, p. 519.

DELEGATED PROMISCUITY
or
"That's all men want"

Rita, a young woman, suffered from a chronic schizophrenic-type syndrome. Breastfeeding was for her mother very distressing: she was able to nurse Rita only if at the same time she herself was being spoonfed by her own mother. Indeed this mother's own unfulfilled dependency needs, which immobilized her on the level of the earliest mother-child symbiosis, compelled her to foster in her own daughter a life-long pattern of dependency. The mere fact of hormonal maturation, however, determined for both generations the erotization of their relationship. "Mother (a violinist) was saying that artists have their own rules. She was—how do you say it?— a bohemian. She would walk around naked." Against her (lesbic) response to her mother's seduction Rita had no way of protecting herself, because of the absence of a father in the oedipal phase: when Rita was barely two, she woke up at night and saw the Gestapo drag her father from his sickbed. She soon learned that he had been killed. Rita was thereafter separated from her mother and placed under another name in a gentile family. Mother, who was running from one hiding place to another, could see Rita only on the street and at the risk of her life. When they met, Rita would walk near her mother as if by chance, pretending not to know her. At the age of three she had to learn never to address her parent as "mother."

To Rita's conception of men as a source of terror (they killed her father and hunted both her and her mother to murder them, without her understanding why), her mother added other negative elements, central to her genetic script. Thus over the years Rita learned from her mother what the latter would repeatedly tell her therapists: "My husband didn't love me. He was a brute and abused me sexually." Bearing out that there was no place for a man in the affection of this woman was the fact that she made only a few feeble attempts to find a new husband for herself and a father for Rita. These attempts ended up, without exception, in the triumphant reaffirmation of what she always maintained, that "what men really want is only to jump on a woman and drag her into bed."

What happened to her husband that fatal night became one of the most important factors in determining a peculiar pattern in Rita when she was in her late teens and early twenties: She had to get up the middle of the night and leave her bed in her mother's home, to wander around in the streets. One night, ultimately, under the threat of a gun she was raped by an unknown man. To bring about this (first) sexual experience in Rita, three main (unconscious) motives participated. One, the need to run away from mother, i.e. from the danger of being seduced by her, resulted from the regressive equation of this danger with the father's being found in bed by his killers. Two, in running out in the night to roam in the street she was moved by her longing and need to find her father. Three, in structuring a rape under the threat of being shot, she re-enacted her father's destiny as victim of human aggression. (The way in which the Germans disposed of their victims outside of concentration camps was mostly through shooting.) Rita's subsequent promiscuity represented typical attempts at restitution: Her deepseated hatred and suspicion of men had to be denied by exploitation of sex, her (unconscious) fantasy being that she had to pay the price for survival through unconditional sexual surrender:[23] the experience that men are ruthless killers had to be, in other words, buried and denied with the help of mother's indoctrination, "men only want sex."

Not having had parents to protect her against the primitive fear of being killed by men,[24] Rita seemed at first doomed to remain a mental cripple for the rest of her life. Yet in dual therapy the relationship with a non-seductive mother substitute and a "safe" man brought about striking changes in this "psychological" orphan. Long before her all-consuming unconscious anxiety subsided, which accounted for what appeared on the surface as typical "schizophrenic" flatness of affect, Rita began to show signs of capacity for emotional attachment. Ultimately she developed an intense transference involvement with both therapists (in disagreement with Freud's contention that psychotics do not develop transference, Flescher, 1953).

In view of her experience with men, it was especially important to observe how she would feel particularly towards me. Though occasionally she had the fleeting concern that I might be a Nazi in disguise, she soon reacted to me, under the corrective influence of the female therapist who promoted her trust in me, with feelings which were transferred from how

---

23. Such a mechanism—or "defense," as it may be—was observed even among the primates. A male monkey who has mounted the preferred female of the head monkey in his absence, will, noticing the leader's return, run towards him and "present himself," i.e. convey his sexual availability. This device for abating fear of castration and death as punishment for incest plays, incidentally, an important role in the dynamics of human homosexuality.

24. See concept of "psychological orphans" (Flescher, 1966, p. 351).

she had perceived her father had been towards her before she lost him at the age of two. Though Rita's father had been a traveling merchant, he appeared to have been warm and loving towards her when he was at home. This deepest layer of feelings in Rita must have been tapped for affectionate attachment to me. Behaviorally, her promiscuity soon stopped, as did her restless running around at night. Her tendency to answer any question with "I don't know," which betrayed fear that any information could seal her doom, slowly disappeared. Only a morbid inclination to self-observation, which transpired in such remarks as "Here I go repeating myself," "I am smiling again," or "Wasn't it stupid, what I just said," seemed for a long time unassailable as an expression of her split in the Ego, approximately but not exactly along the lines of differentiation of the Super-Ego from the rest of the Ego: Rita had to be both child and parent because for long periods during her childhood she had been deprived of parents to watch and protect her. An exasperated dependency on her mother appeared also in her pathetic need, even after she was living away from her mother and earning her own upkeep, to walk long stretches in order to beg her mother for the few cents she needed for a subway fare. Ultimately dual therapy also reversed these consequences of the disbalance which her family constellation and genocidal trauma had enforced on her genetic disposition.

As for Rita's mother, she suffered from the inexplicable appearance of red blotches on her face and neck in the presence of people. There were sufficient elements pointing toward the likelihood that her exhibitionism, as well as her daughter's promiscuity in striking contrast to her own sexual abstinence, enforced this her conversion symptom: the blotches betrayed both her excitement from the unconscious sexual fantasies which she acted out through her daughter, and her unconscious guilt feelings ("blushing with shame").

GROWING UP WITHOUT ANXIETY
or
"I wanted to be fearless as boys are"

A mother saw her seven-year-old boy on the other side of the street. When she caught his eye, he motioned to her and then, on an impulse, started to cross the street. Somehow either she didn't have time to motion him back or he disregarded her warning, but he walked straight into the path of an oncoming bus and was instantly killed. This mother, as my colleague learned, had over-protected her child and given him all the security and acceptance to which *she* felt he was entitled. She had followed with particular zeal the fashion of "progressive education": she freely exhibited herself to him. Thus he learned from her that he could do anything, without restraint or caution: near her there was no room for anxiety, fear, or threat of danger. During the analysis of this mother it emerged that ever since her childhood she had wanted to be an "uninhibited and fearless boy." This wish was the mainspring of her suggestive empathy as a mother.

The boy thus paid with his life for the unconscious agreement between mother and son to disregard completely the restrictive role of the external world. It goes without saying that, in the boy's fatal "slip," an unconscious primitive root of a judging and punishing psychic agency (superego) also participated. The exposure by his mother had aggravated his oedipal conflict and the concomitant guilt feelings. Do we need to add that the wish of this unlucky mother's parents for a boy rather than a girl was another link in this chain of cause and effect? (Flescher, 1966, p. 38).

THE CONFLICT ABOUT SEPARATION
or
"Did mother want to seduce me?"

A daughter in her early twenties living away from her
family decided to initiate psychotherapy. Her parents had
divorced and each remarried. She made her decision after
learning about the mental breakdown of her brother. Her
mother, advised of her daughter's plan, did not react because
she felt "it was up to her." She considered her, as she put it,
"mature enough not to need my blessing and certainly not
my objection." However, as mother had come from another
town to visit her daughter, they decided to spend the night
together. Before falling asleep mother was about to embrace
her daughter. The latter in drawing closer to mother "by mistake" touched her mother's breast. She withdrew in panic,
turned around and cried silently. Her mother did not embrace
her, but withdrew quickly in her turn. Three years later the
daughter confronted the mother in a conjoint session, demanding to know why she had not asked what had made her suddenly turn her back on her mother. It would have reassured
her, she commented, because mother's own subsequent turning away seemed to confirm the thought which had frightened
her. "Did mother want to seduce me—to hold on to me?" As
is usually the case, the mother's explanation, that she had felt
rebuffed by her daughter, did not satisfactorily explain her
own quick withdrawal. She recalled, though only "vaguely,"
that her daughter's hand had lightly brushed against her breast,
and that she had felt uncomfortable at the thought of embrac-
ing her. Actually she was relieved by the opportunity afforded
her by this rebuff of her daughter to put an end to her own
discomfort. Ultimately she came to recognize that she could
have openly supported her daughter's decision to initiate
therapy and from the first could have shown herself interested
in what made her daughter decide to take this step. She could
simply have been ready to take into stride her daughter's possible refusal to answer her, the more so because she had good

reasons to anticipate such a reaction. If the parents had not been divorced, and if the father had been sufficiently interested in helping to keep the lines of communication open between wife and daughter, these complications would have been quickly settled, or might not have arisen at all. (The effectiveness of triadic settings in decreasing anxiety and guilt feelings is well illustrated by this fragment from a conjoint session.)

A CROWDED INFANCY
or
"No, I mean I have bought fruit"

Her younger sister would complain that Hilde (the patient) was always a cold and ungiving person. The sister did not know how much her own birth only thirteen months after Hilde's accounted for this. In reality both suffered from the so frequent lack of sufficient and exclusive mothering, without having to share her with another sibling (twin or close in age). Their oral fixation was aggravated also by the lack of breastfeeding by a hardworking and constantly harassed mother, and especially by the birth a year apart of three brothers. The fixation in the oral phase appeared in both as marked obesity which subsided only after adolescence. Both had underdeveloped breasts[25] in sharpest contract to their

25. On the basis of my familiarity with the genetic history of orally deprived patients, I believe that the effect of the maternal introject and fantasies of attack against it on the hormones regulating a proper growth and attractive shape of breasts deserves a thorough investigation, not only because of the esthetic and erotic value of breasts but also because the function involved, as we have shown, is so essential in the proper development of the child.

otherwise well-shaped bodies. Hilde's other childhood deprivations included the early loss of her father in a car accident, the coldness and hostility of her stepfather (himself orphaned as a child) and finally the prolonged illness and death of her mother when Hilde was in her early teens.

Hilde was mostly taciturn, especially in group situations, and irritated when other women were talking. "They would simply gab about food and clothes." In therapy her inability to look at people's faces revealed itself as due to an avoidance mechanism: her longing and rage against the mother's breast was shifted along familiar lines of investment in so-called "partial objects": first from her mother's breast onto her face and then onto any other human face. A marked character trait of "negativism" manifested itself in her inclination to react with initial opposition to any suggestion made by others and to answer any question first with a "No" (as in the headline quotation). At any request, even if one of obvious advantage to her, she would at best remain silent, so that it was not only not clear whether she agreed but even whether she had heard what was said. For years she was incapable of thanking anyone for a courtesy shown her, and later could say it only with her head turned away, and so softly that her children would chide her for what seemed to them her unpoliteness.

She married a man primarily for economic security, and only through prolonged analysis succeeded in achieving some degree of amelioration of her frigidity. She never could bring herself to show interest in sex, although her husband complained about this. Still she never resisted her husband with only one exception: once in a quarrel over her general attitude toward sex she broke out in a fury, screaming at her husband, "All you want is sex, sex, sex! I feel like pouring cement in my vagina!" In analysis she understood that the fantasy was due to a reversal: she did not want anything to be poured into her sibling's mouth by her mother. Indeed when there was an interruption of a week or so in marital sex life, which occurred only exceptionally, she "missed" her husband's advances. She could not understand why because, as she confessed to her therapist, she without exception reacted with well-concealed hatred to her husband's attempts to initiate love-making. "Why can he have pleasure whenever he wants it, and why does he want it so often?" was always her first angry thought. But when intercourse was well advanced she would suddenly notice her own mounting excitement and then think, "How stupid of me to have so much anger against what is so pleasurable." The only thing she would feel then was regret that the sexual act sooner or later had to finish. She recalled once as a child having overheard her aunt pleading with her uncle not to hurt her, and she had (primal scene) fantasies about cruelties he inflicted upon his wife. Ultimately she admitted that, bewilderingly for her, the fantasies to which she was resorting to reach orgasm during intercourse were of "cruel men" who were hurting and raping her.

In analysis she brought material indicating that all her inhibitions and character traits ensuing from the many psychic injuries suffered as a child, including the previously mentioned primal scene," were telescoped into the experience, not recalled but reconstructed, of seeing her mother *feeding her younger sister*. All the aggressive responses engendered by the repeated oedipal frustration (loss of her father, rejection by her stepfather) had regressively reinforced the trauma of her earlier oral frustration and sibling rivalry. This, however, became clear to the patient only when she recounted a peculiar incident which occurred when she entered the bedroom. She noticed, as she maintained with surprise, that her husband was waiting for her to make love. When she became aware of his erection, to her utter bewilderment and shock she heard herself saying, "I don't want milk." When analyzing this breakthrough from her unconscious, though in denial form, of an infantile wish repressed throughout her life, she understood many things: the reason why she almost killed her sister by accident, her anger against women "gabbing about food," i.e. using their mouths, her taciturnity reaction to her never expressed demand at the sight of her mother bottle-feeding her sister (*"I want milk, don't give it to her!"*), her avoidance of eating at the table both with her original family and now with her husband and her daughter, her accusation that her husband (standing for the sibling brothers) does not allow her to have female friends (her mother), etc.

The impulse to interfere with the pleasure of others and the fear of losing control of her rage, rooted in an utterly exasperated *oral envy,* accounted for her coldness, uncommunicativeness and confusion of sex with feeding. The "cruel man" of her fantasies was not only her "cruel" uncle and her hostile stepfather, but also herself "punishing" her mother for her lack of generosity (in nurturing). Her unconscious need, rooted in oral deprivation and reinforced by subsequent frustrations, made her miss intercourse when it was not forthcoming even though she initially abhorred it, and also wish that the sexual act could be everlasting. This clashed, however, with the oral envy which was so total that she wanted to destroy her husband's pleasure even in the very act in which he was sharing it with her. Hers was a compromise solution: only when she had dissipated in sado-masochistic fantasies the aggression pent up in her from so many frustrations was she able to enjoy intercourse. A breakthrough (in dual therapy) which ameliorated not only her love life but her general attitude towards her husband and then towards other people ultimately came about in the triadic setting of dual therapy. In tears she disclosed that while she had previously accused her husband of being oversexed, what actually threw her into a real panic was when he showed himself affectionate and tender towards her.

IMPROPRIETY TRANSMITTED
or
"What's wrong with a little nudity, Doc?"

The patient, an alcoholic, would add: "This is your hang-up, Doc. You are behind the times. . . . Victorian prudishness, eh?" He had again exposed himself to his two daughters, despite his therapist's cautioning him not to continue in his habit of stripping naked as soon as he got home. His wife was "inaccessible" for the purpose of exploring why she did not object to her husband's exhibitionism. She was in "traditional" therapy, which meant that her therapist found it obligatory to give her the experience of "absolute confidentiality and discretion," so as to preclude any exploration of *her* motivation for promoting conflicts in her daughters, which sooner or later were bound to disrupt their emotional balance. That this wife must have drawn some gratification from her husband's exhibitionism in a state of drunkenness, along with the inevitably incumbent guilt feelings, was undoubtedly true: concurrently with her husband's sexual liberalism, she was the victim of her own addiction, not to alcohol but to food, with the result that she suffered from extreme obesity.

As to the genetic background of her husband's exhibitionistic pattern, it quickly came to the fore after a few sessions of dual therapy. "She (his mother) would often come home drunk. . . . One time (voice quivered) I saw her lying on the floor. . . . She had passed out. There she was, completely naked, dishevelled and wallowing in the dirt."

Evidently the patient had used his two daughters as proxies to master a trauma which he had never worked through. The naked mother was not only an object of his (sexual) curiosity and arousal. He had hated her most of all because she did not mind inflicting upon him the picture of utter degradation and loss of self-control. His father's tolerance of mother's alcoholism was, as is so frequent the case with mates of alcoholics, easily traceable to his own latent disposition to drinking. He himself became an alcoholic after his wife died from a liver disease.

This illustration, like so many others in this book, imposes on us also a re-evaluation of the present trend toward sexual license or, as it is referred to more and more, the "sexual revolution" to which the patient alluded when chiding me for being "behind the times." But to this topic we shall devote a major effort on a later occasion.[26]

CULTIVATING SEXUAL TASTES
or
"She would moan and groan with pleasure"

In exploring her peculiar sexual preferences, Mrs. O. recalled how her mother perpetuated with her the known children's game of "playing doctor" by insisting on "cleansing the body" with enemas, as a cure-all. She would also convey to her daughter impressively and audibly the pleasure she experienced while giving herself a rectal lavage. In the course of dual therapy it became clear that Mrs. O.'s memory had also the function of "screening out" other more exciting and at the same time more enraging recollections of "primal scene" experiences, when she had also overheard her mother's physical enjoyment.

Besides this mother's exhibitionism, there were other elements pointing to her morbid involvement in her daughter, e.g. her habit of showing the patient her naked breasts through tears and holes in her housecoat. According to Mrs. O., her

---

26. Genetic Prevention of Collective Irrationality.

mother insisted on always having the last word, thus exasperating her husband to the point of his attacking her physically. Evidently, the sado-masochistic provocation of her husband was another way of gratifying this mother's urges, rooted in the anal stage.

In connection with Mrs. O.'s complaint about her own husband, who was "not soft and cuddly" as she so much wanted him to be, still another memory about her mother came up. The patient described an incident which had left her utterly bewildered. She could not understand why her husband, during their love-making, became furious when she began, as she said, "to stroke his breasts." He angrily pushed her hand away, cursed her and turned his back on her. While wondering why men do not understand women's need for tenderness, she suddenly recalled that when she was very small, perhaps three or even only two, mother would allow her to play with her breast but then would suddenly slap her hand and push her away. There is no doubt that, by exhibiting herself seductively, only to control and to be punitive re her daughter's sexual arousal, this mother, as so many parents do, attempted to master the anxieties and guilt feelings encumbent on her own sexual needs, immobilized on infantile (oral and anal) levels. It is not difficult to grasp that the re-enactment with her husband of the trauma of rejection by her mother (repetition compulsion) was facilitated by his own psychological allergy: he was evidently too threatened in his masculine identity by the way his wife caressed him.

REBELLION THROUGH PROXY
or
"I could not help laughing"

Mr. A. said this happened after he suggested to his son
Henry that he might want to take a job this coming summer.
Without blinking an eye, Henry answered, "Pop, but I don't
want to work. Who cares to keep a job?" (– – –?) "Why I
laughed? How can I blame him? He is all me. I think our society is too materialistic. Money, money, money, that is all
everybody cares for. People hate each other because of the
cutthroat competition. As for myself, to tell the truth, I could
spend my life without working. The idea of assuring to everybody who wants it a negative income-tax is the best I've heard
for a long time."

Mr. A.'s own father was a man who didn't brook any
opposition in the family. If he decided something, he did not
ask his son if it suited him or not: "He simply ordered and that
was that." With pride, Mr. A. recalled that at the age of ten
or eleven he was earning money by going around with a bag
under his left arm, picking up pieces of paper from the street.
Had it been indispensable that he work at such an early age?
"No, not at all, it was simply that my father had ordered it."

When Henry was found smoking marijuana, his father did
not mind. "After all, it's his life." He only wanted to make
sure that Henry did not, like so many youngsters, become a
"pusher" to make money. Sooner or later he would get into
trouble with the police. It was evident that this father's approach to his son was the exact opposite to the one used
toward him by his own father. He not only did not impose his
will and expect blind obedience; he even enjoyed his son's
complete disregard of any well-meant suggestions or advice.
This father, as is the case with so many parents, was quite
unaware that he was fascinated by his son's denying him any
parental authority, simply because Mr. A. had introjected his
own father and made his son into a proxy of himself. Thus a
situation was created which allowed Mr. A. after four decades

to rebel against his father with the already familiar defense of "introject attacked by proxy."

But was it possible that the paternal introject as such did not leave any trace on Mr. A.'s behavior? I shall not go into all the data proving the contrary. It will suffice here to say that what brought this father to me in the first place was his shock at what had happened a few days earlier. He had inexplicably lost control at the sight of Henry's long hair, grabbed his son and engaged in a physical fight to force him to cut his hair. It was precisely this act, in sharpest possible contrast to Mr. A.'s principles and behavior, which made him decide to enlist psychiatric help.

SONS AS BROTHERS
or
"Why should they not learn to help?"

This complaint was angrily voiced by Mr. C. the boys' divorced father. He was very attached to both his older brothers. For Oscar, the next in age, Mr. C. was not only a faithful companion, but would, after they left home, *cook meals,* advise him on jobs and introduce him to girls. He was financially very generous towards both his brothers and always at their beck and call even if he himself had most pressing obligations to attend to.

"Yes, why did I drop everything to bring Oscar and his bride over in my car and to *help them to move,* drag things up and down the stairs? Who needed all this? He could well afford paid help!" A few months earlier Mr. C.'s father left Oscar (in estate) practically everything. "Now he can live the

rest of his life on what he inherited. And just imagine—I
asked him a few days later for some small favor, but he didn't
have time! (– – –?) Well, I didn't mind it. What the hell, with
his wedding coming up and all." It "just happened" that barely
two weeks later Mr. C. himself had to move from one apartment to another in the same building. On that occasion he had
brought his two sons, both in their early teens, to tears, by
haranguing them most violently: They did not show themselves to be particularly enthusiastic when he asked them *to
help him move*. It is true that they also well knew that their
father, being in the $30,000 bracket, could have easily
afforded hired help. "They could very well make this little
effort. Don't I spend every weekend with them and *cook for
them*, trying to meet every whim of theirs?" When exploring
the reasons for Mr. C.'s sudden need to move and to be
helped by his sons, the patient recognized that he had raised
both his children as substitutes for his brothers. Indeed his involvement in his present charges and those of his youth was
detrimental to his relationship with the opposite sex, a fact
which his "after-divorce bachelor" life only served to prove.
Mr. C. ultimately also understood why his girlfriend of long
standing would only raise her eyebrows when he ranted and
raved about the "ungrateful" sons who did not so much as lift
a finger to help their devoted father.

"SHOCKED" TURNING SHOCKER
or
"I wanted to surprise her"

Raymond had as a child often heard his parents making love in the dark but he could not remember how he had felt at that time. Many years later, he was "shocked" when he learned from a married woman's diary what women expect from their love life. He recalled that as a teenager he had vague feelings of loathing toward his father, a school teacher, whom he suspected of covering with the mask of a respectable citizen his appetite for sensual pleasures. Raymond had a tendency to exploit jealousy in order to endear himself to his girlfriends. One such incident was particularly significant. He had arranged a date in a hotel room with one girlfriend, and then invited another with whom he had previously broken. Neither knew of his arrangement. When the latter came to the door, he turned the light out. He planned to turn the *light* on only after she opened the door. "I wanted to see her face when she suddenly saw me with another girl." He could not explain why he had to go through all this. Ultimately, after the analysis of a dream, Raymond recognized that in staging this scene, he was trying to impose on somebody else the "shocking" experience of surprising a couple. His wish to cause each of his girlfriends resentment at the sight of the other reveals the motive of revenge displaced onto them from his mother who had in the primal scene "betrayed" him with his father. The session in which the patient gained most of his insight into this started off with his remark: "Doctor, I still don't see the *light*."

OEDIPAL TRIUMPH BY PROXY
or
"We don't want to make him feel guilty"

Mr. N. constantly anticipated catastrophes befalling either himself or others. His innumerable obsessional rituals, aimed at averting these disasters, absorbed most of his energies. At the same time, inexplicable guilt feelings and self-accusations preyed on his mind. Recently he had *seen through his window* a man staggering and falling to the ground. The old man had died from a heart attack. The patient accused himself of having caused the man's death by breaking wind shortly before while observing "what was going on in the street."

Before the session, Mr. N. had been found "by mistake" trying to open doors other than the one leading to the waiting room, or lingering in the hall entrance. He did not know what he wanted to see or hear, but recalled that in his childhood he liked to peep at disrobing women when nobody would notice.

In a conjoint interview with his wife, he asked how he could put a stop to a certain impropriety of his son "without making him feel guilty." His wife agreed emphatically, adding that she also was in a quandary. "After all, we would like to do what everybody is trying to do now with their children that is to liberate them from shyness and inhibitions." The father explained the problem: His seven-year-old Benny has the habit of playing under the table. "I caught him looking under the skirt of my sister, I mean of his sisters—" Both parents, rather advanced in their therapy, smiled embarrassedly and then plunged into a pensive silence. Each understood to what degree his own childhood experiences accounted for this "problem." Both had been left unsupervised by their parents, and also allowed to sleep with their siblings so that they ended up by indulging in rather advanced sex play with them. It was their guilt, rooted in their acting out of oedipal strivings displaced onto siblings, which made them hesitate to put a stop to Benny's re-enactment of their past. The guilt feelings had not subsided after all these years simply because the original (incestuous) wish still persisted in them.

Their "quandary" about educational intervention and the setting of limits was therefore also determined by the delegation of their own oedipal wishes to their child (acting out by proxy). Why Mr. N. felt guilt over what he had *seen through the window* became clear once he had recalled his childhood habit of *looking into windows* in order to catch women in the act of undressing. What he wanted to find out was not unrelated to his own son's habit of looking under his sister's skirt: the usual anxiety of the little boy about anatomical differences between the sexes, anxiety rooted in the known castration complex of any male violating the incest taboo. Though his castration anxiety was not per se augmented by the rituals concerning menstruation observed by orthodox Jews, his extreme ambivalence toward his father made him complicate his life unbearably by carrying these rituals to absurd extremes. The man who died on the street while Mr. N. was watching through the window was not only his father, but a phallic symbol in the context of his castration anxiety underlying his scopophilia (overerotization of the act of looking at sexually stimulating objects, the counterpart of exhibitionism).

A LIBERAL MOTHER
or
"I did not want to push her to study"

With these words Mrs. N. explained why she did not want to express her disapproval of her daughter's decision to drop out of college in her second year. Mrs. N. had this to say about her own mother, "She vexes me when she remarks that I never know how to say no. She feels that those rioting students and children in general, who think they have everything coming to them, should have their heads bashed in. I instead said: 'After all, you don't throw your children to the wolves even if they eat your heart out.' . . . I don't know what is wrong with my eyes. I am dizzy and still have those headaches. I went as you suggested to my ophthalmologist. Here's a peculiar guy for you! After he examined me he said: 'I would like nothing more than to tell you that there is something wrong with you, but I don't find anything!' Some statement, no? Then he explained that he wanted in this way to convince me that it is really only in my mind. He and my mother, when she comes to his office, they really enjoy each other. They crack jokes, they (laughs) have a field day. (– – –?) Well yes, she (hesitates), she has a sense of humor. It is only with me that she is tense and behaves as if she fears that I will bring her bad news. And how it bothered her when she saw that my sister had bought a new hat! She remarked to me, 'She must be loaded with money, your sister, don't you think so?' It sounded peculiar when mother just received a diamond ring from father for their anniversary! Therefore when my sister told us how much the hat cost, I said: 'It was a good buy, baby!' Then I got it from my mother. 'Why can you call her baby, but when I do the same with you, you blow your top?!' Somehow I don't feel it's the same, but I could not find an answer. (– – –?) The ring which father bought for mother? Well, only a little envious (laughs). . . . I felt embarrassed at one point. Father was talking to mother while standing near me and stroking my arm. Mother poked fun at him when he told my sister he was proud that I am studying for my master's. (She recently registered for courses in literature at college.) She said, 'He soon will have her studying for her Ph.D.!' Is mother jealous or something? (– – –?) You mean Zelda (Mrs. N.'s daughter) might find it peculiar that I don't object to her leaving college when I after so many years have resumed going to college myself? . . . Yes, I see what you mean. . . . I didn't look at my mother when father touched my arm (see similarity to illustration on p. 166) but I imagine that she could have felt annoyed. (– – –?) They are doing it less often now." (Mrs. N.'s husband and daughter used to joke in her presence about marrying each other, pretending to hold hands and so on, which Mrs. N. did not find very amusing.)

(This case of rivalry between a mother and a daughter comes very close to the one between a father and son on p. 171.)

GUILT FROM REPETITION
or
"Dora always sort of watches me"

Mrs. G. could not explain why it irritates her beyond description when her daughter Dora *"watches"* her. The other complaint was that Dora constantly fights with her brother. "She is always jealous of him. Yesterday we visited my parents. My brother Carl again pretended not to see me and did not even say hello. My supervisor (female) was *observing* how I would handle myself with the counsellor (male). She just *watched*. The counsellor is a jerk and he made me mad. I resented her being there and not saying anything when we quarrelled. (– – –?) Well, she intervened, but not until later. My mother would not even do that when my brother tore into me. She was afraid that Carl would break down or something. (– – –?) What use would it have been to tell her about that other thing (sexual play) between Carl and me? If I had told her, she would have blamed me for everything. When he pretends not to see me he is probably thinking of what happened between us. Sometimes he would beat me, leaving

black and blue marks, and I didn't tell anybody. (– – –?) That
is a good question, why does my husband not interfere when I
beat Dora? He certainly is not blind and can see how Dora
gets my goat. Still he doesn't move a finger when I go crazy
and pound her with my fists. . . . She constantly harps that
I prefer Ronny (son). Certainly I do. Who wouldn't? He is
fun to be with. He doesn't provoke me. How good Dora is at
turning the knife in me! . . . When I see Dora just standing
there and *watching* me, I know that she is thinking, 'What is
she doing again with Ronny?' I see red. (– – –?) You say that
I feel guilty when I am *watched* and angry when I am not
watched? Yeah, if my mother had *watched* me better, then
Carl wouldn't have done those things with me. . . . If only
my husband would be more patient with Dora. Everybody says
that she looks like his mother, and you know how my husband
has fought and still fights with his mother. He has this crazy
idea that she always preferred his younger sister. . . . Now I
understand why nothing helps to make Dora stop fighting
with Ronny. Dora gets it from me and my husband and then
she has to stuff herself with food. Again she's eating as if
there would be no tomorrow. . . ."

A DISTRAUGHT MOTHER
or
"He seems to want to get my goat"

She looked distraught and angry, while listening to the
recording of the previous session. I learned that the question
on her mind was whether she had the right to expect her in-
laws to be more generous toward her husband. "I would not

like to appear too greedy. I have dreamt about my son being killed by an oncoming car. (– – –?) Everything is all right with him except his thumbsucking. As soon as he sees me, he sticks his thumb into his mouth. It is as if he does it only to get my goat. . . . I think that he is frustrated, I don't know by what. It is true he had only ten weeks of breastfeeding, but he is already six! At six why would he still want the nipple? He should have outgrown it long ago. (– – –) Somebody older than he? You mean me? How, oh, well, you mean my nailbiting?" (The connection between her concern about appearing too demanding with the in-laws and her own oral deprivation escaped her awareness, although she eventually understood that her annoyance at her son was due to her own (oral) sibling rivalry, which was as pronounced in her as it was in him.)

AN UNINVOLVED PARENT
or
"Why didn't father do something about it?"

Mr. W. recalled that around the time of puberty he could not stand his mother's leaving the comb she had just used either on the windowsill or on the kitchen table. Though he admitted that his sense of disgust was exaggerated, he was furious that none of his remonstrations had any effect on his mother. "She continued, blimey, to keep that comb full of hair where I could see it." In analysis another memory came up which explained his disgust, that of the sight of his mother standing on a table to fix the window shade on a hot summer day. Somehow she did not have any underwear on, so that her son lying on his bed obtained a full view of her pubic hair. His sexual response to this was warded off through repression. The substitutive "reaction formation" of disgust extended from the pubic hair to his mother's hair in general. This memory came up after he made a sarcastic comment about his wife's habit of appearing at the breakfast table with her hair still in disarray. "What I cannot understand," the patient concluded, "is that father had seen me blowing my top again and again, and yet he never told mother to stop provoking me in this manner. Even if my feelings of disgust were exaggerated, how much effort would it have taken for him to tell her not leave those damned combs around and why didn't he mind my busting with rage?" Mr. W.'s mother also indulged in severely beating her son, who would deftly defend himself by parrying his mother's fist blows with his elbow. This caused her to shriek that her son was *beating her*. But even this was not sufficient to motivate his father to intervene. It later emerged that his "uninvolvement" actually began only when his son was six years old. The "traumatophoric number" was ultimately traced to the fact that Mr. W.'s father had lost his own father at the age of six. An important motive which reinforced this father's need *not* to bring his wife and his son together might have been the fear that a closeness between wife and son would automatically result in his being excluded as a father from the family triad: a fear which the loss of his own father at the height of the oedipal phase must have "concretized" for him. (By now we know what may be the motives of a father for not wanting to stop the fights between his wife and his son or daughter.)

Equally "uninvolved" remained the father of another patient. "My mother had the habit of scratching her anal region and then smelling her hand. It made me furious because I didn't want her to touch anything with her hands when preparing food. She would say that my room was not so clean either. What had one thing to do with the other? My father would stand there and not say a word. Only when I looked at him in anger would he ask mother in a sort of disinterested way if she had heard what I had said, and naturally nothing would change." Significantly enough, not only did the patient retain for many years the belief that children are born from the rectum, but his sexual fantasies and activities bore the mark of a strong fixation on the corresponding (anal) level of his psychosexual organization. The oedipal rivalry of the father with this patient, which was the main reason for his keeping aloof from the clashes between wife and son, came clearly to the fore on another occasion. The son had invited his girlfriend home for the first time. His father made an all-out attempt to impress upon her how much more gallant, charming and witty he was than his son. He did this in such an obvious manner that the patient's older sister had to object to his demeanor.

WARRING GENERATIONS
or
"Father told me that he loved me more than mother"

This is what father would tell Debbie behind her mother's back. This embarrassed her greatly. She recalls that as a five-year-old, every Sunday morning she was allowed by her father to lie near him in the parental bed. Her mother seemed not to mind this. She would masturbate without anyone's appearing to notice. In therapy Debbie volunteered her belief that her mother may have wanted her to lie in bed near father because otherwise he would leave home. Mother suspected father of philandering, and Debbie saw mother beating father with a frying pan. On other occasions father also beat mother. Here Debbie brought up the physical fights she herself had with her husband. Father had taken her out of college to make her work for him in his office. For that matter, mother once beat Debbie when she wanted to prevent her father from taking her sister Cora out of high school a few months before graduation, to help him in his work. "Is it not remarkable that of all our brothers and sisters it was only Cora and I who worked for father and who also had the most peculiar husbands and the most miserable marriages?!" The use of her daughter to keep her husband at home, neither made this mother more appreciative of her daughter nor made him into a more loving husband and father. All parties to the violation of the triadic principle paid heavily for their acting out of irrational strivings: the father died prematurely of heart failure, the mother ended in a psychiatric sanitarium, Cora's depression required hospitalization and electroshock therapy and Debbie herself needed many years of analytic help with her multiple marriages. She entered dual therapy at the time when the transference-countertransference bind with her last (female) analyst aggravated her depression to the point of danger of suicide. A few months later she greatly enjoyed a trip to Europe and noticed that, contrary to her previous pattern of attracting men who were cruel and demanding towards her, she now seemed able to interest kind, considerate and helpful men.

RATTLING THE CHAINS
or
"All that I ask is to be treated as a person and not as an object"

This is what Eliza, a young widow who had recently begun to read books on psychology, was telling her mother in a conjoint session. But what emotions accompanied this request? Not only was she crying desperately so that her face was all bathed in tears, but somehow she seemed unaware that copious material was swaying from her nose. But Eliza's mother noticed—as more than likely her daughter wanted her to—and asked me for a tissue to "wipe her little girl's nose," as she sarcatiscally said. Neither mother nor daughter was equipped for such an emergency. Evidently the need to be taken care of by a mother was something which they both still shared. As far as Eliza was concerned, her declaration of independence was belied by the infantile form of her delivery.

It was true that the mother was at fault, though not as Eliza charged. It was Eliza's own childish and helpless leaning on her mother which accounted for the lack of respect for her daughter's individuality. Therefore the accusation, at other times formulated by Eliza as her mother's "controlling my every movement, my every breath," disguised what I have the habit of alluding to with my patients as "rattling the chains": The noisy rebellion against the parent is actually obscuring the child's own unconscious incapacities, i.e. unwillingness to grow up and to give up the ties with his parents.

EXERCISE IN MATERNAL SADISM
or
"My oven exploded, I was careless"

The accident, from which she suffered severe burns, was
her own fault. Years later she had a dream about men walking
upstairs which reminded her of her brothers sleeping upstairs
and the repulsive *smell* of sweat. Mother preferred her brothers. From associations to the oven, she came to talk about
sculptures like busts and statues being baked in ovens. Baking
reminded her of children being pushed in the oven and eaten
by witches in fairy tales and of the opposites wishes to *burn*
and *devour* her mother because she had deprived her as an
infant of loving nutrition. Her mother compounded the feeling of (oral) deprivation by shaming her through letting
others know that, at the age of thirteen, she once expressed
the wish to suck her mother's breast.

When the patient returned from her first dates, this mother
would jump out at her from the dark and beat her on the head.
This occurred after the death of her father when she was in
her early teens. (As she described her mother's punitiveness,
she was unaware that she was constantly touching her nose.)
. . . "My nose? Yes, I have always been sensitive to *smells*. I
could not stand the terrible smells after father left the bathroom. Every day he would give himself a colonic irrigation
after taking a bottle of magnesia, a box of Ex-Lax and a glass
of Russian mineral oil.[27]

"I suffered from some kind of *breathing* difficulties.
Throughout a whole year from nine to ten, my mother would
take me to a doctor who would stick a big metal tube in my
nose with a long rubber hose connected to two bottles, to
flush out the sinuses. He would then push gauze into my nose
very hard. It was painful, but even more so when he cauter-

---

27. The patient's exaggeration on this point (her father could possibly
not have taken all these laxatives and purgatives at once) reflects her
unconscious objection against his oral indulgence.

ized the inside of my nose. *The smell of burned flesh was terrible.*"

With the rage this daughter had against her mother who was directly and indirectly punitive towards her, it is not surprising that she used her "maternal introject" to retaliate against her mother. Unfortunately, what unconsciously was the wish to hurt her mother resulted in her own injury, as in the explosion of the oven, because of her "carelessness." The need to attack her mother in herself, which compounded both crime and punishment, became ultimately eroticized and imbedded in her personality as a therapeutically most resilient masochistic pattern. Mother's interfering with her interest in boys had a historical antecedent: the parents would often fight terribly, to the point of attacking each other physically. The daughter played an important role in this conflict because it was her parents' pattern that each of them would come to her to accuse and complain about the other. Each would then leave her in the conviction that she sided with the complainer, although she "actually did not say very much." The guilt feelings about having in this way contributed to the unhappiness of her parents' marital life deepened her masochism by linking it with a guilt-inspired need for punishment. (This illustration is paradigmatic of the mixture of elements from the oral and anal phases in the patient's traumatic experiences.)

PROXY-DESTROYER
or
"Did I say that?"

Mrs. E., a depressed patient and severe nailbiter in her early thirties, was greatly puzzled by a dream she brought up during the previous session. Contrary to her suave and subdued manner, in her nightmare she had been extremely violent. She had cut up somebody's arm. But the dream remained unanalyzed because, as patients so often do, she recalled it only at the end of the session. This time she began by commenting on the quandary she was in: should she put her foot down with her five-year-old Benny, and make him stop destroying his own toys and those of his younger brother? Then she said: "I always like to take things apart." When I asked her what she meant by this, she did not understand my question. She said it was only that she didn't know what to do with her son's habit of taking a car, for example, and dismantling it. She did not believe me when I told her that she had just mentioned *her* liking to take things apart. Fortunately, she was still in the phase of "process cross-recording,"[28] so that it was possible for me to play back for her what she had said. She then brought up the fact that she is irritated that her mother is not willing to have her cousin as a guest. Yet she also quickly recalled how she resented the fact that her mother had burdened her with the care of her youngest sister, while their parents left the country for a trip. Mrs. E. reported how once when her mother had said, "As it is on your way, Rena would you drop me off there?" She had answered, "Mother, it is not on my way, but I will gladly take you there." "Don't be fresh!" was the angry retort of her mother. Mrs. E. remained silent.

At the next session she laughed, recalling how her son

---

28. In this phase of dual therapy the first half of the session is devoted to listening to the recorded second half of the previous session (with the other member of the dual team), while the second half is devoted to the recording of the current analyst-analysand interaction.

Benny blackened the white shoes of his older sibling. When asked how she handled that incident, she said she did not want to be strict like her mother. She then blithely said, "Whenever he does a thing like that or damages the things of the older ones, they practically kill him. For that matter, the next oldest one, Paul, told me that he wishes Benny would die." (– – –?) "I told him that he might want it, but that Benny would not die." Rena recognized the misapplication of what had been previously conveyed to her: that unconscious wishes cannot kill. At that time the therapist's aim was to make her aware of her unconscious wishes, by assuring her that wishes per se don't hurt anybody. She eventually understood the danger of the frustrated and angry older sibling's acting on the challenge implied in his mother's response to his expressed death wish. She then brought up an incident which had occurred the day before: "Paul rolled up the car window, catching Benny's hand in it." Evidently Paul wanted to punish Benny as much as Benny wanted to be punished for his habit of destroying his older brother's toys.

The sibling rivalry between the brothers was due not only to this mother's using her sons as proxies for her own unreleased aggression but to the oedipal conflict: Benny was extremely demonstrative and constantly kissed his mother, who tolerated it because she "did not know what to tell him." It was in this context that Mrs. E. came to talk about what a happy period her high school years had been. In sharpest contrast with her present inability to raise her voice, with her depression and general tendency to avoid people, she had been gay and most popular with her peers, had enjoyed many sports, acted in school plays and so forth. At first she could not trace the drastic change in her personality back to any particular occurrence, until the therapist suggested from the context that it might have been the birth of her younger sister (by fifteen years), the very object of her previously mentioned reluctant hospitality. She then recalled what a "shock" and "cause of shame" it had been for her that her mother gave birth to her younger sibling when she was already a teenager.

The reader can easily guess what price Benny and Paul would ultimately have to pay if their mother's using them for the alleviation of the aggression which underlay her depression was not stopped before the acting out of hostility (their mother's and their own) became imbedded in the personality patterns of her children.

THE SELF-ELIMINATING MOTHER
or
"Is it fair that I should come along?"

"Today I need a tranquilizer. It is the *first time* in my life I have considered taking one. I never believed in drugs, but I cannot stand this tension. . . . I don't know where to go this weekend. I hate not having anybody to go with on a trip, to a museum or something. . . . I have to rush after this session and pack the suitcases for my husband and my daughters. They are going to the mountains for a few days. (– – –?) Well it will be the *first time* that they have gone away with my husband. They enjoy Randy and don't make any bones about it. I am no fun to be with. Besides *I feel too old.* It is only natural that he finds my daughters more exciting. I would not blame any father for preferring a young chick to an old woman. *I leave them alone.* When he comes home they practically forget that I exist. They run towards him and look into his pockets to see if he has brought something for them. Nobody even looks at me. . . . If I could only understand why both daughters, especially Maria (the elder), are so nasty with me. When I have my usual rages *she looks at me* as if to say, 'Here you go acting crazy.' . . . Yesterday father and mother visited. I have not seen *him* for about two weeks. He ran towards me to give me his usual bearhug. It makes me nervous. I don't know what to do. I don't want to push him away. . . . My mother? Yes, what did she do? In her thoughts she seems not to notice what is going on. She is forgetful. *She has aged.* (– – –) You mean that I am doing what she did? I eliminate her by cutting myself out? You really think so? But if I give them my husband why do they all hate me? They should all three be happy. (– – –) Do you think that it is fair to tell them at the last moment that I am coming along?"

The negative dyad prevailing between this mother and her daughters had the purpose of acting out through proxy her own oedipal wish.

RECIPROCAL DEPENDENCY
or
"I went out of my mind"

Both Mrs. D. and her much older husband struggled with deep-seated dependency needs, each in a different manner. She was a hardworking dressmaker who was compelled constantly, though completely ineffectively, to nag her husband to do some work, because he was lazy. He justified his avoiding any such effort by an elaborate philosophy about leisure and the "real values" of life. It soon became evident that Mrs. D. gratified her dependency needs by the use of the "introject gratifies proxy" defense. She gave to him what she (unconsciously) wished her mother had given and would still give to her. (This defense is identical to the one used by children in their play with dolls. They shower them with the tender care and affection that they expect from their mothers.)

Mrs. D. has a poignant memory from when she was six, of running down the street one winter night to meet her mother
coming home from work. Instead of hugging her daughter and
understanding that she acted under the overwhelming longing
for her mother which forced her to risk the cold and dark in
the street, the mother hit her and scolded her severely. Now
a mother herself, Mrs. D. still would become panicky when
she had to wait for her husband. She was therefore greatly
upset a few days ago when her husband announced that he
was going to spend some time in a bar with a friend instead
of coming home. Still she controlled her anger, even when he
came home after midnight. Indeed he expressed surprise that
she did not make a scene when he made the same announce-
ment the next day. While waiting for him this time, however,
Mrs. D. simply "went out of her mind." She had already discarded his explanation about the company of his friend as a
big lie. Instead she pictured him in the arms of a "motherly
looking" but also very attractive neighbor across the hall,
whom she for a long time had wanted to befriend but somehow "had not dared to make the first move." The thought of
her husband's being embraced by her neighbor unleashed an
indescribable fury in her. Again and again she thought of
"biting off his penis" and of "plunging a knife in his chest."
When he finally came home at five o'clock in the morning,
he told her that in a recent session with his analyst, they had
discussed his longing for his father, who died a chronic alcoholic. Evidently the husband made his friend into a father substitute and acted out a long-repressed wish to find his father
in the bar (see similarity to case, p. 209). At the same time
he inflicted on his wife the very feeling of desertion he must
have experienced as a child at the hands of his father. Mrs.
D.'s fury at the thought of his being in the arms of the neighbor was unleashed by her unconscious envy that he as a man
could still be embraced by a woman, as she herself longed
for the warm arms of a mother. Hence she had the fantasy of
castrating him, a fantasy which she tried to implement by her
habit of denying herself to him sexually.

CHAPTER EIGHT

GENETIC CHILD-REARING

Scope of General Principles

The variations through which a genetic disbalance in the family triad, as exemplified by the preceding genetic scripts, may translate itself into immediate or delayed disturbances in the development and function of the child are infinite. This does not mean that genetic rules capable of preventing the most common alternatives cannot be formulated. Similarly, there are a thousand ways in which one can ruin a watch yet there is no need to specify each of these ways; the general rule of avoiding any mechanical and chemical damage to the watch covers the most common possible accidents.

This is true also for the prevention of mental illness. For that matter, neither did the analytically oriented psychic prophylaxis of the past aspire to cover all the possibilities through which the innumerable variables present in the environment of a child can exert a detrimental influence on him.

Valid Traditional Guidelines

While proceeding to present the general rules of preventive education in accordance with the philosophy of genetic psychoanalysis, let us refresh our memory about the prophylactic rules offered to parents in the past which are still valid today. As these guidelines are of a different category than those derived from the triadic principle, they are not superseded by the latter. However, we would not do justice to the importance of genetic-analytic findings if we failed to emphasize at the same time that the triadic principle in its personality- and destiny-shaping influence overshadows any other hitherto offered psychoanalytically inspired child-rearing suggestion.

In reference to the traditional rules of psychoanalytic prevention, it may be recalled that the child's initially inadequate
capacity to discharge tensions was to be taken into consideration. Hence the stimuli which impinge on his organism at
the dawn of infancy should be measured out carefully. Noise,
violent movements, strong lights, forced awakenings, etc., are
to be avoided. The recommendation that quiet and long sleep
is necessary for the newborn, and that the number of waking
hours should increase very slowly, takes adequately into account the infant's limited capacity to cope with the external
world at this early age.

Importance of Physical Contact with Mother

It goes without saying that this rule should be comple-
mented by the infant's experiences of physical contact with
the mother as his needs are taken care of in an atmosphere
of warmth and loving acceptance. Indeed, the suggestion that
a mother should not avoid close contact with her child covers
a whole range of circumstances, among which the most important is breast-feeding.[1] The practice of "self-demand" feeding, widely followed for some time, is today moderated by
consideration for the mother. In general the mother's own
comfort and pleasure in performing her nurturing task cannot
possibly be separated from her general emotional attitude
towards the child. One cannot expect a mother to have a constantly accepting attitude toward her child if she caters exclusively to his (changing) needs and ignores her own. On the
other hand the pleasure of providing the child with physical

---

1. The movement promoting breast-feeding sponsored with intelligence
and tact by the "La Leche League International" in Chicago (*Time Maga-
zine,* July, 1968) is therefore greatly to be appreciated.

The group therapeutic experiences (see p. 200), where the importance
of touching and being touched, of communication in the nude, of collective
bathing in warm water, is promoted in order to "break down barriers
between individuals," center on the unconscious hope of making up for
what was missing in the early mother-infant relationship.

and emotional gratification depends also on what the mother receives from her husband in love, consideration and support. This points up the frequently overlooked influence which *father exerts on the raising of the child* even in earliest infancy.

Admittedly, in the first months of a child's life the father's influence on the genetic atmosphere exerts itself mostly via the mother. And here also there are innumerable alternatives to be considered. Thus a father may be hostile toward both wife and child, yet in different ways and for different reasons in each case: unresolved (anaclitic) dependency, normal or inverted oedipal rivalry, rebellion against increased responsibilities, and so forth. The frequent *deterioration of the marital relationship with the birth of each new child*—contrary to the myth that children make the marital relationship more meaningful and deepen the bonds between the parents—is a fact which I feel has not been touched, let alone integrated into the theory of human psychopathology. If husbands realized how much assurance, consideration and love mothers need (both before and after they have given birth to a child) to help them discharge the task of proper "mothering," they would less often and less strongly react to the mother-infant psycho-biological symbiosis with frustration at being relegated to the background.

Setting of Limits

The formation of habits is due to repetition of the same, or approximately the same, condition. In this connection it has to be mentioned that there is a growing awareness, in the field of mental prophylaxis, of the importance of the child's acquiring the capacity for self-control. Hence it is recognized that a pre-eminent task of parents is to provide *limits* for the child's self-regulative needs and impulses. The nursing and feeding situation provides the opportunity for the first application of this parental function. Excesses of indulgence in the areas of bodily contact and feeding should be avoided. There are mothers who, overanxious lest the child starve, engage in forced and excessive feedings, as there are mothers who, at the slightest whimper of a child, frantically pick it up and cuddle it. Both these patterns condition the child to an aggravation of his "ego-cosmic" (Ferenczi) self-centeredness, laying foundation to an irascible demandingness and to the expectation that the rest of the world will be at his beck and call.

Overindulgence Covering Hostility

Since errors in this most vulnerable stage of the infant make for an infinite variety of clinical pictures which sometimes appear only after many years, it would be most useful if certain findings and insights could be common knowledge. They could thus be put to good use, without the intervention of a psychiatrist or a child guidance clinic. For example, the area of feeding provides the point of encounter between mother and child, and is prototypical of everything which the adult later expects or dreads from another person. The quickest way to make such mothers desist from exaggeration in their ministrations to the child is to make them realize that *every excess* in feeding, cleansing and caressing *is merely a denial of the opposite wish,* operating in the unconscious. Indeed, a mother who is obsessed by the anticipation that her child may starve, is the victim of a "wishful fear": for certain unconscious reasons (usually unresolved sibling rivalry of the oral phase or oral deprivation per se) she wants her child *not* to be fed, but rather to starve. It is the guilt about this "unmotherly" attitude which forces her to prove the contrary by her exaggerations. The excessive use of oral stimulation which quiets the child when he feels uncomfortable or in distress is certainly most convenient for the parent, but it promotes oral fixation.

Addiction to Oral Pleasure

Pacifiers rightly deserve the reputation they have. They should not be abused, however. Parents should refrain from providing them when uncomfortable bedding conditions or

temperature, wetness, draft, noise and similar disturbing conditions can be corrected. Actually such distressing stimuli in
the environment, and primarily deprivation by mother and
later by both parents, will make the child use many other
objects for oral consolation or for numbing of pain, frustration, anxiety and depression (the pillow, the "security" blanket
and most frequently the thumb).[2] The exploitation of oral
gratification lays foundation, as much as does complete oral
deprivation, to general *oral fixation,* which then lays foundation to a tendency toward *addiction* to food, alcohol or drugs.
The entrenched habit of always having recourse to the
"anaesthetizing" influence of oral-erotic gratification creates
a special vulnerability to overreaction against and refusal to
cope with any type of increased tension or, more specifically,
any type of displeasurable feelings in later life. Why indeed
should he cope with these when he has learned that by oral
indulgence he can always drown them out? Clinical experience shows us daily that a regression to this infantile level in
search for relief, however, always entails a heavy toll physically, emotionally and financially.[3]

Still, once the external sources for the child's discomfort
have been eliminated, or as long as they cannot be identified
and eliminated, there is no reason why the child in distress
cannot draw solace from sucking on a pacifier to his heart's
delight. If the need for a stimulating contact with the parent
is the basis of the child's unhappiness, this need should be
satisfied, again with consideration for moderation and for
mother's comfort.

I have elsewhere shown how frustration aggression can pre-

---

2. A frequent result of oral frustration and ensuing (oral) fixation and
regression is *nailbiting.* It results from deflecting the frustration *aggression*
from objects and directing it toward the Self. It corresponds to K. Abra-
ham's division of the oral stage into *oral-erotic* and *oral-sadistic* subphases
(1927).

3. I do not have a sufficient number of cases to support my impression,
but even in addictions of any kind dual therapy seems to be effective. For
the possible reason for this see 1966, p. 331ff.

vent gratification of the very wish which has been frustrated. I consider as a prototype the situation of a hungry infant waiting impatiently for the bottle. If the hunger and waiting period are too long the child will typically hit out against the bottle. The impatient or thoughtless adult trying to feed the child frequently concludes that "it is evident that he does not want the milk" and removes the bottle. This naturally only aggravates the infant's frustration aggression, and perpetuates his angry and vindictive rejection of what he so badly needs when it is again offered to him[4] (Flescher, 1953, p. 433). This situation is paradigmatic of certain transference-countertransference impasses in classical analysis arising from the absence of a third person as a possible mediator—I almost said "pacifier."

It is pertinent to mention here that children in hospitals, exposed to prolonged separation from their mothers, regularly lapse into a listless or depressive mood. They have been observed not to run happily to their mothers when they finally appear, and to the contrary, evidently under the influence of accumulated frustration aggression, they either attack their mothers physically or withdraw completely from them (to prevent such an attack no doubt).

Anal Stage and Sado-masochism

Toilet training, as already suggested, should not be too harsh, too early or too abrupt. The attitude of the training person (usually and preferably the mother) should not be too impatient or too anxious. A parent who is himself free from fixation in this phase will confidently expect the child to acquire the capacity to control his sphincters.

The promotion of *sublimation* of the pleasure which the child derives from the narcissistic investment in his bodily

---

4. It may sound banal, but I have often seen a pacifier with a drop of honey put an end to the vicious circle of an exasperated mother's attempt to quiet a child and the latter's ceaseless screaming and rebuffing of her ministrations.

(waste) products is something which cannot be gone into here. It should suffice, however, to stress the importance of praise and reward for the child's attempt to sublimate the phase-specific needs of his age in drawing pleasure from play and creative activities with objects and material, activities centering on difference of form, color, consistency and texture (sand, paint, fingerpaint, clay, coloring books, toys, etc.). Freud and later Ferenczi (1916) discovered that the emotional investment of possession (notice the etymological root *sedere,* "to sit") in general, and of money in particular, is supplied not simply by the realistic value they carry but from an anal-erotic root, i.e. from their unconscious identification with bodily (waste) products. Hence the many expressions in which money and scatology are combined (*pecunia non olet—* "money does not smell," a dirty miser, filthy lucre, etc.).[5] A morbid investment in money from sources here discussed may go from one extreme of hoarding and avarice to the other of waste and extravagance.

In agreement with the established fact that developmental phases do overlap, traces of the anal stage are to be found in the subsequent urethral-phallic and genital stages. Here is an illustration from the associations of a male patient.

"When I heard noises at night I knew that my parents were meeting in the bathroom. . . . First I did not know what they did there together. When Sally and I played doctor-patient I tried to give Sally an enema, but she screamed and didn't let me. Later I heard that she did it to a neighborhood girl. . . . I thought that father stuck something from the back into mother and that Sally was born after that. I believed that babies were carried in the stomach and born in the bathroom. . . . Before and after I approach (sexually) my wife, I have to go to the bathroom. . . . I have a sensitive stomach.

5. I have found a recent confirmation, if such is still needed, of this connection, which every psychologist could easily verify, in the philosophy of a Texas millionaire: "Money is like manure. When it stacks up it stinks, but when you spread it around it makes things grow." *Time,* June 27, 1969.

When I *eat* something which disagrees with me I begin to worry: Will I get an ulcer or even cancer? . . . When I worry I forget about sex. . . . I recall my mother insisting that I *have a bowel movement* every morning after breakfast. When I couldn't produce one, damn it, she pushed the enema bone into me. . . . Once—gee, I completely forgot about it!—I saw my mother sitting on the toilet. I saw something dark there between her legs. I had a peculiar feeling. I don't know what it was. Later I saw blood *in the toilet*. I somehow knew then, though nobody told me, that it was from mother. Since then I cannot stand the sight of blood. . . ." The serious impairment of the patient's love life was traceable to his fixations in both the oral- and anal-erotic stage as a consequence of his mother's just-described toilet training, the effect of which was superimposed on traumatizations in the oral phase (not mentioned here).

The mechanical procedures which a mother adopts in feeding and toilet training a child in terms of too early or too impatient control or hostile neglect cannot be separated from the *basic attitude* of the mother toward her child. This attitude is again determined by the kind of role she unconsciously assigns the child in her psychic economy. Yet a genetic exploration of the infinite variety of possible psychic injuries to the child in the oral and anal stage has proved that the operating detrimental agent can be isolated, evaluated and eliminated by using as frame of reference the *genetic script* according to which *both* parents expect the child to live.

In other words, pertinent clinical observation extended over two decades established that occurrences in the early mother-child relationship are greatly influenced as to their consequences by later vicissitudes of the genetic triad. In fact both are intimately linked to the kind of relationship *which existed between mother and father* from the moment of conception—actually even before this—until the offspring's ties with his parents are superseded by extrafamilial investments. (This my opinion has to be relied on, since it cannot be disproved as long as other investigators will not apply the triadic ap-

proach of genetic psychoanalysis to the study of etiopathogenetic problems.)

Hence it is my considered judgment that it is not fruitful
to study—as is increasingly the trend—the minutiae of the
"individuation" processi of the child by observing mother and
child exclusively, without the third member of the genetic
triad, the father. To streamline research down to the details
of the child's gradual demarcation of his Self from the symbiotic mother-child image, in the hope of finding the answer to
questions concerning therapy and prevention, must lead to
failure and for the following reason:

The most ominous mental diseases, which are traditionally
traced back to man's earliest stages of mother-child interaction, are seemingly determined and maintained by a detrimental influence exerted only by the mother over the child.
This influence, we most emphatically repeat, can still be decisively modified for the better or for the worse by the *father's
action and attitude,* commission or omission, *toward both
mother and child.* The two implications of this thesis should
not be overlooked. The first consists in the assuring prediction
that prevention may still be effective at later stages of development when the father comes to play a more direct and more
important role in the psychic economy of the child. This however can take place only if the triadic principle of genetic
education is consistently adhered to. The second implication
derives from the first. It is no longer a prediction but an em-
pirically validated fact: even the most ominous clinical conditions are capable of striking improvement and even radical
cure when the patient is offered the opportunity to "correct"
his past experiences in a setting mirroring the original genetic
triad. This fact in turn militates strongly in favor of the proposed genetic approach to neurotic prophylaxis.

We are stressing this point at this juncture on the basis of
the following suggestion extrapolated from a host of clinical
observations: The triadic principle entails a *father's awareness of mother's procedures in the area of nutrition, body care
and toilet training.* His most constructive role and attitude is

easily determined by the other rules, proposed in accordance with the maturational needs of the child. The principle set forth here excludes automatically, to take an extreme example, a husband's preventing his wife from nursing their child because he maintained that her breasts were his alone[6] or because he worried about their becoming unshapely. It also excludes the more common opposite occurrence, i.e. that a father, out of *denial* of his oral envy, allows his wife to force their child by holding his nose to swallow food though he vomits it again and again. He may also for the same reason close his eyes to his wife's pattern of tempting their obese daughter with the most fattening cakes. A constructive participation in the raising of the child also prevents a father from overlooking his wife's habit of inflicting daily enemas on their child or taking rectal temperatures of their teenage son and, again an extreme example, will also avert his joining with his wife to force the enema syringe into the rectum of their daughter, terrified and screaming to the point of hoarseness. (These fathers' errors by omission or commission are all drawn from our patients' childhood histories.)

Freud has, in one of his most important papers on the limitations of psychoanalysis as a method of therapy, "Analysis Terminable and Interminable" (1937), pointed out that masochism is of all clinical conditions the most refractory to analytic resolution. As sado-masochism is certainly an inherent characteristic of the anal phase, it behooves us to delve a

---

6. This extreme manifestation of infantile claims was present in a man who insisted: "My wife's tits are mine, and mine only." However, it exacted a heavy price on the one who was indulging his infantile wishes to such an extent as to almost delusionally confuse his wife with his mother and his little son with his younger brother. While repairing his car, he lifted his head "by mistake" and fractured his skull; not long after he was involved in an armed robbery (evidently he was not only unusually selfish but believed that "what is mine is mine and what is yours is also mine") and drew a heavy prison sentence. If somebody had been attuned to his claim at the time when he labored under the trauma of oral deprivation at the sight of his mother's feeding his younger brother, he might have been spared all these self-destructive experiences and the resulting calamity for his family.

little more into the preventive avenues which are open to parents in this stage of their children's development.

What has been said about deprivation inherent in every *overstimulation* is particularly applicable in the anal-sadistic stage where the child's ego has an extremely limited capacity to cope with any type of tension increase. Overstimulation of the child through physical care by the mother can occur either through seductive manipulation or through impatient, angry and outright sadistic harshness, and not rarely through alternation of both.[7] Depending on the degree of such a parental approach, it may lay foundation precisely to sado-masochism which, every clinician will agree with Freud, is one of the most difficult sexual and characterological aberrations to reverse. But first a generalization: Adults as a rule forget what were the most exciting physical pleasures when they were themselves children. The body of the infant has its own erotic pleasure sources which do not involve the sex organs per se, at least not significantly in the early stages of development. A mother can therefore be overstimulating and physically seductive by the manner in which she feeds the child (oral stage) or teaches him to acquire sphincter control (anal stage). That proper nutrition and good digestion are essential to the child's physical health and normal growth has been known practically since parents began to care for the well-being of their offspring. What was not known before Freud is that these physiological functions are used as discharge channels for variations in the libidinal tensions centering mainly on the corresponding (oral and anal) zones of the body.

As toilet training is usually the task of the mother, a special effort of enlightenment is necessary here to prevent overstimu-

---

7. What makes coercion in this phase particularly frightening is that in this contingency the child for the first time is being confronted with the requirement *to give,* i.e. with the separation from himself of what is psychologically considered part of his body. The reaction of *rage* and especially *fear* to this request explains why in so many languages extreme fear is associated with loss of feces. (This connection has a phylogenetic antecedent in the reaction of animals to extreme danger.)

lating the child's incumbent (anal and sado-masochistic) ero-
geneity. The detrimental consequences of the fact that mothers
can and do gratify in the toilet training of their children their
masculine penetrative or *frankly sadistic* impulses, rooted in
their own experiences as children, has not yet been fully realized. In fact, the resulting sado-masochistic dyad between
mother and child is hardly given up by the latter, but at best
is transferred in toto for the rest of his life into subsequent
relationships. This again entails especially serious repercussions on the *sexual identity* of both the subject and the object
of such relationships, according to which one has been conditioned to passive-masochistic and which to active-sadistic
penetrative patterns.

There is still another way in which a detrimental attitude
on the part of the mother in this area can affect the personality
of the child (illustration drawn from the case material of a
patient in his thirties):

> He would derogate whatever he did. No achievement of his
> was good enough for him. "I feel that whenever I try to im-
> press people with something they could say, 'Put it in your
> back pocket.' I am really only bullshitting all the time. I'm
> impatient with whatever I undertake. I tell myself, "When
> will you start to *produce* instead of sitting there on your fat
> ass?' I think this is the reason why I cannot stand to be with
> people. I behave in such a way that I make them despise me."
>
> His mother had been extremely impatient and irritable
> when she toilet-trained him. By introjecting this attitude of
> hers, he ended up by looking at himself through her eyes,
> i.e. dealing with himself sadistically, corresponding to the
> level of his sexual organization at the time when anal-erotic
> pleasure had to be curtailed to meet his mother's demands.
> Though she succeeded in exacting conforming submission
> from her son, her attitude made it impossible for him to relin-
> quish that specific developmental phase, to the detriment of
> his self-respect and his general relationship with people.

Relevant to this topic is the popularity among children of
the game of "playing doctor." The most obvious motive is the

opportunity it provides for looking at, displaying and generally coming in physical contact with sexually significant parts of the body, including pregenital (oral, anal, etc.) zones. It has further the purpose of mastery of a frightening experience: an actual consultation with and/or intervention by a physician. Besides, we have seen that mothers' own sadism can manipulate some doctors, who are eager to oblige because of their own inclinations. They are likely to treat their young patients with the same or even greater insensibility and cruelty than their mothers have shown (see p. 240). These children are likely to inflict upon their siblings or playmates (see p. 158) what they themselves have suffered at the hands of adults. Finally, "playing doctor" can serve as a convenient vehicle for acting out sheer sibling hostility or (after erotization) sadistically patterned oedipal fantasies, either heterosexual or homosexual (see p. 199). Forgotten (actually repressed) though the memories of these single or frequent occurrences may become, they provide an important motivation for some of these children to become real doctors later in life. Among these there is naturally at least some proportion of physicians whose behavior is similar to that of certain mothers who gratify their sadism in the early training of their children. These doctors indulge their unconscious sadism by inflicting on their patients superfluous painful procedures or surgical interventions with the alleged wish to help, without realizing that they obey certain compelling forces traceable to their own experiences as children. Sometimes there prevails a combination of these unconscious motives, with the so-called "secondary gain" in this case of lucrative nature.

A mother would boast of how she "cured" her son's inflamed sore throat. "I simply got hold of an alum bar (used by barbers to check minor bleedings) then I simply rubbed the back of his throat with it, real hard! He screamed bloody murder, but within a few days there were no longer complaints about not being able to swallow and all that and the fever had gone." Decades later, after her son was married, he still was overcome by choking sensations and inexplicable anger whenever his wife dared to touch his collar or tie.

His mother evidently had repeated with her son some of the "doctor play" in which children like to engage so frequently, although not exclusively at this end of the digestive tract (see p. 205). Her preference for the mouth was explained during her therapy: as the oldest child she saw all her younger siblings being breastfed by her mother. For this she had plenty of opportunity, as her mother was blessed with thirteen children besides herself. Was it surprising that she wanted to punish (orally) her son, her first child, when she was nursing him? She could not help confusing him with her siblings, and thus had to deny him what she had been over and over again taunted with by her mother. Her milk suddenly stopped, and her mother, who just was nursing her own last child, had to intervene to help nurse her grandchild. It was indeed an unusual confirmation of the known unconscious equation, child=sibling, so frequent in genetic scripts.

But to come back to our main topic. The *hostility* and *sadism* to which the pregenital (oral and anal) sexual organization contributes so decisively is frequently turned against the Self (actually against the introject). This then provides willing objects for the kind of doctors described above and especially for surgeons, which explains the statistically established appalling number of unnecessary operations. What concerns us here is that each parent should be alert to his own and the other parent's unconscious ambivalence and sadism toward their children, which make them either become cruel samaritans for their offspring or unquestioningly go along with suggestions of neurotically or psychopathically motivated (unscrupulous) physicians. Actually this warning refers to an inclination of parents not too far removed from that which leads to the phenomenon of the "battered child," though it is a better disguised and often well rationalized product of parents' self-deception.

In conclusion, it is worth re-emphasizing that the triadic principle is here also safeguarded by the father's general relationship with the child's mother, because her attitude towards the child and her procedures in this area, although determined by her own genetic experiences, can be greatly modified by the nature of the intramarital relationship.

Importance of Child's Gender

Regarding the problem of *sexual identity,* modern psychoanalytic research, and especially *genetic* psychoanalysis, has shown that one of the most frequent traumatizations of the child arises from the parents' conscious and unconscious attitude about the sex of their newborn child. Analysis of prospective and actual parents points up the many ways in which a child's sexual gender can gratify a mother or father and yet not necessarily provide a solid basis for the proper raising of the child.

Here is a typical illustration of a mother who badly wanted a girl. Mrs. R. was incapable of separating from her chronically sick mother. Therefore she raised her first son with the fantasy of his being a small girl, as she herself in her unconscious still was,[8] and wanted to be. At the same time the mother assumed in the genetic stageplay the role of an all-giving and always available parent. When her next child happened to be a girl, it was only natural that she turned, with greater emotional investment, towards her daughter because she corresponded to her fantasy more objectively than did her son. One would be inclined to think that while this mother might engender serious difficulties in the development of her son, this would not be the case with the daughter. In reality the daughter was also deprived, because Mrs. R. could not genuinely be a giving and loving mother as she herself did not have such a mother. Also she did not make it rewarding enough for her husband to be warm to his daughter. This mother's incapacity to separate from her own mother made it thus impossible for her to give her daughter the amount of freedom and opportunity *to share* which are indispensable

---

8. Here projective identification is likely to turn into *objectivation;* in such a case the son becomes feminine, adjusting to the mother's expectations.

to a child in the oedipal phase. The daughter eventually developed food fads which later resulted in a tendency to overeat and to alcoholism.

How a father's wish for a boy can distort the sexual identity of his daughter is well illustrated by the case on p. 118.

The "acceptance" of the objective sexual gender of a child is usually not in itself a guarantee that the parents' attitude will be a constructive one. A son, for example, may fit into his mother's fantasy of being her "phallic" extension. From this alone an unconquerable separation anxiety may result. However, as in such a fantasied bond the phallic element is decisive, it is very likely that both partners to this type of symbiosis react to the prospect of separation, even if a short one, with *castration anxiety*. Sometimes along with this "phallic extension" symbiosis the son experiences his mother, because of her pronounced masculine strivings, as being stronger than the father but at the same time more threatening. The introjection of such a mother may then lead to the establishment of a "pseudo-masculine" identity, which in its turn may lay foundation to masochism or to the homosexual solution of the oedipal conflict.

We shall return later to the sources of developmental disorders involving confusion of sexual identity, because of its particular weight in mental prophylaxis.

Sexual Curiosity

The handling of the child's *sexual curiosity* requires special attention. It is certainly in the parents' power to stunt or promote the child's innate curiosity and this may affect his total learning capacity. The child's inclination to ask his parents many questions is the most natural of his rights: the parents brought him into this world and for a long time mediate and interpret to him the realities of life. The questions which children raise most frequently bear out quite patently how early sexual drives begin to stir in the young. These questions either pertain directly to pregnancy, birth and anatomical differences between the sexes or aim at this topic but are, through displacement and sublimation, modified into allusions or symbolic references. A benign, supportive and even outright praising attitude on the part of the parents for the child's showing a need to know and for his formulating intelligent questions is indicated. One might be inclined to think that few parents would deny the child such a response. But closer observation reveals clearly how often overtones of impatience, more or less superior amusement or even direct derision are discernible in the way parents give or withhold answers to the young one, even when the parents have had plenty of opportunity to notice the child's intelligence and sensitivity.

In general, as I have stressed elsewhere, parents take liberties with children which they would not dare take with adults unless for one reason or another the latter are in no condition to retaliate. We shall return later to this topic.

Children's Wish to Learn

That the child's willingness to learn and his pleasure in enlarging his knowledge about people and things depend, like so many other inclinations, on the earliest environmental influence, does not need to be belabored. It is also understandable that a genuine interest on the part of the parents in the child's progress in school and his intellectual development in general can come about only if it does not go counter to the specific genetic script which each parent is compelled to write for the child. The other condition is that the *current* triadic constellation must allow for a spontaneous expression of the parents' admiration and pleasure in the child's achievements.

For the first requirement we can use the example of a mother who because she was a girl was not allowed to go to college, in contrast to her brothers. Such a mother cannot possibly draw genuine pleasure from her children's school achievements. Even if she frequently uses them as proxies for her own unfulfilled scholastic ambitions, the original frustration will inevitably appear in a disturbing ambivalence toward her children's intellectual progress. For the second condition we can use the case of a father who, because he fears that his wife's admiration of his son will alienate her affection for him, is likely to minimize or even frankly derogate his son's accomplishments. In both cases the children's motivation to study may suffer severely. The extent to which the influence of the school can modify, for better or for worse, the child's genetically determined learning problems and his attitude toward the school in general, including the spreading phenomena of truancy and dropping out, will be dealt with in the second volume.

Special consideration must naturally be given to the child's need to know which of the possible relationships between the sexes are the most satisfying. Even the earliest answers about sexual life should contain elements which give evidence that the very existence of the questioning child is an essential part of the marital relationship. This is at the same time a first illustration of the application of the triadic principle in child-rearing, to which we will return shortly in a much more fundamental context. Sexual information should naturally not be overstimulating. In this regard the rule of thumb may suffice that one should not go beyond the scope of the child's question and in general should preferably assume, as I have suggested, a "passive attitude" here.[9] (In presenting practical guidelines we shall come back to this issue.)

Excessive Masturbation

Masturbation must be considered as the child's privilege of his age, provided it is not engaged in excessively. If there is evidence that the child feels guilty or worried about the consequences, he should be enlightened by the parents, preferably the one of the same sex, or the one who feels more comfortable

---

9. See Chapter on "The Onset of Sexual Curiosity," Flescher, 1951, p. 486.

about discussing such matters with the child. Otherwise the help of a professional should be enlisted. While postponing suggestions concerning the problem of *sex education in schools* to the discussion of extrafamilial educational influences in general, I shall mention here only that schools should provide parents with the opportunity of becoming enlightened themselves about sexual life *before* children can be exposed to "double bind" information from home and from school. Conflicting attitudes and explanations of those who provide them only add to the alienation of the child from the parents and that of the parents from the school.

Excessive masturbation is not always a response to overstimulation by parents or (older) siblings, though this is frequently the case. Again, its compensatory and anaesthetizing effect, in the same sense which we indicated in reference to excessive autoerotic gratification in general (see p. 251), has to be kept foremost in mind. When it is not a response to overstimulation, masturbatory relief is most typically sought as an antidote to feelings of distress and displeasure from various sources like pain, frustration, anger, anxiety, guilt and particularly, though it is often well disguised, *depression*. In this sense excessive masturbation comes dynamically close to other types of addiction (food, alcohol, drugs).

Primal Scene Experiences

Pertinent to the topics of sexual curiosity as well as of children's masturbation are the "primal scene" experiences. I have found that many traumatic experiences, occurring both before and after the oedipal phase, are most frequently telescoped in the fantasies about and reactions to witnessing the parents' love-making. In this connection I want to be very explicit: The tendency of misinformed parents who are rather influenced by a certain trend in the psychoanalytic movement, now mostly superseded but taken over by the present atmosphere of "sexual revolution," has disastrous effects. It does not meet the child's "healthy" curiosity about sexual matters if parents make a habit of exposing their sexual activity to their children. The children will not become, through their parents' verbal or—even worse—physical exhibitionism in this area, more "free" and more "naturally conditioned" to enjoy in later life the emotional and physical aspects of love. They instead inevitably fall victim to all the previously mentioned consequences of exacerbated but unreleased sexual tension and frustration aggression which render impossible a smooth course of the process of maturation. The same detrimental consequences naturally ensue from experiences of overstimulation when the child's relatively weak and undeveloped ego is exposed to intimate physical contacts with siblings in direct sexual play, for example when put together in the same bed, or to erotic stimulation by adults who are not members of the family.

Here is what one mother of a teenager had to say about her approach to sexual education:

> "I cannot understand it. My daughter becomes more and more shy. How different she is from me, and for that matter also from my husband. Ever since she was a baby, I didn't mind her seeing me or my husband without clothes on. I even let her hear how much I enjoyed making love with my husband. Still when we have guests she avoids meeting them. When she is with me or in general in the presence of other people, like in a store or a waiting room, she never lifts her head, but keeps her eyes glued to the floor. . . . Most of the time she closes her door and sits for hours in her room alone. She even prefers to eat alone. When we ask her why, she says she hates 'noises, people talking, the radio, and so on.' " (It is not difficult to grasp how her daughter's psychic allergy to the physical proximity of people in general and noises in particular resulted from the planned and "well-meant" exhibition of her parents' naked bodies and of their sex life.)

In the above illustration, I hope it is not necessary to prove that such traumatizations would be impossible without the active or consenting participation of the other parent. To take another pertinent example, this is what I learned was going on between a married couple before they entered dual therapy.

They quarrelled terribly about their miserable sex life. The husband accused his wife of denying herself to him for most flimsy excuses. She in turn had resolved not to have anything to do with him because his sexual habits were driving her crazy: He would engage in foreplay and then would suddenly leave her because of some "urgent" matter he allegedly had to attend to. She called him a sadist who delighted in exciting her and then leaving her terribly frustrated.

Again the genetic background of each party to the marital drama revealed a striking similarity in terms of early seduction. The husband was allowed, actually prodded by his mother, to share his bed with his younger sister. He ultimately engaged in most intensive sex play just short of intercourse. His wife, for her part, at about the time of puberty, was left alone at home for long hours. The men who boarded with her family would come into her room and expose themselves. Though she was "furious and frightened" she did not complain to her parents because, as she said, she felt "too embarrassed." She also was seduced by a sibling, an older brother with whom she was sleeping "because mother wanted it," although there were other rooms and beds available.

The husband's accusation that his wife rebuffed him sexually revealed itself to be directed unconsciously at his mother who could not attend to his needs, overwhelmed as she was by a too large family. Indeed his pantomime of arousing his wife, herself the harassed mother of several children, only to leave her suddenly in order to take care of something else, was a vindictive re-enactment of the behavior of his mother, whose quick and impatient ministrations to him were too frequently and suddenly interrupted by her having to take care of his siblings.

The anger in his wife in turn corresponded to her re-experiencing the rage against the adults of her childhood (the boarders) who had overstimulated her by their exhibitionism, leaving her with as much unreleased sexual tension as unconscious guilt. Guilt feelings ensue from the fact that every temptation by an adult is reacted to as a seduction by a parent, i.e. as an experience which exacerbates the oedipal conflict.

Here is another illustration from a dual session, the first part of which the patient shared with his wife. While walking in front of me towards the office he suddenly began to sway, knees slightly bent, from one side to the other. His rather masculine wife objected sharply against his "clowning." Her husband explained to her that in this way he was alluding to my comment in the previous contact with me about his walking very slowly as if impersonating an old man. When his wife left, after the conjoint part of the interview, the patient expressed frustration that his nightmares had returned. He thought that they had left forever when he (against my advice) had interrupted his (dual) therapy after a few months because he had felt sufficiently improved.

"Yesterday I had a frightening dream: a gorilla was chasing me. I was scared out of my wits. In order to escape I flew, in a sort of superhuman effort, over a fence. . . . The fence reminds me of being chased by my father for making too much of a racket on Sunday afternoon when my parents liked to take a nap in their bedroom. When escaping from father I knew that I should not run through the gate of our fenced-in garden. This brings to my mind an incident when I was about eight and was standing in front of our house: I suddenly saw an enormous truck coming towards me. I was paralyzed with fear and could not move. Just at the last moment I ran and thus avoided my being crushed to death by the truck. . . . I was sleeping frequently near my mother, actually between her and my father; I was sickly, you know. I recall when I had to go to the bathroom, I always had to crawl over my father. Once he woke up in anger and beat me. (– – –?) Maybe—Oh yes, now I remember. One night I woke up and I was frightened. There was a great commotion in bed, my parents did something which I didn't understand. . . . I don't remember if I cried."

The caricatural walk of the patient was ultimately understood as imitative of a gorilla which stood for the sexually powerful father, as did the "enormous truck." The patient's

flight over the fence alluded (typically) to difficulties in his
sex life. "Flying" stands in the symbolism of the unconscious
for intercourse (the *winged* Amor and Cupid) and appears
most frequently in dreams of men with impaired potency. The
"fence" stands for the father over whom the patient had to
crawl on his way to the bathroom, and in a more essential
sense for the father's interfering role in the oedipal constellation.

His fear of being caught by his father, and yet his provocation of him as well as his panic at the prospect of being
crushed by the truck, were traced back to his identifying
with his mother in the primal scene and to his passive
wish to be loved by father. The conflict about this wish accounted for his choice of a masculine wife, but also for the
infrequency of his sexual approaches to her. It explained also
his avoidance of male company and his pronounced tendency to provoke men in authority into attacking him, which
resulted in serious setbacks in his career. The "wishful fear"
of being chased and attacked, which disturbed all essential
areas of his life, was rooted in the sexual indiscretion which
his parents inflicted upon their son at his most vulnerable
age, by allowing him, with the excuse that he was "sickly,"
to sleep in the same bed with them.

Apparently there is a definite trend toward a change in our
sexual mores. Not only the young seem to be committed to the
so-called "sexual revolution" but, judging from literature and
the performing arts, so do their elders. Regarding this type of
liberation the following can be said, for reasons now well
known and also made explicit in the course of this writing:

Sex in the human race is burdened with deep-seated feelings
of *guilt*. This is most patently reflected by the concept of
"primal sin," which derives from the ever-renewed and inevitable potential inclination of each new member of the
human society to commit the oedipal crime. The incest is seen
to be the most dreadful of all crimes because it involves, in its
expression of extreme and homicidal selfishness, the very two

people to whom man owes not only his survival but life itself.[10] Freeing the emotional and physical love from the incumbent (oedipal) guilt feelings is *not* achieved by taunting the child with the display of what he cannot have, at first because of his physiological incapacity (prior to puberty), and later on only at the price of that most dreaded crime.

The current encouragement of sexual license in public testifies to the pathetic attempt of mankind to free itself from what throttles man's capacity *to love* other people and *to feel* for them. This kind of attempt, however, not only fails in its endeavor but aggravates the problem insofar as the younger children *now are exposed, from sources outside the family, to overstimulation during the crucial years of their development.* They inevitably must develop neurotic patterns in response to the heightening tension which they are not equipped to cope with, thus initiating new extra-genetically determined chains of transmission of psychic disorders from one generation to another. The failure of mental health prophylaxis through the trend toward increasingly "frank handling of sex" is perhaps best proved by the apparent increase in abuse of drugs, in excessive drinking, in breakdowns and general antisocial and destructive patterns, precisely on the part of teenagers (and those "below thirty") who think that they have found the solution of their and society's problems in the total surrender to the pleasure principle. (Other more constructive motivations in the rebellion of the young that has swept through schools of higher education will be gone into when we deal with group psychology.)

Children as Scapegoats

A more general observation pertaining to a topic which has been already, though only fleetingly, touched upon concerns the inclinations of parents to take out on their children the

---

10. Incest with other members of the family like siblings or children is no more than a displacement: the underlying fantasy is still the original oedipal striving for the parent.

frustration and anger engendered in them outside of the family. It is known that married people do indulge in this type of displacement onto each other. They often even knowingly justify using each other as scapegoats by saying that at least from these quarters they don't expect the type of retaliation with which a boss, a co-worker or a neighbor would be likely to respond if they were to give free rein to their irritation or resentment. This, however, is incomparably more true for the role of children whom parents use as "whipping boys" for frustrations suffered in their contacts with other adults. It naturally combines with the already emphasized need of parents to make their children (via their genetic scripts) into targets for vindictive and cruel impulses the history of which goes back to their own childhood.[11] The disastrous effects of this urge of parents to scapegoat their children, arising from *both* these sources, is well exemplified in the following disclosure of a greatly agitated mother who came to my office asking urgently for help:

> "Whenever Jonathan opens his mouth, my husband calls him stupid or idiot. With the customers in the shoe store who drive him crazy, he is sweet as honey. The boss can walk all over him and he swallows everything with a smile. With everybody else my husband is kind and helpful, a real angel,

---

11. The syndrome of the "battered child" refers to a phenomenon which has only recently begun to arouse public indignation: There are brought to the attention of the police and of physicians children who have been beaten to the point where not only their health but their very lives were endangered. Though the high incidence of such occurrences, as those who are studying this problem maintain, is much greater than the number of cases of child abuse reported or discovered by chance, it is still infinitesimal as compared with the children who are *psychologically* "battered" by their parents. To take a recent extreme example, only because it occurred in my vicinity, there cannot be a very bright future in store for the two children who were brought by the police emergency squad to plead with their father not to jump from a roof. This was done after their mother's desperate appeals to her husband proved useless. The mere existence of the children in this father's life was evidently not sufficient to dissuade him from wanting to take his life; probably in these last moments he hated his wife, paradoxically because of the children, more than he hated the children themselves.

but at home with Jonathan, it is insult after insult.

"He spends his evenings playing cards. I beg him to remain with us. I say, 'You've been away three days in a row with your pals and you come home late at night. You know that I can't fall asleep when you're away from home. Am I not desirable?' (– – –?) No, but I give him sex whenever he wants. He says I am cold. When I beg him to remain at home he says 'What do you need me for, you and your son?' I say, 'Why don't you want to lie down near me?' But he doesn't even want to listen to me. So I finally lost my patience and told him, 'It's either the cards or me.' He left without saying a word. Now we are separated. But this is not the reason why I came to you. I feel much better without him. Now I can sleep without him being around. What did I get from him? He was unable to embrace me warmly. He would say I was a cold fish. How can I be different if he leaves me every evening? How can I be warm to him?

"It is for my son that I am here. After two years living on campus he returned home when we got the new apartment. He was so attentive and affectionate to me! One night I came home during a snowstorm. I hardly made it. My husband as usual was out playing cards. Here was my son offering me tea. A really good kid. He really cared. He knew what was going on between me and my husband, and it was that evening that he asked me, 'What do you need all this for? Why don't you get rid of him?' I said, 'You know that I cannot live alone.' He said 'What's the matter, don't you have guts?' *My son actually helped me to make up my mind.* After the separation everything seemed to be perfect. I did my work, the house was quiet. There were no problems. Also with my son everything was all right.

I think it was a year ago that Jonathan confessed to me that he smoked marijuana. I was surprised because before he didn't even smoke regular cigarettes. I don't know why, but I put it out of my mind. A few days ago he returned home dishevelled and trembling. 'Please, Ma, help me, something terrible has happened to me! I took LSD. Help me, please! You don't know what I am going through, I am going crazy! Those fears may come back. They are terrible. Please take me to the hospital!' . . . He took LSD four weeks ago.

His friend who stood by told me what had happened. Jonathan was out of his mind, falling all over the place, he felt like vomiting and tried to rip his tongue from his mouth. He is now in a psychiatric hospital, because he feels that he is going crazy. He looks like a ghost and has those anxiety attacks, screaming again and again, 'Please help me, help me! I don't want them to come back,' meaning those fears. The psychiatrist doesn't know when he will release him from the hospital. He called me and said that Jonathan badly needs therapy and, for that matter, I should look into myself, and here I am. . . ."

It turned out that Jonathan *had taken LSD the day after his father had separated from his mother.*

From the father's side, Jonathan was a target for his displaced hostility. He was a scapegoat not only for what his father was currently enduring from the boss and his customers but also for father's sibling hostility. Indeed, his boss' demand that he be nice to customers was experienced as his parents' exhortation to be nice to his younger and "preferred" brother. As a matter of fact, his wife reported (in a subsequent interview) that her husband insulted his younger brother just as he did Jonathan, calling him stupid and idiotic. That jealousy was the common denominator of this father's attitude toward both brother and son was obvious.

Moreover, the mother's own genetic script-writing came through clearly in this interview. She invested in both her husband and her son only from the level of her *dependency needs.* Jonathan's willingness to be more affectionate toward his mother and her appreciative response to it was experienced by the father, typically, as conspiracy of his wife and son against him. To make sure that what he assumed would really come about (objectivation), Jonathan's father removed himself from the home situation, thus enacting his own oedipal wish to triumph over his own father. Jonathan's impulse to rip out his tongue as (oedipal) punishment for having suggested that his mother get rid of father is typical of the excessive cruelty of that part of our moral conscience rooted in the most unmitigatedly destructive layers of our unconscious. It was excessive, just as it was excessive when King Oedipus tore out his eyes as punishment "for not having seen" that he was committing incest. Similarly, our young man did not know, as for that matter none of the parties to the breakup of this family knew, that unconsciously they were enacting the Sophoclean tragedy, each with his own share of guilt.

In conclusion, Jonathan not only was berated by his father but also was deprived of his company and was irresponsibly pushed into a position where the pressure of guilt, need for self-punishment and ensuing depression forced the youngster to resort to the use of dangerous drugs. Like so many who attempt to numb themselves with drugs against feelings of desperation, Jonathan also believed in "expanding his mind," when in reality he ended up by losing it: the attempt to rip out his tongue proved that his self-destructive impulses had succeeded in forcing their way into his consciousness and overwhelming his ego.

Expression of Frustration and of Anger

The need of the child to express his feelings of frustration and anger when he is disappointed, threatened or punished should not be curtailed. However, parents also should not unnecessarily provoke the anger of the child. While this caution may seem superfluous, the frequency with which parents, no matter how well-meaning, engage in teasing and provoking their children fully justifies it. As it is, during the child's maturation there exist innumerable occasions for the expression of his frustration and anger, to which parents should react with patient understanding and warmth. Also, if they notice that the child's (frustration) anger is displaced onto any substitute animate or inanimate object, or denied altogether by his withdrawing with a blank face from contact with those who, in reality or in his conviction, have hurt him, a special effort should be made to reopen the lines of communication. The incident or grievance should be discussed, most suitably *post facto,* i.e. after the child has had the opportunity to let off steam. Naturally the parent should avoid sitting back and watching the child's display of anger with a smile of superiority. Children are quick to perceive not only signs of condescension, but in general anything which adds to the inevitable frustration that they are considered "only children" when their most passionate, but also most conflicted, aspiration is to belong to the same generation as the parents.

The discussion with the child should be engaged in within the broader *context of the frustration* which engendered the angry outburst in the first place. The accent of the parental intervention in general is thus shifted decisively onto the realm of *communication* between parent and child, the former having the important, if not essential, task of initiating and sustaining the dialogue. This naturally requires a basically accepting and warm attitude on the part of the parents, that is that they be free from an unconscious compulsion to write a detrimental genetic script for the child.

Capacity for Self-control

The issue of *discipline* and the means of inducing the child to control himself and to acquire desirable social habits—both are obviously interrelated—can also be quickly dealt with: The parent should be able to convey the necessary standards and limits with an attitude which communicates clearly to the child that his obedience is expected as something natural. Parents are likely to assume such an attitude only if they themselves do not rebel, *even unconsciously,* against the very requirements they impose on their offspring. Contrary to the recent advice of some, that parents assume an authoritative "because I say so" attitude,[12] a hint as to the advantages which

---

12. With a child who is too argumentative a more authoritative approach may occasionally be indicated, except that one then foregoes the opportunity to understand the underlying need of the child. A friendly explanation may easily induce the child to express his disappointment that the parents spend so little time with him, revealing that litigiousness and patent infractions are often disguised ways to get the parents involved with the child who longs for their company. One could define such a pattern as one of "flouting parental limits." Indeed, it explains why parents are often faced with the painful fact that their offspring have succeeded in overstepping the limits of their most liberal standards. In our experience, however, such occurrences are as a rule determined by the operation of some more detrimental factor within the genetic triad.

will accrue to the child from following socially accepted codes and behavior is to be preferred. Such explanations should increasingly accompany parents' demands, and should start rather early with an inquisitive and sensitive child. That some parents have the habit of themselves becoming quarrelsome or petulant in their explanations does not argue against this approach. There are always many ways in which sound rules can be made ineffective by faulty implementation.

Again, what mostly safeguards the success of mental and moral training of the child is the total interaction between parent and child. Though much has been written on the all-important question of what best insures a "good" relationship between parent and offspring, a most important aspect has been left uncertain and controversial. My own opinion about this is actually the main reason for writing this volume.

Imbalance in the Genetic Triad

Our effort has consisted chiefly of defining the concept of the triadic principle of human maturation in such a way as to point out a basic condition for insuring the offspring's mental health: *The child needs first and foremost a balance within the genetic triad.* Such a balance is missing when the child is (unconsciously) emotionally invested in and experienced by one parent as if he were his (or her) parent, sibling or mate, while the other parent is seen to be either a rival or an object of competitive wooing. A faulty genetic constellation also prevails if the child is considered merely the rightful object of the parents' sacrificial, renunciatory and self-effacing strivings. Conversely, the "common front" imbalance (Flescher, 1966, p. 361) prevails when both parents refuse to shoulder their child-raising responsibilities. Such parents experience the son or daughter merely as a burden and a nuisance. The fact that the "unwilling" parents often are so openly vocal about it seems to justify the suspicion that the parents' patently rejecting attitude is rarely genuine, but a manifestation of a commonly shared defense. Indeed, genetic psychoanalysis proves unequivocally that in such cases the child is most frequently merely used as a convenient scapegoat for intramarital hostility.

Another important generalization pursuant to the basic source of a genetic imbalance is appropriate here. This basic source is to be found in what Freud has discovered to be the core of human psychopathology, i.e. the *Oedipus complex*. Even if the child might have been severely traumatized in the pre-oedipal stage of development, dual analysis has found that sexual maturation adds to the preoedipal traumata the ultimate and most decisive quota of instinctual and emotional energies. The oedipal strivings which draw their energies from current and past developmental stages, are the ones which, by involving the parents in the child's needs, give rise to the known variations of the oedipal complex. It is these very oedipal strivings which tip the scale between control and release and between tension and discharge. It is these same (incestuous) strivings which, by clashing with the demands of reality or the moral values of the individual, provide the driving energies for intrapsychic conflicts. And finally, it is via these conflicts that the oedipal position determines the infinite variety of inhibition of normal or exhibition of abnormal behavior patterns as well as attitudes, emotional reactions and moods. In other words, it is the Oedipus complex which ultimately accounts for the whole gamut of clinical pictures of neuroses, from simple neurotic manifestations to impulsive and compulsive character disorders, up to the most severely incapacitating and ominous breaks in reality testing which occur in psychotic afflictions.

The re-evaluation of the oedipal conflict as a central issue both in psychopathology and in mental prophylaxis is of such crucial importance that I deem it necessary to enlarge upon this point a little further.

Preoedipal Versus Oedipal Traumata

During therapy of a patient who is beyond the age of five or six, any attempt to undo traumatizations which are pre-oedipal and pregenital in nature *without* using the oedipal constellation as a frame of reference is doomed to failure. This the reason why I am convinced that no analytic therapy in the foreseeable future will be found adequate if it does not in its design (setting) and function conform most unequivocally to the triadic principle of maturation. This is because, as has been explained, therapy is committed to carry the patient's maturation to its completion.

This conviction will, I hope, be more easily shared when on a later occasion the issue is presented in the broader context of our phylogenetic past. In doing this, the reasons for our opposition to the growing tendency to minimize the oedipal conflict in favor of preoedipal traumatizations may become more cogent.[13] Usually such an underestimation is rationalized by the purported need to widen the scope of analytic inquiry insofar as etiopathology is concerned. Yet such an attempt is fallacious because it is based on an artificial separation between the repercussions of experiences occurring in the phase of (self-preservative and erotic) dependency (on the mother) and those of oedipal, i.e. sexual-genital, involvement. Even when the trauma has very clearly been inflicted prior to the oedipal stage, its most serious consequence is the telescoping of the impact of the trauma into the oedipal situation. For that matter, I would be surprised if any clinician were to show me a patient whose incapacity to free himself from an oral dependency on his mother could be proved with certainty to be only preoedipally and not also oedipally determined.[14] A therapist, therefore, who confines himself to observing and registering experiences of his patient in the preoedipal phase,

---

13. More detailed exploration of erosion of the belief in the overriding pathogenetic influence of the Oedipus complex, and the causes and consequences of this phenomenon, will be presented in the volume about mental prophylaxis on a collective level. There the fact will be elaborated upon that the separation between the preoedipal and oedipal strivings, i.e. in essence the nutritional-dependent and genital-sexual stages, reflects a phylogenetically rather late distinction between nutritional and sexual drives.

14. I have shown elsewhere that the frustration aggression of the preoedipal stage in more ways than one exacerbates the oedipal conflict to render it traumatic (1950, p. 408, 1955, p. 415).

without pursuing diligently their extension into the oedipal stage and without making a special effort to solve the corresponding phase-specific conflict, is in for a deep disappointment: after a breathing spell in his clinical condition, the patient will sooner or later revert to the previous array of defenses. Such a turn is then typically understood by the analyst to be simply an expression of "unusually intense pre-oedipal and pregenital fixation." Much more can be said in favor of an integrated approach to both oedipal and pre-oedipal positions in human development. But this has to be postponed, as just mentioned, for a later occasion, because a certain aspect of the issue has clear bearing on the fact that the triadic principle is applicable and actually should be urgently applied also to the prophylaxis of *collective* psychopathology.

Child as Separator

Under the influence of the instinctual and emotional needs of the Oedipus complex, the human child cannot help wanting to *separate the two parents*. This is always true for every child between the ages of three and five but very often is discernible at a much later age. It remains true even if the child gives the impression of simply wanting one or the other parent for himself, exclusively or prevailingly out of unmet dependency needs. Indeed the dependency position usually cannot be given up or else is regressively reactivated, because of a dead-end immobilization of the developmental process at the inception of the oedipal constellation. The child and adolescent arrested on this level of his psycho-instinctual organization seizes eagerly on anything which he can construe as a dissension between his parents. This naturally is facilitated in those cases where the aggressive or victimized parent becomes the vocal critic of the other parent.

The typical tendency in children of such parents is to aggravate the intramarital friction by *playing one parent against the other*. They also have an overwhelming need to monopolize the attention of one or both, with the thinly disguised or manifest intent of disrupting the parents' being together. Such children's patterns may become the subject of clashes between the parents and finally result in one or the other deciding to leave the family for a short while or forever, which is precisely what children unconsciously are aiming for when they have not learned "to accept the parents as a couple." On this issue an important clarification is in order. That such an outcome is neither gratifying nor free of most traumatic repercussions on the child derives from two facts: One, the oedipal position is without exception a conflicted one, simply because the child has just as many motives and needs to *keep the parents together*. Two, the separation of the parents is naturally nothing else than the "genetic disbalance" carried to the extreme. With all the stress laid here on the ubiquity of the Oedipus complex, the fact remains undebatable that *the resolution of the oedipal conflict is entirely dependent on the attitude of the parents*. It is they who have the power to help their children pass through this crucial phase without permanent impairment of their emotional and intellectual capacities, just as it is in their power to make the solution of this core conflict in the human race more difficult or even impossible.

Role of In-Laws

Parents ultimately have to achieve the last and most difficult task of education: to still be helpful while making themselves expendable to their offspring. The capacity and willingness to help the latter free themselves from the original family bonds entails, in the first place, tact and discretion in judging the choice the son or daughter has made, or is about to make, of a life companion. Such an attitude will be present if the parents have adhered to the triadic principle in another very similar situation: We have in mind their attitude toward each other's family. In our experience with married couples, when squabbles, enmities and derogation of in-laws are an important source of marital unhappiness, they are as a rule the outcome of a conscious or *unconscious rejection of the spouse* and frequently a source of genetic imbalance. A repudiation of the husband's or wife's family, we repeat, even when it appears as a clamorous siding with the mate against his relatives, is usually a sign of an intense unconscious ambivalence against the mate himself: the hostile component of the ambivalence is displaced onto the spouse's family.

There is, however, a more basic point to be made regarding the "new family" of which one has become a member by marriage, or to which one's son or daughter is about to belong. The need for "more perfect parents" is at the basis of the intense involvement in in-laws. To this fact I have been alerted by two observations: the first pertains to the so-called "family romance," consisting of fantasies that one is not really the child of one's parents, but of other, usually more elevated and "better," parents. These fantasies or daydreams are spurred by experiences of frustration with one's own mother and father, and have to be understood as an attempt to explain and also compensate for the rejection suffered. The second observation concerns the ideology of genetic psychoanalysis itself, and especially its original prototype. Dual therapy actually can be seen as meeting this need for a new set of "psychological parents," i.e. "better and more understanding" ones.

Dual therapy, however, *differs basically* from the family romance. The difference lies in that what family romance fantasies cannot achieve, dual therapy optimally can. The patient has the opportunity in psychological transactions with real people (transference) to work through the actual and imaginary wrongs suffered. He achieves this in the first place by becoming aware of the difference between repressed and/or denied *legitimate* claims and those which are not only indefensible *per se* but *unacceptable* even to the individual himself. Coping with the ambivalence of patients who come to us emotionally bruised or deeply wounded by their parents—our "genetic scripts" explain why it cannot be otherwise—has long been known to be part and parcel of the analyst's work. But this is especially true in dual analysis because of the opportunity given the patient to relive his past experiences in a setting which reproduces the original genetic triad.

Unconsciously the same is expected from the in-laws. The latter naturally are neither equipped nor inclined to take in their stride the ambivalence of the newcomers; after all, they also expect, as the old saying goes, "not to lose but to gain" by their offspring's marriage.

> "In-law" jokes tend to use as an almost exclusive target the mother-in-law; their crudeness is proportionate to the intensity of the hostility harbored against her. Here is a typical joke: What would be his greatest Christmas gift?—To find his mother-in-law hanging on the tree. The fact that the mother-in-law is preferred to the father-in-law as a target of aggression bears out how much more painful and traumatic the frustrations suffered at the hands of a mother are, as compared with those from a father. And indeed I have not yet found a case of deep depression whose history does not go back to what occurred between the mother and the infant. This naturally, as we have had opportunity to stress, and in agreement with the triadic principle, does not eliminate the weight of the father's contribution to the problem.

To come back to our main topic, it ensues from the above that unless the parents have reached that degree of triadic maturity which has made their relationship with the relatives of their spouses a gratifying one, they cannot possibly be very constructive when their own children have to make their final choice and, more crucially, have to learn to accept the prospective bride or groom in the context of her or his family (see pp. 106-107).

It is pertinent to mention here, because it further highlights the over-all applicability of the triadic principle, that raising a child in the tradition of one's own family, with ostentatious disregard for the customs and beliefs of the in-laws, is as a rule experienced by the child as a prohibition against loving the other parent and expresses in this indirect way the parent's wish to monopolize the child. Like every other violation of the maturational principle, a hostile attitude of parents toward the in-laws disrupts the child's psychic development via an apparent feedback. The requirement of total allegiance interferes with, among other things, identification processi which we have found to be so essential to an integrated concept of the Self.

The schizophrenic "split" of a teenager who has been in and out of psychiatric hospitals was traced back by her therapists to the manifest hatred of each parent toward the family of the other. The hostility was not limited to expression of disparagement and denigration. "Whenever I came back from visiting the family of my mother or father," the young woman recalled after emerging with the help of dual therapy from her months-long state of catatonic mutism, "they'd be disgusted with me as if I had brought home dirt from the other side. They made me change my clothes down to my underwear every time."

Another boy's schizophrenic condition was dominated by obsessive ruminations about courts, prisons, escapes and police abuse. He was raised by his mother, who had always feared that sooner or later he would become a criminal. She firmly believed that he had inherited such a tendency from her husband's family, one of whose members was killed in a gang reprisal (Flescher, 1966, p. 314).

A female patient was instilled with her mother's rejection of the spiritual aspirations of the father. She presented him to her daughter as "narrow-minded and pedantic," overly concerned with intellectual achievements, typical of his family background. The daughter, in order to conform with her mother's implicit injunction against loving the father, defied him constantly by "playing stupid" and failing in school. Ultimately the exasperated father gave up with her and displaced onto his son all his aspirations and hopes of perpetuating the intellectual tradition of his family. This naturally aggravated further his daughter's alienation from him and influenced her choice of a husband who corresponded to her mother's expectations. Yet this did not make her any happier: Her mother's attitude did not decrease her daughter's oedipal attachment out of existence. It merely frustrated it and relegated it to the unconscious. Repressed and frustrated, it still exerted its influence. Through comparison with her father it devaluated her husband in her eyes and made it impossible for her to really love and respect him, until in dual analysis she learned to distinguish between what she herself wanted and what her mother wanted. How the latter violated the triadic principle does not need explaining.

The attitude of parents toward prospective suitors and their concern about the *right choice* is usually exaggerated in proportion to their ambivalence about the necessary separation from their son or daughter. It is without fail empathically understood by the latter as the parents' wish to "hold on." This may lead to a stubborn, vindictive, and anxiety- and guilt-induced precipitation of a "fait accompli." Sometimes attempts are made to cut the Gordian knot through elopement or some other rash act. ("Young lovers" who commit suicide in protest against the "tyrannical control" of their parents are usually the victims of dyadic binds in which anger towards their parents by far outweighs their love for each other.)

Seemingly unsurmountable difficulties as a rule arise from parents' gross violation of the triadic principle. The juncture of separation from the offspring often brings to a head all the irrational motivations which participate in the parents' "genetic script-writing." A frequent outcome is that the son or daughter never marries or (more frequently with the latter) after an unhappy marriage moves back to the original family. Typically a dyadic tie then ensues or is resumed between parent and offspring, who is incapable of extricating himself from his bind and all the ambivalence and sado-masochism which such a tie inevitably entails.

Another typical constellation derives from the application, to the contingency under discussion of a pattern already encountered: the provocation of a parent in order to attract his attention and to get him involved. We described this maneuver as "flouting the parental limits." It manifests itself in the tendency under one or another aspect to engage in activities contrary to parents' standards, to insist on having more free

time and "more freedom" in general, to shirk progressively all
responsibilities at school and at home, and to choose most in-
appropriate friends. Even the most liberal and understanding
parent may be forced to conclude, to his chagrin, that his son
or daughter seems to engage in outright provocation of him.
Indeed, in most cases this is the unconscious aim toward
which the various motives of the youth converge, all deriving
from this conflict: the wish to free himself from the bond with
his parent, but at the same time the rebellion against the
necessity of breaking this bond. As the reality principle in-
exorably tips the scale in favor of the latter, we shall give a
closer look to this conflict. We shall do this especially from the
viewpoint of the triadic principle at the juncture when the
capacity for emancipation from the original family is put to
its ultimate test.

In the case of conflicts around the final extra-familial object
choice, the son or daughter is often inclined to choose for love
object or mate somebody who by virtue of background, education, religion or race will hardly meet the preference of the
parents. The oedipal complex always accounts for this trend,
though disparate mechanisms may be involved on different
psychic levels. In the first place there operates the *exogamic
defense:* the need to choose somebody strikingly dissimilar
from the parents has the aim of protecting oneself from guilt
about violating the incestuous taboo. But as is usually the case
with any defense, this one at the same time gratifies the very
strivings which it aims at warding off. Indeed, the difference
between the unconsciously loved and consciously chosen object allows for the perpetuation of the oedipal attachment in
fantasies completely removed from one's awareness.[15] Finally
there is the role of the parents' inevitable objection to the improper choice. To a substantial degree—at least on the sur-

15. I realize that no less frequently it is the similarity of the chosen
to the oedipal object which (through unconscious identification) facilitates
the perpetuation of the oedipal position. The existence of the endogamic
and exogamic object choice, elsewhere explained by me as two opposite
alternatives imposed paradoxically by the same prohibition, the incestuous
taboo, is pertinent here.

face—this takes care of the guilt feelings inherent in the oedipal position, and at the same time it unconsciously gratifies the "culprit" because the parents' objection is translated by the offspring as evidence of *their* involvement and *their* not wanting to let go.

This last motive should, indeed, not be undervalued. It explains the so frequent angry reaction of the young to any encouraging advice or the most friendly suggestion offered by parents who want to be helpful when their sons or daughters are facing the problem of meeting members of the opposite sex. The parents' wish to be of help is inevitably taken to be a sign of their rejecting their offspring, of considering them merely a burden, of impatiently waiting to get rid of them, and so on. What complicates the matter, but also offers valuable opportunity for effective prevention of clashes between two generations engaged in the act of separation, is the fact, established via analysis of patients in the triadic setting, that such difficulties usually arise when at least one parent actually sees in the child, albeit unconsciously, a rival threatening the stability of the marriage. Thus the conviction of the offspring, who is "helped" to find a mate or is criticized for the way he goes about it, that the parents want to get rid of him, often contains a substantial component of truth: one parent, believing or actually noticing that a (positive) dyadic tie prevails between his mate and his son or daughter, may want to eliminate the reincarnated rival of his childhood.

In less dramatic cases a frank discussion between the parents, and at this age level also including the offspring, can reveal which parent contributes most to the genetic disbalance. In the case of entrenched separation difficulties, however, where self-destructive behavior (promiscuity, delinquency and abuse of alcohol or drugs) threatens to destroy the young ones and to turn the parents into victims of everlasting guilt feelings, professional help should be enlisted as soon as possible. The son and daughter are likely to display opposition to this step and obstinately rebuff their parents' efforts. If, however, the latter are capable of recognizing the operation of frustration aggression in their children in this contingency (see p. 252), they will not resentfully cease in their effort but will persist until their children's frustration anger is finally dissipated. Only then will their constructive attempt be appreciated and their advice acted upon.

Here is an illustration of difficulties encountered upon separation from parents:

> A young patient could not make up her mind whether she really loved her boyfriend and whether she should marry him. In a conjoint interview, her twice-married mother, Mrs. Z., volunteered the circumstances of the breakup of her first marriage. As the divorce would have been by her default, she expected her son to be assigned to the custody of her husband. She therefore wanted her son to have a companion, and arranged to become pregnant with her second child. The daughter thus heard from the mother's own lips how she came to be conceived. The wish to give a child a companion is not unusual for parents who live together. But making it part of a planned divorce adds one more to the array of peculiar motivations for pregnancy which women may have (see p. 53).
>
> What is, however, pertinent here in terms of the communication to her daughter, herself in the process of weighing marriage, is Mrs. Z.'s complete lack of consideration for her husband in her manipulatory design. The evidence that this pernicious attitude toward the male sex had been only slightly muted in the second marriage was actually my reason for suggesting conjoint sessions with Mrs. Z. and her daughter. My hope was to make this mother aware of how she was discouraging her daughter from loving her fiancé. I knew that in the process Mrs. Z.'s present marriage would also improve. In separate exploratory interviews with Mrs. Z. I learned that her tendency toward manipulation went back, as is usually the case, to her own genetic past: her mother also well knew how to interfere with her daughter's wish to marry. Indeed, Mrs. Z.'s mother was very effective in promoting and facilitating her daughter's sexual affair with her boyfriend, with the later admitted aim of "curing her daughter of her silly infatuation." Given the overriding influence

which mothers have in such matters, especially with daughters, she was very successful in the stratagem: the "silly infatuation" ended in separation.

The "genetic scripts" of parents bear out most tangibly the reinforcing but also determining influence which parents exert on the nature of their children's oedipal fixation.[16] A child may thus prefer the parent who prefers him over his mate. The intensity of the child's wish to separate the parents derives from the relative weakness of the ego in comparison with the powerful instinctual demands which impinge on it. The child's ego is weak in the oedipal phase because it has not yet benefited from the integrating and consolidating influence of the respite offered it by the decrease of instinctual energies in the latency phase. There prevails in the child a heightened emotional tension, even at rest periods, because the psychosexual organization of the child in the oedipal stage does not offer him adequate modes of discharge: the autoerotic activities provide insufficient relief. This is the most compelling reason for parents to pool their good will, as well as their emotional and intellectual resources, to assist the child in his predicament. This phase is the more crucial as the vicissitudes of this conflict will determine not only the life style of the adult and ultimately his destiny but, decades later, the nature of the *genetic script he in turn will enforce on his offspring.*

In conclusion, in sharpest contrast with the precepts of *psychoanalytic education,* which has hitherto overlooked or underplayed the oedipal phase in favor of the anaclitic dependency on the mother, we consider the oedipal conflict of more decisive pathogenetic influence. Hence we hold the handling of the *oedipal phase to be central* to the function and

---

16. This explains the fallacy of the outworn and yet still used argument of "anti-Freudian" colleagues and psychologically sophisticated intellectuals who triumphantly point out that if the Oedipus complex is ubiquitous, as psychoanalysts maintain, it cannot possibly be the cause of emotional disorders. The validity of this reasoning is hardly greater than if somebody were to maintain that as delivery is the normal outcome of pregnancy, deliveries cannot possibly cause dangerous complications for either mother or child.

duty of parents and to *genetic prevention* in general.

The triadic principle of maturation has at its core the fact that two members of the genetic triangle must, by playing adequately the role of parental figures, help the third member to become independent from the primary family to the degree compatible with his capacity to love and care for a member of the opposite sex, and to be capable of friendship toward members of the same sex. This double-pronged capacity of the offspring in turn entails the willingness and aptitude to lay foundation to a new genetic triangle, again governed by the triadic principle of maturation.

In the human race, because of the uniquely prolonged dependence of the child on his parents, a dependence which is *biologically as well as culturally determined,* the sexual function has become complicated by powerful interfering emotional factors. These basically go back to the reality of sexual urges which must have as objects the parents themselves. Because of the incest taboo, these urges are ultimately doomed to failure. Hence the need for objects of love has to turn elsewhere. Four powerful reactions in man—*anxiety, guilt, shame and disgust*—make the process of changing the direction of the sexual urges toward post-oedipal, i.e. extra-familial, objects rather difficult and conflict-laden. The triadic principle safeguards the essential function of parents, to assist the child through action, words and attitude in coping successfully with the above ego reactions. It consists in the first place of the parents' sparing their children experiences which are *traumatic,* i.e. precisely those which exacerbate feelings of anxiety, guilt, shame and disgust.

On the basis of this consideration we shall attempt to be as specific as possible in assisting the parents during those phases in which they are objects of the child's most intense emotional involvements and conflicts. Here are a few basic guidelines which we consider most important for parents to observe. They are, as is to be expected, in essence only illustrations for the practical application of the triadic principle in raising children.

CHAPTER NINE

PRACTICAL RULES

Rule 1 *WARM AND LOVING ACCEPTANCE BY ONE PAR-*
ENT CANNOT MAKE UP FOR THE LACK OF IT IN
THE OTHER

A child needs warmth and tenderness from *both* parents. When these are provided by one parent, the other parent should give evidence of his approval and support. Optimally, there should be a constant alternation of this role between the two parents: at times one will have the function of "providing" and the other of "approving"; at other times the roles are exchanged. This is necessary to offset the anxiety and guilt arising from the child's anticipation that an affectionate and accepting attitude on the part of one parent will expose the child to hostile envy and jealousy from the other parent. The loving warmth of each parent is necessary not simply to avoid the disruptive repercussions of conflicts about divided loyalty, but primarily because in normal development one parent is needed to consolidate the child's capacity to love the opposite sex and the other parent to consolidate the child's sexual identity.

If each parent genuinely approves and promotes closeness between the child and the other parent, this will be easily seen from the way he reacts when the other parent and child are engaged in an *activity* or a *project*. Violation of the triadic principle may betray itself in a parent's habit of suddenly recalling some urgent task which must be attended to. The motive for such an interference must be cogent, lest it seem to bear out the parent's tendency to separate rather than promote closeness between the other parent and the child. If there is no real urgency, parent and child typically tend to disregard completely, or at least for some time, the "separator's" prompting. Yet they do not escape guilt feelings which put an end to the emotional atmosphere of closeness that had prevailed.

Rule 2   *BODILY CARE AND TOILET TRAINING OF THE INFANT SHOULD NOT BE HARSH OR OVERSTIMULATING*

Improper physical care of the child can impair greatly, even fatally, his development and maturation. This can result either from seductive manipulation or from impatient, angry or outright cruel harshness, often from a combination of both. Depending on the degree of these parental approaches, such treatment may lay foundation to one of the most difficult sexual and characterological aberrations to reverse—sadomasochism as shown in the introduction to the rules (see p. 256).

There we have mentioned that the capacity for sexual excitement in children is not confined to the genital organs. Indeed, before these organs acquire this capacity, they are overshadowed in their importance as "erotogenic," that is sexually excitable, parts of the body, by the *oral* and *anal zones*. The erotic component of nutrition, digestion and elimination makes it possible for unenlightened and neurotically motivated mothers to traumatize their children in feeding, cleansing and teaching them bowel and bladder control. The consequences of improper handling and attitude in this area of child-rearing not only render the acquisition of normal habits difficult if not impossible, but may also determine symptomatic and characterologic complications ranging from mild to most severe.

Not only because of anatomical proximity, but also because of factors pertaining to man's phylogenetic and ontogenetic history, there exists an intimate relationship between the terminal part of the digestive tract and the genital apparatus. Freud's discovery of the "anal" stage in the child's sexual development refers to the psychological side of this relationship. Since the time he first made it public (in the "Three Essays on Sexuality," 1905), it has been confirmed by an overwhelming wealth of data drawn directly from observation of children and from their verbalizations. Memories of patients in dual therapy pertaining to the anal stage speak cogently in favor of the extension of preventive measures into this area as well. Whether the sadism of mothers who force-feed their children is less detrimental to the latter in its traumatic repercussions than that of those who initiate toilet training too early and implement it too harshly cannot be decided at this stage of our knowledge, although, again, a sadistic mother will probably not be radically different in either of these pregenital stages.

The child is spurred into giving up the pleasure of gross sensual gratification which he derives from his bodily functions and its products chiefly by the desire to *emulate* the adult. But, as I have mentioned, taking the parent as a model is not an automatic occurrence. The child's feelings about the parent and, again inevitably, the parent's attitude toward the child are decisive here. (There is no doubt in this case that the chicken came before the egg.) The disposal of bodily excreta in conformance with exigencies of time and place and the general acquiring of lasting habits of orderliness and cleanliness, character features rooted in the phase under discussion, depend most specifically on the *relationship of the child with the mother.*

These desirable habits will not become solidly entrenched in the character of the child if the mother has not offered him the necessary amount of warm acceptance and security. In this stage a manifest tendency toward *stubbornness* and *negativism* also finds its most important drive-energetic source. These character traits complicate the relationships of the child with others when he grows up. The responsibility of the father usually lies, if he is not substituting for mother in the child's toilet training (rare), in his active participation and endorsement (less rare), or in his tacit consent (most frequently) and abstention concerning this aspect of child rearing. Yet if *other favorable factors concur,* even personality features ensuing from too impatient, harsh or neglectful handling by the mother can be sublimated into their equivalents, persistence and tenacity in socially valuable pursuits. Of these factors a balanced interaction within the mother-father-child triad is the most decisive, as previously explained and as exemplified in the present rules.

Rule 3 *PARENTS SHOULD REFRAIN FROM OVERSTIMULATION OF THE CHILD, EMOTIONAL AS WELL AS PHYSICAL*

Excessive kissing, tickling, swinging, roughhousing, pushing and pulling create in the child as great an overload of tensions as do constant frightening, threatening, taunting and teasing. The parent is likely to undervalue this source of traumatization because he has forgotten his own childhood vulnerabilities and because as an adult he is able to accept a greater dose of stimulation, both active and passive, without a heightening of his psychosexual and aggressive tension beyond the threshold of tolerance. Not realizing that this is not the case with the child, adults often irresponsibly ignore the child's comfort and shower him with kisses, fondling caresses and other displays of physical signs of "love." They are surprised and often outright hurt when the child tries to fight them off. If they instead would look closer into what compels them to engage in the excessive demonstration of physical affection for the child, they might then discover that here also the over-all rule that *every exaggeration betrays the hidden opposite emotion* holds true: the overly affectionate behavior of a parent is similar to a child's frequent display of "love" towards his sibling by squeezing him in an embrace until it becomes painful. It simultaneously denies and gratifies the underlying hostility.

Though children in play with others (usually siblings) may have learned to draw erotic pleasure from physical stimulation and may ask their parents for more, the latter should refrain from granting this wish. On the contrary, the parents should be alert to the kind of play that goes on between the child and his siblings or friends, should *avoid letting children sleep together in the same bed* and in general should prevent any situation which may lead to detrimental sexual overstimulation of the young.

Observation of how mutual scrutiny of attitudes in dual analysis by both therapists facilitates the process of *undoing* the traumatic experiences responsible for the patient's problems, compels us to stress the importance of heeding our principle of maturation, especially in the area under discussion: each parent should take care that neither he himself nor the other parent overstimulate the child. It would be most helpful here, we repeat, if parents would recognize that excessive display of physical signs of love usually disguises unconscious hostility towards the child.

Rule 4 *EACH PARENT SHOULD CONSIDER HIMSELF INDIS-
PENSABLE TO THE CHILD DURING HIS DEVELOP-
MENT*

To consider oneself less important to his offspring than the
other parent is actually an infringement of the first rule. Indeed, opposition to one parent's closeness with the child may
paradoxically express itself by the other parent's removing
himself ostentatiously from the family situation in order to
"leave them undisturbed," or "not to inconvenience them,"
yet all the while nursing a smoldering anger at being forgotten,
superfluous and excluded. The incapacity of parents to fulfill
their maturational role within the genetic triangle lays foundation not only to the *positive* symbiotic dyads, but also to the
negative dyads (see p. 108). Though the detrimental consequences of each have been sufficiently illustrated, the understanding of this issue is extremely important and therefore
requires further clarification.

Elimination of any member of the genetic triad is a violation of the triadic principle of maturation. This is true also
if a parent excludes himself. Self-effacing and self-exclusion
of a parent has as its inevitable consequence his *conscious*
hostility against his mate in alliance with his child. It is always
based on the repressed fantasy of facing again a "couple"
standing (unconsciously) for his parents: he recreates the
situation of his childhood, when he was exposed to the painful but inevitable human experience, the *oedipal defeat*.

Self-exclusion of a parent is in general a very traumatic
factor in the genetic history of a child. This most startling
mechanism, laid bare in genetic-analytic therapy, usually leads
to a variety of self-destructive symptomatic and characterologic patterns in the parent. It is actually an expression of
self-directed aggression: the parent turns onto himself what
he originally wished against his own parent.

There are many good reasons to maintain that the powerful
driving force of *repetition compulsion* enters there, by promoting the inception of a hated emotional and erotic alliance

between mate and child: The self-induced *negative* dyad gives him the opportunity of reliving consciously, and this time with "justification," his rage against being the defeated and excluded third party. But at the same time the original wish to eliminate the hated and feared rival—the father for the boy, the mother for the girl—in the triangular oedipal conflict[1] asserts itself. In other words, one uses oneself as a substitute for the hated parent.

It was one of my most distressing discoveries that men especially have a tendency to carry their self-elimination pattern to the point of sabotaging their role as providers, or otherwise responsible fathers and husbands, by ruining the economic security of the family through gambling, drinking or addiction. Moreover, in extreme but not infrequent cases, they play brinkmanship with physical illness and death. When the latter occurs, the original wish to eliminate father is realized. This would be the most ominous example of the irrationality of the unconscious—the killing of oneself while wishing another's death—if this mechanism did not also play a decisive role on a more massive scale in group psychology. (For the *collective* "death instinct," see second volume.)

To return, however, to our genetic rule concerning the "self-eliminating" parent, it is evident that the right to do whatever he wants with his life, including planned suicide, is forfeited by any adult who becomes a parent. I think it is not too much to ask, that he who has brought a child into this world should feel responsible not only for the child's well-being, but also for his own. This is incompatible with the mechanism of psychological or physical self-elimination. For though we have shown that he aims (unconsciously) at punishing his parental introject, ultimately, however, and again via the genetic script he compels his child to live by, he psychologically injures his son (or daughter) by depriving him of his presence, which is indispensable for a triadic balance.

---

1. In the inverted variation of the oedipal constellation, the other-sex parent is the one whose elimination is sought.

The theme of how much parents are responsible for their wayward children's problems was given a most sensitive and dramatic expression in F. Perry's film "Last Summer," after the book by Evan Hunter. One of its highlights is the poignant confession of a girl to her friends of having spat on her mother's grave. She had drowned after accepting in a state of half-drunkenness a challenge to swim out to a sandbank. "She had no right to do it," was how the senselessly orphaned daughter explained her act of desperation and utter contempt for her mother's irresponsibility.

Rule 5 *CHILDREN SHOULD NOT BE LEFT ALONE WITH-OUT ADULT SUPERVISION*

A prolonged absence of meaningful adults is usually stressful for the young child and *"primitivizes"*[2] his needs. Sexual and aggressive impulses, mostly from frustrated emotional hunger for contact and communication with parents, impinge upon the infantile ego, pressing for immediate discharge. Under such inner pressures, sexual exploitation and seduction, usually along sado-masochistic lines, are often invited or indulged in by emotionally deprived children. The tension engendered in the young child by sexual stimulation or hostile attacks, or a mixture of both, transcends his tolerance at that stage and thus inevitably becomes traumatic.

Once again the triadic principle is helpful in clarifying this

2. I would define *primitivization* as a mechanism whereby sublimated emotional patterns are, under the influence of too persistent frustrations, regressively replaced by the primitive sexual and aggressive patterns from which they originally evolved.

issue. The hostility of older siblings toward the younger ones and motives of intense rivalry, envy and jealousy among children in general are usually proportionate to the degree to which their parents have forced them, through neglect or over-stimulation, into genetic role-playing incompatible with their maturation. Therefore the advice against depriving children of the tension-relieving and reassuring influence of parental company and supervision should not be taken lightly. It should be followed until the young have reached a level of maturity and responsibility that will make them instinctively avoid traumatic experiences. This will spare them the alienation through guilt and shame from their parents and, by displacement, from other people.

Parents should also prevent children from being molested or victimized by adults who, because of fear of failure or for other reasons, are incapable of finding sexual gratification with grownups and impose their physical attention on those whom they can easily abuse through force or deception. Seducers and rapists can exploit the naïveté and even unconscious willingness of victims simply by offering candy or a ride in a car; others may resort to more subtle and empathically highly effective baits, like the man who persuaded a five-year-old to follow him to where "his daughter lay sick in bed, longing for company." For her compassion the victim paid by being raped and murdered.

Recently the allegation has been made that among children who are lured or abducted, only those who unconsciously invite sexual crimes will allow themselves to be trapped. Such an extreme position looks very much like an attempt to shift the blame for the crime onto the victims. In reality, the few cases which have come to my attention through the therapy either of the prey of criminal assaults or of their parents, have compelled me to draw a different conclusion: the *unconscious of the parents,* i.e. again their genetic script, was mostly responsible for the child's experience. This holds true even if the last link in the chain of cause and effect was provided by the child's unconscious cooperation with the abductor or rapist. But precisely because such attacks can also take place completely independently from the parents' unconscious motivations, children should be protected through adequate measures against sexual and aggressive abuse by peers or adults. Parental neglect in this area has to be considered as a violation of the triadic principle by omission, willed for one or another reason by one or both parents.

Rule 6 *THE CHILD SHOULD BE TAUGHT EARLY TO RE-SPECT THE PRIVACY OF HIS PARENTS AND HIS SIBLINGS AS WELL AS HIS OWN*

A sense of privacy and modesty is easily adopted by children if their parents themselves give evidence of accepting the rule of mutual respect for privacy and discretion.

The child's inclination to indulge in exhibitionism and voyeurism should not be encouraged or exacerbated by exposing him to unnecessary overstimulation. Mutual display of any state of undress between parent and child overexcites the latter, aggravates his preoedipal and oedipal conflict, increases his guilt feelings and forces him sooner or later to resort to a variety of defenses which then become the core of immediate or delayed emotional, functional or psychosomatic disorders. When a parent has exposed his body to the child, he should soon, but casually, be made to understand that the other parent has been advised of this. Thus no room is left in the child's mind for the exciting but also guilt-inducing belief that he shares a secret (attempted seduction) with one parent behind the back of the other.

With the growing preoccupation, admittedly justified, over

the tendency of the young to withdraw, and with the so common confusion *of being alone* with *feeling lonely,* parents have a tendency not to allow their children to be by themselves. It is true that children who have given up trying to establish meaningful contact with their parents are inclined to close themselves for hours in their rooms or to avoid sharing meals with the family. No less frequently, however, parents, to prove that they are interested in their children or for some other reason, may have a tendency to impose their presence on their children as soon as they come home from school—to barge into their rooms, scold them for isolating themselves, for disparaging in this manner the company of their elders and so forth.

It is characteristic of modern life that its tempo overtaxes our nervous system, so that some time should be granted to each individual for quiet and undisturbed relaxation. Special consideration in this respect should be given to the young, who have yet to find a balance between their strong urges and the confusing combination of stimuli and strictures presented by external reality. They should therefore be granted the opportunity to reintegrate themselves and to dissipate the conscious and unconscious sensual, emotional and intellectual reverberations of contact with people, without being made to feel guilty of rejecting those close to them. We have this in mind, and not only the intimacy of one's physical care and physiological functions, when we advise that the young should not only learn to respect the privacy of their parents and siblings, but also know how to protect their own. Naturally the recognition that this is their privilege will be conveyed to them only if the parents have instilled in them respect for their own privacy and comfort. The latter includes teaching the children as early as possible that both activities and respites of parents should not be interrupted except for urgent reasons. It is less difficult than it seems at first glance to time and dose the process of conveying to the child the limitations and stringencies of life *in relationship to his capacity to endure* frustration without having to repress his anger and then turn it against his siblings, against those outside of the family or against himself. There exists in each parent, my experience with a sizeable number of different family constellations has taught me, an instinctive knowledge about this matter, a sort of inborn tact and sensitivity. It is brought to bear optimally, however, only if the parental drive has the opportunity to deploy itself freely. This, as we have again and again stressed, goes hand in hand with a sustained balance within the genetic triad.

Rule 7   *SIBLING RIVALRY, THOUGH INEVITABLE, SHOULD BE NEITHER DRAMATIZED NOR AGGRAVATED*

Rivalry feelings between brothers and sisters are exacerbated by the parents' partiality toward one child over the other. One's first-born child is typically but not always identified with oneself, while the next are assigned the (genetic) role of rejected siblings. A first child may be preferred just because of his age, since it is easier to communicate with him and he is better company. At other times, the sex of the child accounts for the preference: a parent may have wanted a girl rather than a boy or vice versa. Such a preference may disregard the actual sex of the child and result in a type of rearing which distorts the sexual identity of the child, who then is favored on the basis of the role assigned and not on account of his objective gender. This often, but not exclusively, happens after parents have had several children of the less accepted sex. A child may also be preferred because of his position in the sequence of children, if it is similar to that of the

parent in relation to his own siblings, e.g. a parent may identify and then be partial toward his third child if he himself
had two older siblings.

On the other hand, the younger or youngest child may be
preferred because he is more dependent and easier to handle,
mobilizes the parental drive to a greater degree, does not yet
elicit feelings of rivalry and competition and is less apt to
criticize the parent.

Middle children, finally, may lose out in the affection of
the parents because the latter are, for reasons explained above,
likely to be partial to the oldest and the youngest. Sometimes a child's special gift may induce the parents to concentrate their attention on him to the detriment of other siblings,
but usually it is the other way around: the favored child re-
sponds with some admirable talent or interest, which the parents' admiration furthers, and this in turn perpetuates the
parents' overinvolvement.

A child may, on the other hand, also absorb the concern,
affection and overprotectiveness of guilt-ridden parents because of some physical or mental handicap. The other, "the
forgotten sibling," then resents both the discriminating parents
and the "preferred" recipient of their attention. Yet the pertinent feelings of hostility are typically kept in abeyance by
the "overlooked" child. This is possible for him to achieve
because he benefits from his conviction, supported by the implied or explicitly stated opinion, that he is, in the eyes of his
parents, the healthier and more mature child, the greater
source of joy for them and so forth. This prevails until, by
some improvement in his condition or removal from home,
the spoiled sibling ceases to enjoy his privileged status. Almost without exception the hitherto neglected child then develops problems which urgently seem to require the same
devotion which the parents had paid to the first.

Another factor may complicate even more the dynamics
involved.

A schizophrenic boy's sister was considered by her mother to be mature, reliable and "strong as the rock of Gibraltar." The mother, who had never succeeded in relinquishing her dependency on her own mother whom she described precisely as being "strong as the rock of Gibraltar," during her son's illness had assigned to her daughter the role of a substitutive mother to herself. As to her son, she used him for projection and objectivation of her own dependency needs. Indeed, dependency on his mother played a decisive role in his clinical condition. When he markedly improved in dual therapy to the point of moving out of the home of his widowed mother, taking on a job and generally showing that he was able to take care of himself, the mother had to make a new kind of adjustment. She needed an object on whom to project her extreme dependency on her mother, which also had the function of assuring her against the guilt feelings about her oedipal attachment to her father and older brother. As now only her daughter was available, she invested her with the role her son previously had played. From both these roles the daughter became the target of a "double bind" injunction: "Be strong like my mother, the Rock of Gibraltar, and be weak and helpless like myself." From the impossibility of meeting this contradictory empathic suggestion of the mother, the daughter suffered a psychotic break in her turn. The extreme rivalry between this brother and his sister was the inevitable concomitant of the genetic script of their mother.

But let us come back to the main topic of the present rule, sibling rivalry. *Proper communication* between both parents and the parties to a conflict will quickly put an end to an argument or run-in between their children, provided that the parents' "genetic script" does not impose repetition of their own unresolved hostile competition with siblings. As these most frequently center on the accusation of preference and discrimination by one or both parents, the participation of each parent in the discussion of the problem with their children can easily correct and dispose of either any mistaken impressions on the part of the aggrieved or any objective partiality or injustice. By "proper communication," we mean the willingness of the parent to listen without impatience and to make the effort of finding the proper elements and wording so as to turn the conflict into an emotionally enriching experience. This will be achieved when the incident ultimately results in a genuine acceptance of the other's rights and privileges by each of the contending parties. Sensitive parents may soon discover that rarely is there a greater pleasure than that which rewards them for their effort of reconciling conflicts between two human beings. Each of these experiences convinces one about the basic pliability of the human mind to the exigencies of reason and justice, and by extension about the applicability of the same principles to clashes of interest between more powerful contending groups of every dimension.

Rule 8   *CHILDREN SHOULD NOT BE CONSIDERED PALS OF THEIR PARENTS*

Parents should not allow their children to use them as lightning rods for the tension and anger engendered in them by others. It is not "ego-building" or "morale-lifting" if parents exchange their role as educators for that of scapegoats.

A patient who had never been able to control her verbal abuse of her parents recalled how they would tell her every time she insulted or provoked them, "Look, we're taking it, but don't count on others to do the same." The end result of this kind of parental "permissiveness" was a lifelong dependency of the patient on her mother and father, with her unbridled sadism and incumbent guilt feelings providing the fettering chain which left her free only for promiscuous and ephemeral involvements with men.

Children need their parents as mediators of reality and of its demands and restrictions. They are the first and usually the chief source of behavior-regulating values. By putting oneself persistently on the same level as one's children, one renders them "psychological orphans." They do not learn to control their impulses, to acquire moral standards or to act on the incentive of becoming in the process of maturation like the admired and envied grown-ups. (In play it is the privilege of parents and of their young to erase transiently the difference in generations or to "swap roles," the former reliving their own childhood and the latter enjoying a foretaste of the future.)

The difference of generations between parent and child should be maintained, mutual respect being the ground rule for communication between the two. The superiority in physical strength, capacity, skill, knowledge, self-control and wisdom which the parent has, or normally should have, over the young child should be conveyed to and experienced by the child as qualities operating for his benefit. Parents should avoid bringing their superiority to bear on the child in such a way as to emphasize his shortcomings. Only thus can the child be motivated to model himself after the adult. This also precludes parents' presenting themselves as weak, self-effacing and willing to sacrifice themselves on behalf of the child. It is known that genuine respect for others can be maintained only if it goes hand in hand with self-respect. This is true also for the parents' attitude toward their children.

Rule 9   *A PARENT SHOULD REFRAIN FROM COMPETING
WITH THE CHILD FOR THE OTHER PARENT*

Parents' competition with the child for each other betrays
to him the weakness and vulnerability of their marital bond
and deprives him of an adequate model for identification. It
also exacerbates the child's guilt feelings inherent in the assumption that he presents a threat to his parents' marriage.

> A mother who would run to the car in order to wedge
> herself at the last moment between her husband and her
> daughter would also have a temper tantrum whenever the
> daughter put her toothbrush between those of her parents.
> Though this mother correctly perceived her daughter's com-
> petition, her overanxious reaction certainly did not facilitate
> her daughter's relinquishing the oedipal position. The latter
> had every right to think, and, as her analysis revealed, uncon-
> sciously did, "You have father in a more meaningful way,
> why do you not even allow me to sit next to him? Just be-
> cause you won't allow me to have a little of him, I will not
> surrender my hope of taking him away from you."

Equally self-defeating are parents' habits of "putting down"
their sons or daughters when they try to impress the other
parent with some physical asset, intellectual feat, evidence of
wit, pleasing appearance, good taste, or the like. The best
course for a parent to take is first to see what reaction the
wooed parent exhibits. Only when the child's competitive
aspirations appear successful, so that the oedipal conflict runs
the risk of being exacerbated by the evidence of the other
parent's seductibility, is intervention necessary in the form
of a discussion between the parents in the *absence of the
child*. The impropriety and detrimental consequences of the
parent's reaction to the child's maneuver should be pointed
out without recrimination, and always bearing in mind the
biblical saying about "not throwing the first stone." Without
the other parent's benign and watchful participation in the

triadic interaction, we are all liable to enjoy excessively being "preferred" by the child and, conversely, to resent equally excessively anyone who is preferred over us.

Rule 10 *EACH PARENT SHOULD BE A BENIGN CONCILIA-
TOR AND MODERATOR BETWEEN THE CHILD
AND THE OTHER PARENT*

Even if the child's complaints and accusations betray grossly the motive of wanting to separate the parents, he should be listened to with calm and genuine interest. Communication should be established with the purpose of bringing the child back to the parent. This is not too difficult, provided the parent does not fall victim to his wish to monopolize the affection and allegiance of the child. A more subtle caution pertains to the parent's attitude in the very act of conciliation: one should not arrogate excessive merit to oneself. In other words, the parent should avoid presenting himself as more loving and more understanding, thus betraying his competition with the other parent for the child.

A parent's shirking his task of peace-making intervention in a quarrel between the other parent and the child *is an unmistakable sign of his hostility against either or both.* It is one of the most frequent violations of the triadic principle, violation by omission. A mother may excuse her absenteeism by her concern over being too "controlling" or "critical" in the face of her daughter's constant provocation of her father. Such a mother betrays that she has a stake in perpetuating the quarrels. A mother who instead induces her daughter to respect and accept her father makes it possible for the daughter to draw closer to him without hurting him or being hurt. Such an attitude of the mother never escapes the grateful awareness of both the other parties. The same is true for the role of a father in the clashes between a mother and a son and for the role of either parent in those clashes, no less frequent, between a child and a parent of the same sex.

The prospect of closeness between the mate and the child is intolerable to a parent when it unconsciously activates in him repressed hostility residual to his having witnessed closeness between father and mother or parent and sibling. Such a constellation usually leads to the inception of a *negative dyad* where the self-eliminating but onlooking parent enjoys the fights between the other members of the genetic triad, because it not only assures him that he is not being discriminated against but also not rarely affords him a sadistic pleasure.

A parent may even actively incite one or both parties of the family triad to quarrel. This is most typical of a mother who seems unable to limit a child's unruliness during the absence of a (working) father. She then eagerly seizes the opportunity to report on the child to her husband as soon as he enters the door. The unfailing result of this frustrating reception of a father who, fatigued and/or worried, had hoped to find at home peace and repose from his daily struggles, is that he becomes quickly verbally or physically punitive toward the transgressors. Often there prevails a combination of two alternating negative dyads: both parents make sure that they are not the discriminated-against third party and consequently the child, instead of coping with only one hostile parent actually must contend with two.

Giving the child the opportunity to express his disappointment should not, however, be construed as encouraging an endlessly complaining, nagging, critical pattern. This holds true also if the accused one is the parent himself. Indeed I found one of the most common examples of "genetic scriptwriting" pertinent here, precisely in those cases in which a parent *promotes* in the children abuse of himself, while on the surface he appears to be simply the pathetically helpless victim of their harassment. Analysis, especially in the dual setting, quickly reveals that the underlying fantasy is one of attack against the maternal or paternal introject: The "helpless" and "abused" parent confuses himself with his own mother and father and delegates to his children the attack against the (introjected) parent, in the by now familiar "introject attacked by proxy" defense. (This is as a rule the case with parents who, when they were themselves children, did not dare express any criticism against their own parents.)

If the child expresses criticism against the very parent who has wronged him, the participating and moderating presence of the other parent is most useful in preventing the "frankness" and "spontaneity" from degenerating into endless arguments and ending in alienation between the contending parties. The mere presence of the non-incriminated parent acts soothingly here. This is because, in an overwhelming proportion of cases, the fights which result from complaints and criticism are of a *defensive* nature: not only the child but also the parent is likely to use expression of anger to ward off overly positive feelings and sensuous impulses rooted in unresolved oedipal conflicts.

Disciplinary action or questions of granting or denying certain privileges are the most frequent occasions for parents to implement the task of dealing constructively with their children when they feel wronged by the demand or decision of one of the parents. In general the exigencies of education, which parents genuinely believe in, the prime-moving concern for their clashes with their children, provide an excellent opportunity for the parents to put under scrutiny and self-control their temptation to violate the triadic principle, i.e. to enforce a particular kind of genetic script on their children.

It ensues from the above that the attitude of a parent toward the child who complains about siblings, playmates and classmates, teachers, doctors, traffic officers and people in authority in general, should be no different from the one described above. In other words, the parent should not automatically side with the aggrieved child, but should be an in-

terested and also *objective* listener who will avoid sacrific-
ing the criteria of justice and fairness when asked to take a
stand on the validity of a complaint.

Parents should in general be alert to the child's need for
ventilating his anger, and seize upon clues betraying such a
need without waiting for direct verbalizations. If the child
was wronged in reality or in imagination, he should be assisted in learning from his experience to better understand
others and/or himself. Disappointment is either somebody
else's fault or one's own, or (most frequently) a combination
of both. In each case the parent is in a better position to evaluate the incident from a distance and, *post factum* to help the
child benefit from increased insight into his own motivations
and those of others.[3] But parents should always keep in mind
this basic tenet: The attitude of the child in dealing with frustration over his disappointment in others will be predetermined
by what *he has experienced and learned*—or, if one prefers,
been conditioned to—*within the genetic triangle.* In other
words, the child's approach to the whole problem of extra-
familial relationships, which will concern him increasingly
as he grows up, has its inception in this specific kind of
genetic experience in childhood.

---

3. Even an expert can overlook the weight of suggestive empathy and
thus be easily misled in advising a parent on how to handle the complaints
of a child. For an illustration, see H. G. Ginott's *Between Parent and
Child,* p. 38.

Rule 11   *PARENTS SHOULD NOT TAKE OUT THEIR FRUS-*
          TRATIONS AND ANGERS ON THEIR CHILDREN

The rule that children should not use their parents as lightning rods for what they have suffered outside of the family is even more valid in the opposite direction. Indeed, the misuse of children as scapegoats for their parents' unreleased hostility, engendered in intercourse with other adults, is an incomparably more frequent occurrence. The physical and emotional superiority of the parent over the child who is so essentially dependent on him makes possible an unlimited abuse of the child. An adult, unless he is dealing with somebody who is in a vulnerable position, is likely to control his anger out of fear of immediate or delayed retaliation. With his children he can behave as he pleases. If a child has become the displaced target of a parent's angry disappointment or irritated apprehension, he cannot possibly take revenge on the parent except by running away from home or by direct aggression. Such retaliation is by far more costly for the child than for the parent.

Concerning the implementation of the triadic principle in this contingency, the following can be said: in making one's mate aware that he is taking or about to take out on his children his "extra-familial" setbacks and disappointments, great tact and sensitivity are required. Displacement is a defense, and nobody is particularly grateful for suddenly being deprived of the relief which a defense provides to his ego. Special care should be taken not to do this in the presence of the child. To appear as the "protector" of the child, that is, to seem the "better" parent, violates Rule 10, which aims at avoiding precisely this outcome.

Rule 12 *CHILDREN   SHOULD   BE   SPARED   WITNESSING
QUARRELS BETWEEN THEIR PARENTS*

This experience should be especially guarded against if the
child is, as is frequently the case, the cause of the parents'
disagreement. Constant quarrelling between father and mother
exacerbates the child's oedipal conflict in the sense that, while
his wish to separate the parents seems about to come true, he
must at the same time feel frightened and guilty about this
very hope. (Usually both these reactions are quickly repressed
and covered by a variety of other defenses.)

Some of the most frequently overlooked traumatic experiences are those pertaining to the battles between parents. They
occur usually, though not exclusively, at the end of the day
or late at night, when infantile conflicts are most likely to
rise to the surface from the parents' unconscious. Understand-
ably, these quarrels break out at the moment when each parent expects the other to offer "love without guilt," as if this
were in his power. The child overhears the clashes of the
parents even when he is asleep: he simply weaves what he
unconsciously perceives into his dreams. Awake or asleep,
he invariably confuses the angry exchange between father and
mother with primal scene experiences. Indeed the "interpretations" in the child's mind (conscious and unconscious) of
what is going on in the bedroom of his quarrelling parents is
highly tinged with sado-masochism. In such cases the child's
own (frustrated) aggression directed against one or the other
parent, as well as the ensuing guilt feelings, endow the primal
scene with an especially violent and frightening meaning which
may leave an indelible mark on the child's future love life.

A recent publication, *The Intimate Enemy* (G. R. Bach
and P. Wyden), might be mentioned here. Its authors declare
themselves committed to channel the ambivalence inherent in
all human relationships, but especially in those of an intimate nature, i.e. most typically between husband and wife,
into what they call "constructive aggression." Unfortunately
they have disregarded the detrimental repercussions on the

child of constant fights between his parents. On the contrary, these authors believe that it is constructive even when the child himself fights with his parents, because it promotes "establishment of the child's identity."[4] They have overlooked the fact that what makes family life so unhappy in our most affluent of modern societies, and what makes our youth resort to the use of drugs and other types of self-destructive behavior, is certainly not their docility or obedience toward their elders. Display of aggression against any type of authority, the one against one's parents acting here as a conditioning pattern, is in a sizeable proportion of the youth of today not only boundless but endlessly repetitious, that is, really without any cathartic effect. This is because almost without exception the open aggression against parents or parental substitutes is used as a defense, i.e. aims either at denying anxiety about (preoedipal or oedipal) closeness and passivity or at securing punishment for objectionable (unconscious) wishes rooted in the known irrational infantile positions.

Rule 13 *EACH PARENT SHOULD GIVE EVIDENCE THAT HE APPRECIATES AND ENJOYS THE COMPANY OF THE OTHER PARENT*

To say, as one mother did to her daughter, "You can have him," referring with derogation to her husband, is a typical example of conveying opposition to the mate's closeness with the child. It acts as a prohibition by conveying to the child

---

4. This reminds us of the rationalization of certain militant groups who substitute racial equality with "racial power" and justify the use of violence by presenting it as a means of "finding one's own identity." It is this kind of condoning indulgence in aggression that accounts for much of mankind's predicament.

that one parent deprecates the other as a love object.[5] Showing oneself to be unwilling, disinterested or bored at the prospect of sharing in the spouse's work or diversions, or in general spending time with him alone, has as great an antimaturational effect as direct derogation through words or attitude of the other parent's professional interests, avocations, tastes, etc. Both deprive the child of an incentive to overcome the anxiety and guilt incumbent on the oedipal conflict. In reality genuine love usually leads to a convergence and blending of one's interests, enthusiasms and preferences with those of the loved one.

It may sound far from trail-blazing to suggest that both parents show the child that they cherish each other. Yet the truth is that most parents believe that to show that they hold each other in deep affection is less important than to show love and tenderness toward the child. In reality, by acting on such a mistaken belief they violate the basic tenet of the triadic principle; parents, through their attitude and behavior toward each other, provide the child with a blueprint for his own capacity to feel love for the opposite sex and friendship toward the same sex.

> This explains why it is not enough that separated or divorced parents avoid denigrating each other to the child. Even if they were to stress the positive qualities about each other, which in reality they most rarely do, the child would notice the glaring contradiction between such utterances and the drastic step which the parents have undertaken in breaking the marriage. If any communication could be helpful, it would be one in which the parents admit to the child of a knowledgeable age that they themselves have, through errors of judgment due to unrecognized influences from their own past, contributed to the disruption of the marriage. Such an explanation would especially counteract the most destructive consequence of the separation of parents in the life of chil-

---

5. Indeed in one such typical case the daughter ultimately became promiscuous, i.e. "had men" indiscriminately and meaninglessly, just as mother's permission to "have her father" was meaningless.

dren, i.e. that each parent expects the child to prefer him and reject the other. This increases the child's inevitable guilt feelings rooted in the conviction that he was the cause of the parents' separation. Resolution of the oedipal bond with the parents then becomes impossible without analytic help.

A "child-centered" family does not promote maturation of the young. To be considered by one or both parents as the most important member of the genetic triad deprives the child of the wish to emulate the adult. To prefer the child over the husband or wife is not an expression of genuine maternal or paternal love, but a sign that in the parent's mind, for his own infantile reasons, the difference between two generations is blurred or even non-existent. Tempted as either parent may be to appear in the eyes of the child as more understanding, more affectionate, more self-sacrificing, more intelligent or, under whatever aspect, the "better" parent, he should not indulge this wish. Even if not accompanied by direct derogation of the other parent, it is, though not the most destructive, one of the most frequent infringements of the triadic principle.

Rule 14 *PARENTS SHOULD SHOW RESERVE REGARDING THEIR LOVE LIFE*

Children should not be allowed to invade the privacy of parents in their bedroom, whether intentionally or "by mistake." The earlier the infant is removed from the parental bedroom the better. *Primal scene experiences* have been found to be traumatic even during the first year of life, when they certainly cannot be recalled by the patient, but were in a few cases reliably reconstructed from the material patients have produced in analysis. Traumatic primal scene experiences are often the core of very serious clinical conditions.[6]

A mother of four who suffered from anxiety attacks whenever she had to face new situations spoke about her difficulties in her intimate relations with her husband: "Somehow we never seem able to have privacy. In the old apartment our bedroom was like Grand Central Station. The children on the way to the bathroom and back could hear and see us when we were making love. There was no other way but through our bedroom. Now we are in a new apartment, but again the glass door to the bedroom lets every noise through. (– – –?) Until I was nine I slept in the bedroom of my parents. I heard everything and knew when they engaged in sex. My mother objected. I heard her saying, 'Stop it, stop it. Bonnie might hear.' I must confess that I would often interrupt what they were doing; I had to go to the bathroom. (– – –) You mean, we could have prevented all this? Yes, but my husband. . . ."

Thus this mother's difficulties revealed themselves to be simply determined by the known mechanism of *repetition compulsion*. She did not know that in the attempt to master the past primal scene trauma, she unconsciously enacted with her husband her own parents: With the help of her children's interference she still unconsciously interrupted not her own love life but that of her parents ("introject attacked by proxy"). Naturally this could not have occurred if her husband, whose deep religiosity was equalled only by his stinginess, had not for his own (genetic) reasons gone along with his wife's "inability" to secure privacy for their sex life.

---

6. I had the opportunity to study the muffled way of speaking and the habit of emitting peculiar sounds in a teenager who was in residential therapy because of her states of withdrawal, alternating with violent angry outbursts against her parents at home. The speech symptoms disappeared as soon as she understood that she re-enacted in this way what she had overheard when her parents made love, while sharing the same bedroom with them.

When children betray their silent or noisy but usually in-direct[7] protest against their parents' being alone together, comments to the effect that the same privilege will be open to them once they are married, are more than enough to stimulate healthy expectations and desires in the young. At the same time, this attitude furthers the process of emotional and sexual emancipation of the offspring from their infantile bond with the parents, and promotes a more mature, warmer and definitely less ambivalent relationship between the two generations.

Rule 15   *PARENTS SHOULD BE ALERT TO, AND AVOID ABETTING, THE CHILD'S OPEN OR UNCONSCIOUS WISH TO SEPARATE THEM*

Playing into the child's conflicted needs to interfere with the parents' being close to each other should be avoided. The child's tendency to put one parent in a bad light in the eyes of the other should be recognized for what it is: an attempt to sow discord between the parents in the hope of monopoliz-

---

7. A twelve-year-old boy had the habit of using his parents' double bed for trampoline exercises. He did this with such zest that the bed ultimately collapsed. (This was his way of retaliation against his parents who, by leaving their bedroom door half open, imposed on him the evidence of what he should not have been so crudely confronted with.)

Incidentally, marital love life can be enjoyed by the parents without suddenly removing themselves from their children and closing the door behind them. Empathically, if not from the parents' demeanor in these circumstances, children easily guess that the incommunicado is not for a private "discussion." Married people have plenty of opportunity to engage in physical intimacy without flaunting it before their offspring.

ing the attention and affection of one or the other. Therefore the parent, without hysterics, but also without triumphant or condescending enlightenment to the child about his "Oedipus," should refuse to countenance the child's manipulation. This can be achieved without making him feel guilty. The benign attitude of a parent who shows himself not to be threatened by the child's designs, and who recognizes the child's privilege to make a "good try," will ultimately be rewarded by evidence that the child feels gratefully relieved. *Indeed, as much as the child wants to separate the parental couple, he is equally strongly motivated not to succeed in this undertaking.*

The resolution of the "core" conflict in the life of man is made easier if the parent has a clear conception of the difference between the irrationality of pre-oedipal monopolization and the oedipal quest on one side and the "legitimate" claims, i.e. what the child is entitled to expect, on the other. These legitimate expectations can and should be spelled out here: The child has a right to expect from his parents warmth, acceptance and interest in his maturation. Maturation for its part includes gaining of self-respect and self-reliance as well as capacity for achievement, mastery of skills and acquisition of knowledge. In the first place, however, the child should be helped by his parents in forming good relationships with playmates, classmates, friends, relatives and people in authority, and above all in acquiring a genuine interest in *non-familial members of the opposite sex.*

Rule 16 *PARENTS SHOULD BE ABLE TO ENLIGHTEN THE CHILD ABOUT SEX DIFFERENCES, CONCEPTION AND CHILDBIRTH, AS WELL AS HIS OWN BUDDING SEXUAL DRIVES*

The clarification provided concerning sex and procreation should be simple and commensurate with the child's age and intellectual development. It should be *passive,* that is, it should not go beyond the confines of the child's questions. An exception may be the case where there is a striking contrast between the child's mental capacity and his ignorance in these matters. Answers to the child's questions should be benign and supportive and neither intellectually nor emotionally overwhelming; parents should avoid going into details of their own sexual patterns, as this would go counter to the rule of preserving the privacy of their love life. Also helpful here are the many publications which offer an integrated and simple presentation of the information needed.[8] The triadic principle would favor the joint procedure, i.e. that both parents be present when pertinent information is given to the child, preferably with the parent of the same sex staying in the foreground during the exchange. In those cases where external circumstances make joint enlightenment impossible, for example with separated or divorced parents, it is again desirable that the child be given the opportunity to obtain the answers to his questions from the parent of the same sex.

Admittedly there is the possibility that discussion of sexual matters between parent and child can be overstimulating to the latter and can turn into an opportunity for acting out reciprocal (oedipal) seduction (see illustration p. 126). Yet here again, following the triadic principle is the best safeguard. The rule that a parent should not have any secrets with his child behind the back of the other parent should be applied

8. The books of K. de Schweinitz (*Growing Up*) and of S. Hegeler (*Peter and Caroline: A Child Asks about Childbirth and Sex*) can be mentioned here, as well as other books and pamphlets on this topic published by the Child Study Association of America.

most strictly in the area of sex education. This obviates charg-
ing the atmosphere with undue erotic tension during the
verbal exchanges between the parent and the inquiring child,
and thus averts exacerbating the oedipal conflict. A mere hint
to the child that the other parent will be informed of the communication acts preventatively here by freeing it from guilt-
ridden secretiveness. But even more decisive is the fact that
genuine adherence to the triadic principle, as expressed in the
implementation of the "rules" suggested, also makes the enlightenment a reassuring and reciprocally endearing experience, instead of a frustrating, alienating and remorseful one
for both parties to the exchange.

In general, the way in which the parent relates to the child's
need to know about the source of man's greatest emotions
and of his physical and spiritual enjoyment, but also of his
greatest vulnerability, will reflect the extent to which the
maturational need of the child is supported by his elders'
parental drive.

Rule 17   *MASTURBATION AS THE NORMAL OUTLET FOR
          THE CHILD'S SEXUAL ENERGIES*

Self-gratification does not present a problem as long as it
is not excessive or openly displayed. Sexual energies are generated in the child long before he has reached full sexual
maturity in the biological sense. They are usually discharged
through self-stimulation. The parts of the body used for this
purpose are preferably those designated by Freud as "erotogenic" zones. The importance of each of these zones changes

from one developmental stage to another. The sequence oral-anal-genital corresponds to the normal shift of "libidinal primacy" and expresses the fact that ultimately, when maturity is reached, the genital zone is the main area for both sexual stimulation and orgastic discharge. The child's masturbatory activity therefore involves the genital organ itself only in the last (oedipal) stage. Preceding this is stimulation of the mentioned "pregenital" erotogenic zones (oral, anal), though not exclusively so. Indeed, erotic pleasure is drawn from any kind of contact with love objects, i.e. through sight, touch, smell or movement, and may, as we know, involve non-genital parts of the sexually desired object. This explains why rythmical hair-pulling, finger-twisting, scratching, grimacing or rocking can be substituted for direct masturbation and related *frustration aggression*. This is because the need for such patterns of release is without exception due to unresolved conflicts rooted in chronic emotional deprivation or over-stimulation (physical and emotional; see rule 3) of the child by his parents and the concurrent introjection of the ambivalently loved object.

A twenty-year-old college student could not control his scalp-scratching. For years he had had another habit, in spite of father's objection yet with mother's concurrence, that of spending hours on her bed twisting her hair. His early childhood was a bleak one: his mother was utterly dependent on and submissive to her own mother. The latter would daily visit her daughter and completely absorb her attention, so that little if any interest was left for our patient and his sister. After the grandmother died, it was only natural that this mother recreate her symbiotic relationship with her daughter rather than with him. When the daughter, who for years was at the brink of a schizophrenic breakdown, was ultimately enabled through extensive therapy to move out of the family and live independently, the mother fell back on her son in her need to recreate the early mother-child relationship. Lying on her bed with her son, as described above, corresponded to a substitutive fulfillment of this need. The son was already in his twenties when he and his mother got into the habit of having conversations late into the night, which would be ended abruptly by the enraged intervention of the father. The latter had many years of analysis, and only in dual therapy became aware of how his tolerating the earlier goings-on between his wife and son had brought about the present source of his bitterness. He was a father in a typical negative dyad with his son. The son paid for his own disregard of father's objection and his mother's violation of the triadic principle with intolerable tension, guilt-induced sexual difficulties and failure in school. He eventually dropped out of college and became a hippie, with a most personal motive for liking long hair.

As mentioned earlier, only open display or excessive indulgence in masturbation requires parental intervention. In the light of the above considerations this should not be limited to inducing the child to curtail his masturbatory activity: the parent must, through close scrutiny of his relationship with his child and of the genetic constellation in his family in general, find the reasons for the child's loneliness, sadness and depression which result in abuse of sexual self-manipulation. Indeed, uncontrolled masturbation shares its cause with addiction to food, alcohol and drugs: the feeling of frustration and anger, originally directed against the parents and then turned against the Self, which underlies the tendency towards depression, requiring instant pleasure or instant numbing.

Rule 18 *A PARENT SHOULD NOT HAVE SECRETS WITH A CHILD*

Nothing which concerns the child should be withheld by one parent from the other, nor should a parent accede to the child's request to hide or distort the truth.[9] A secret between a parent and a child implies the lesser importance of the other parent and plays into the child's fantasy of oedipal separation of the parents. It fosters an unhealthy closeness between the two partners to the secret and unfailingly turns into a source of guilt feelings and need for punishment in both.

A four-year-old girl ran in panic to her mother: a neighbor across the hall who had asked her to keep him company tried to pull her panties down. He let her go when she began to scream. The truth of her daughter's story did not interest the mother, who was only worried about her discretion. "Don't tell Daddy, because he will *kill* that man." This secret kept by the daughter until her early twenties (when her father died), became too great an emotional burden on her. It led her to initiate meaningless sexual activities with male friends while her widowed mother was in the next room. This pattern seemed to aim at recreating the past childhood event but also at carrying to completion a sexual experience which her mother's reaction had linked with unspeakable shame and even with death as punishment. In other words, here was an attempt to overcome, through repetition, her mother's traumatic injunction that she remain close only with her and that she reject father as a too violent and dangerous man. The resulting dyadic symbiosis between mother and daughter led, as dyadic bonds frequently do, to a sado-masochistic pattern; it became evident after father's sudden and "obliging" death (see p. 151) in frequent fights with fists and fingernails, during which they would tear the phone out of each other's hands and scream for the police, each

---

9. Of course, discretions which involve pleasant surprises or gifts about which the recipient is kept in the dark only for a short while are exceptions to this rule.

accusing the other: "She is killing me!" Thus in their
violence towards each other, they enacted also the role of
destructive male—enacted, that is, in consequence to introjection of the husband and father. This introjection became
inevitable after he was, and allowed himself to be, eliminated
from the two overlapping triangles, the one with his daughter
and the other with his son (*ibid.*).

Rule 19 *PARENTS SHOULD REFRAIN FROM DECEIVING
THEIR CHILDREN*

Though white lies aimed at sparing the young some unnecessary anxiety or shock are easily forgiven if discovered,
parents should limit these to a minimum.

It was, for example, an understandable and justified deception when a father signaled to his wife to distract the
attention of his two children, aged three and six, from seeing
the body of a man being recovered from a lagoon, and whom
the father ultimately succeeded in resuscitating. There are,
however, many other situations which children could have
been spared deception if those who tried to protect them had
paid attention to the possible consequences of their act. An
eleven-year-old child who lost her mother after a prolonged
illness should have been told about her mother's death and
should have been allowed to go to the funeral, sharing the
grief of, and being comforted by, her relatives, rather than
being faced later with the fait accompli, that her mother had
been buried without the child's having been allowed a last
glimpse of her.

Children will also understand with time that parents need not reveal the details of the family finances. Children, at least up to a certain age, are incapable of evaluating realistically the parents' financial assets and obligations and are likely to make unwarranted inferences about the parents' lack of generosity or even their stinginess. Yet too much concealment and outright deception in this matter should also be avoided, because children for their own reasons are too eager to notice inconsistencies and self-contradictions on the part of their parents. This is the situation when an inadequate allowance is explained as justified by "hard times," while the son or daughter has had plenty of occasion to see the parents spend large amounts of money on superfluities.

The child's anger at the discovery that his parents have lied to him is usually disproportionate because it stems from sources outside the contingent issue. These are intimately linked with conflicts and crises which are part and parcel of the parents' task of mediating to their child the demands and limitations of external reality, while at the same time trying to preserve the image of "ideal parents" in his mind. The child for his part is torn by two contradicting wishes: he would like to be independent and self-reliant, yet at the same time is unable and unwilling to surrender the protective and supportive parental buffer. In view of this it is inevitable that the child is inclined to find his parents at fault. For precisely because of his need to emancipate himself, the child may be prone to believe, and often with some justification, that his parents tend to exaggerate the exigencies, liabilities and perils of external reality. From the level of the usually more concealed, even to himself, wish to retain the dependence on his parents, he may go so far as *to blame them* paradoxically *for the very existence of the external reality*. There is, however, an objective and psychological core to what seems at first glance a completely irrational accusation: the child was actually brought into this world by his parents alone and they also have been for a long time the child's "whole world." This may sufficiently explain why he holds them responsible also for the other, the real world which sooner or later even the most protected child must face.

The exaggerated vigilance of children for their parent's untruths has its most important root here for the following reason:

The external world is in the first place the one created by men, by their urges and needs, and by the outcomes and compromises resulting from the clash of one individual's wishes with those of others. There are innumerable life situations in which wishes and aspirations will have to be subordinated in favor of those of other people. Cardinal here is the one within the history of *every* genetic triad: for the first time the child faces the painful truth that his wishes are not the most decisive forces in this world, as his infantile feelings of "omnipotence" let him believe.

What we have in mind is, naturally the contingency when more thoughtful parents conceal from their children, out of consideration for their sensitivity as much as for the parents' own comfort, the details pertaining to their love life. Moreover, children themselves betray a most bewilderingly contradictory attitude toward this situation. They are without exception curious about the sexual life of their parents, as their reactions and fantasies about *primal scene* experiences undoubtedly show. Yet, and this can easily be verified, in the starkest contrast to this fact, there prevails in man a marked incapacity *to imagine his parents in the sexual act*. In other words, the parents' inevitable concealment of their sex life goes hand in hand with a self-deceiving blindness on the part of their children, a blindness which protects the young from recognizing that their oedipal wishes are doomed to defeat. It is here also that the original ego-cosmic self-image of the child finds its most distressing and rude awakening.

The image of the parents, which because of the necessity of restraining the incestuous urges has been kept pure and asexual by the child, suddenly appears in his mind in its "true light," that is, they are seen as liars and deceivers who covered their lustful activities by the pretense of propriety.

This is the main reason for the curious mixture of idealism and cynicism in the picture presented by the youth of today. The "sexual revolution" finds here its constant feedback: the truth about their parents' sex life can no longer be hidden from today's children, who are intellectually much more precocious than those of past generations. Children now have a tendency to quickly "see through" what they consider "a lie," and therefore proclaim *urbi et orbi* that all adults are not to be trusted. How this belief is intertwined with the objective and more ominous truth about the "world of grown-ups," which leaves realistically very little hope to the younger generation, will be gone into on a later occasion. Here we only attempt to show that the necessity for parents to be as truthful as possible to their children is imposed by the oedipal conflict which is central to the interaction within the genetic triad. It derives from the essence of the triadic principle that each parent must prevent the other from telling untruths to their children, a temptation which parents, for reasons again related to their own genetic experiences, rarely can resist.

Rule 20   *PARENTS' ENCOURAGING CONFIDENCE IS ESSEN-
TIAL TO THE CHILD'S MASTERY OF PHYSICAL
AND INTELLECTUAL SKILLS*

The emulation of the adult is a prime spur to the child's wish to learn, be it when he takes his first steps, or when he has to acquire the ability to ride a bicycle or drive a car. This is also true for learning in the intellectual sphere. To induce the child to *want* to emulate the adult and to succeed in this, it is not sufficient that the parent show himself physically or mentally competent. The parent's own excellence is no safeguard of the child's willingness to use him as a model or, as analysts define it, as an *ego ideal* for a specific learning task. The *nature* of the total parent-child relationship is the decisive factor here. If the child is for one reason or another frustrated by the parent, he will turn against what he experiences as an unwarranted imposition or an unreasonable expectation. He then often has the conviction that the parent is moved only by his wish to impress others with his child's performance and achievements. And according to my experience, the child more often than not is right in believing this.

> The use of the child as an *extension* (phallic, feminine or narcissistic, or a combination of these), and, for that matter, also the use of him as a *proxy,* is the last manner still available to the parent to build the relationship with his child into his own (the parent's) psychic economy, when he is not moved by the parental drive. The use of the child as an extension (or proxy) is in fact the last point of retreat of a parent who is in the process of completely withdrawing his emotional investment in the child. Or else, it is the last point of advance when the parent is incapable of solid investment of any kind. In both cases the *spiritus movens* here is the same which enforces a parent's genetic script-writing, such as motives of anaclitic or oedipal rivalry or defense against oedipal involvement, etc., in a parent.

A slow or sudden decrease in the child's performance, i.e. in his willingness and capacity to gain command of what his parents would like him to learn, is a reliable indicator of a violation of the principle of maturation as described and illustrated in the course of this writing. This is not at all surprising; we know that even animals teach their offspring many skills necessary for their survival. As we have derived the parental drive in men from what we call the *nesting instinct* of the animal, it is only natural that we trace the capacity of parents to teach and of children to learn to the parent-child interaction, that is, as repeatedly stressed, to the interplay between the parental drive of the first and the maturational drive of the second. The "encouraging confidence" of the caption to the present rule actually refers in simpler terms to what we have learned to know as the "suggestive" empathy of a parent in whom the parental drive is *not* obstructed. "Parental empathy," as this kind of empathy deserves to be termed, can deploy itself freely and optimally only if the parent is no longer under the influence of the genetic script prepared for him by his own parents.

"My father is a genius. (– – –?) Well, he begins to see it my way. I am flunking in math. But he doesn't seem to mind. (– – –?) He also takes it easy. . . ." (Henry's father was preparing his master's thesis in sociology, but had again interrupted his work because of what seemed a deeply entrenched philosophy about leisure versus work.) "I don't know why I am so down. At least this time I am not rushing to smoke grass. At a party yesterday everybody else did. . . . You know those two fellows I worked for. They went off just like that to the Virgin Islands. They didn't pay me. You know I worked on their boat, repairing, painting and all that. I liked this kind of work. (The boat was the very one on which they went on their pleasure trip; one was divorced and the other separated from his wife and children.) (– – –?) "I guess, but it is not so much for the money. I had asked them for very little, because, you know, I would sometimes sort of fool around or not come for work at all. Besides, they were friends of my father. You know . . . I was surprised." And yet Henry should not have been surprised, precisely because they were his father's friends.

The reader is already familiar with the genetic script Henry was forced to live by (see p. 226). Here we see that his father's experiences within his own family triad make him ally himself (unconsciously) with Henry in opposing scholastic achievements, to the intense disappointment of his wife (Henry's mother). Henry, instead of feeling relieved of the burden of work by his father's "understanding," as one might expect, reacts with depression, as he does to the sudden departure of father's friends who had come to play a father role in his unconscious by allowing him to "fool around" and by the ease with which they shirked their responsibility (as husbands, fathers, and employers). Henry evidently senses not only that his father is disinterested in his son's achievement, but also that father on the contrary has an active interest in preventing this achievement. At the time of the interview from which the above excerpt was taken, the son had not yet recognized what he soon would realize: the father could not tolerate Henry's being more successful insofar as scholastic performance is concerned. The risk was too great that the son might please mother more than father did.

From the same motivation, competition with a son or daughter (see Rule 9), and similar infractions of the triadic principle, another detrimental parental attitude may emerge: a parent can directly or indirectly blunt the child's wish to learn by performing tasks which the young one should do by himself, thus making it impossible for him to learn by trial and error. The overprotective parent who, because he "can do it quicker," buttons the coat of his eight-year-old or does his youngster's homework, the father who supplies his son with household money after he is married or, to take one last but not infrequent example, the mother who is eager to bring up her daughter's children, are all motivated by sources far removed from the one that feeds the parental drive.

Rule 21   *PARENTS SHOULD NOT HESITATE TO INSTILL IN THE CHILD MORAL AND OTHER VALUES TO WHICH THEY THEMSELVES ADHERE*

It is essential that parents *act* in accordance with the values they cherish, and not simply "believe in" and verbalize them. One of the most frequent reasons for alienation between children and parents is that the latter too often preach what they themselves disregard in practice. The truth is that children would rather imitate their parents than behave according to their demands. But there are also innumerable occasions when standards of behavior have to be clearly stated and, what is particularly important, conveyed in such a way as to avoid a double bind: too often parents make a demand while unconsciously expecting and wishing their children to do the opposite.

One would think that parents who really care would not need encouragement in this respect. After all, it is the acceptance, in belief and in action, of parental values which ultimately will enable the young to become constructive members of society, assuming naturally that the values to be impressed upon the child are constructive. Yet, paradoxically, "progressive" education, instead of spurring the parents' educational effort and making it easier for them to succeed in their endeavor, has actually made them more confused. The modern approach to raising of the young has had this effect not only on the method but on the very goal of education. In fact, parents now wonder whether they have any right at all to raise their children according to their own values.

On this point we do not hesitate to state our position clearly: If the values to be instilled in children do not go counter to basic moral principles, one can see no reason why parents should not raise their children to love what they themselves have learned to enjoy and cherish in their life. Why should incidental influences coming from other sources have a greater hold on the child's mind than those of loving parents who wish their offspring to develop their assets to the fullest

and to lead happy and rewarding lives? Parents thus motivated will be most unlikely to have to experience what so
often occurs with parents who have imposed on their children
antimaturational (genetic) role-playing and attending psychological mutilation. They will not have to watch helplessly
while their children make choices out of sheer rebellion and
vindictiveness, the reasons for which are unknown to both
parties to the alienation. Within the framework of a mutually
gratifying relationship between the two generations, there is
plenty of room for parents to show flexibility toward the particular sensitivities and endowments of each child.

As I see it, the problem of transmitting values is complicated by the dim recognition by the young that they have
been victimized by their elders' genetic script-writing. A no
lesser part play here the guilt feelings, equally dimly perceived
by parents, who because of their own infantile conflicts were
forced into the role of blind "personality and destiny shapers."
Uncertain as this awareness may be, it is very effective: it
accounts both for the youth's questioning today the right of
parents to want to influence them at all, and for the puzzling
hasty surrender of this right by parents.

Rule 22 *PARENTS SHOULD NOT SURRENDER THEIR AU-
THORITY, WHICH IS ESSENTIAL TO THEIR RE-
SPONSIBILITY TOWARD THEIR OFFSPRING*

The restlessness and rebelliousness of a significant portion
of today's youth in most progressive countries is not due to
their attempt to throw off the yoke of repressive and tyrannical
parental control. On the contrary, these adolescents are the

offspring of parents who decided to apply the principle of "progressive education" in raising them. In reality, children with problems of truancy or dropping out, of sexual promiscuity or perversion, of addiction, vandalism, shoplifting or delinquency in general are children whose parents allowed them an inordinate amount of freedom and independence. An examination of the "genetic scripts" in such cases proved again and again that the parents' liberality was nothing but a cover-up of their disinterest in the welfare of their children, if not an outright expression of their hostility and wish to get rid of them. The unconscious and sometimes even conscious wish operating here is to dump the "unmanageable" or "ungrateful" children into the lap of the police and courts and/or the welfare and psychiatric facilities of the community.

A "common front" inclination of parents to want to get rid of their wayward children as soon as they can earn their own living, or even earlier when they are still economically dependent on their elders but become eligible for custodial care by the community, is a most frequent violation of the triadic principle. This parental pattern produces in the youngster unconscious feelings of rejection with conscious depression which he is usually unable, because it would be too painful, to trace back to its source. On the contrary, it forces him into a clamorous display of an "as far as I am concerned, my parents might as well get lost" attitude. The depression, and its inevitable guilt feelings over the fantasies of attack against the parental introject, cause the young's incessant search for "ups" or "downs," that is, stimulants or sedatives, to drown out feelings of depression, with all the encumbent hazards to their health and performance.

Another no less frequent pattern is that of allowing one parent to take over completely the role of the one who sets limits and imposes socially acceptable standards of conduct, while the other conveys through action, words or attitude that he is sympathetic to the child's unwillingness to accept parental authority and judgment. Here the dyadic collusion between the child and one parent against the educational measures of the other results inevitably in alienation between the parents and in a harshening of the requirements of the parent who carries alone the burden of raising the child. A vicious circle finds its inception here: the opposition to this task leads to ever more exacting, excessive and punitively imposed parental demands. These seem only to justify the other parent's open support of the child's rebellion, which in turns leads to further deterioration of the marriage. In such a situation the child cannot help falling victim to exacerbated guilt feelings, which engender serious and sometimes suicidal depression. Though based on different dynamics than the previously described depressive constellation, this type of depression results in the same self-destructive abuse by the young of the artificial means mentioned above to alleviate their suffering.

Responsibility of parents toward their child entails caring and insisting on knowing the friends with whom he associates and whom he dates. It includes also the parents' being informed about parties, outings and trips in which the young partake—their location, their nature and, up to a certain age (an important factor here is the child's capacity for responsible behavior), whether they have adult supervision or leadership.

This caution is to be heeded especially in countries where there is a growing tendency of the young to use alcohol, drugs and psychotropic smoking. It is the parents' duty to protect their sons and daughters from the destructive pressure of those who, because of their own guilt feelings over any kind of dependency on artificial stimulants and concomitant incapacity to meet their educational and other requirements, have a strong motive to convert their peers to their way of thinking and doing. Analysis of such proselytizers (if they are not "pushers," who do it *also* for the money they need to feed their addiction) reveals without exception that they are acting under the powerful pressure of an oedipally motivated wish to separate the children from their parents, pupils from their teachers, employees from their employers, etc. They don't know that if they succeed in this, they only aggravate their (unconscious) guilt feelings, which will sooner or later exact punishment either by their own doing (car accidents, fatal overdose and so on) or at the hands of others (police, criminal courts, accomplices, gang warfare, etc.).

Rule 23   *PARENTS SHOULD TAKE INTO THEIR STRIDE SOME DEGREE OF NOISY DEFIANCE BY THE YOUNGER GENERATION IN THE PROCESS OF SEPARATING FROM THEIR ELDERS*

Parents should actually be interested in the child's extra-familial relationships long before he is capable of serious and consistent involvement. In this respect quite a number of parents show themselves surprisingly "uninvolved," often with the rationalization that they don't want to "snoop" or "invade" the private life of their child, as if there were no happy medium between complete disinterest and nagging intrusion with wish to control. They overlook the possibility that a friendly and encouraging attitude may very well convey to the child that the parent does not expect any exclusive emotional commitment from him, but draws pleasure from his maturational need to reach out beyond the confines of the family. The parents' obliviousness to this need of the child may be interpreted, and often rightly so, as their opposition to his emancipation. Hence both parents should show themselves warm and supportive of their child's developing interest in contacts with members of *both* sexes outside of the family.

One patient, entangled in a succession of unhappy affairs, reported, "When a girlfriend of mine had a nice figure my mother would ask, 'What's wrong with her, is she consumptive?'" Another mother, who had the pattern of always listening in on her eight-year-old daughter's phone conversations with her friends, said, "When they finished, I would open Linda's eyes to how she was a fool to believe that Jane was really friendly with her. I told her not to be a patsy and fall for it. Jane was only pretending that she wanted her over to play with her." (Possessiveness toward her next youngest sister, displaced onto her daughter, was this mother's driving motivation here.)

The parent who tends to monopolize a daughter or a son is also the one who gives vent, under the influence of his own guilt feelings and usually in an inordinately pressing manner, to his desire that the offspring move out of the house. The striking ambivalence thus swaying the parent may escape his own awareness, but usually not that of the children.

"My mother is very peculiar. On one side she says she cannot wait to see me married and out of the house. But as soon as I become interested in somebody she starts to criticize that person. I had an excellent opportunity to marry. I wanted my mother's approval. I tried to be very nice towards her over the weekend. But when I finally came around to tell her about this man, she found the same faults with him as she did with others. Usually she would find that they were too old for me. This made me immediately lose interest in him. I don't know why; what is wrong with marrying a man who is a few years older than myself?" (The "double bind" communication to the daughter consisted in the remarkable fact that her mother had married herself a *much* older man.)

In the attempt to become emotionally independent from their parents, children often project onto the parent their own clinging and possessiveness of which they would like to free themselves. Attempts of a parent to understand the teen-ager by asking about the sources of his distress are not rarely rebuffed with irritated impatience or derided sarcastically. Instead of experiencing these attempts as signs of a genuine interest in his aspirations, the teenager evidently experiences them merely as another disturbing interference which must be repulsed at any cost, i.e. irrespective of psychic injury to oneself and to the parent. A break in communication inevitably results, which bears the mark of some kind of *self-traumatization* of the adolescent. The latter for his part either withdraws completely or covers his conflicts about separation from the parents by clamorous proofs that *he does not need them*. In fact sometimes the attitude and demeanor of the young seem to convey that their elders deserve at best a compassionate contempt for their attitude of being hurt and misunderstood. Yet parents could easily reach their young ones if they would only be more sensitive to the adolescent's psychological predicament around the problem of emancipation, as already presented (p. 284).

Parents should also afford a supportive but at the same time discrete attitude, especially toward the offspring's final disengagement from his bond with them. This recommendation applies to the parents' attitude towards those who will ultimately become for the young their loved and cherished life companions. The contingency of the ultimate choice of a mate includes so many aspects that a general rule cannot possibly cover all of them. The precept of adherence to the triadic principle is the best counsel one can give parents regarding suitors. Indeed not only the young, in the process of making a definite move away from the family, are under emotional stress. The well-known assurance proffered to parents on the occasion of the marriage of their offspring, "You're not losing a daughter, you're gaining a son," or vice versa, points up the fact that the parents also have to adjust to the new situation.

To facilitate this last step in the process of emancipation from the original family, the parents must steer clear of two extreme positions, both in contravention to the triadic principle. The first extreme is to betray too much fear about "losing" the son or daughter by exaggerating the precautions around the "right" choice of the mate.

The second extreme attitude, often assumed on a denial basis, is that of expressing so much enthusiasm and admiration for the prospective son- or daughter-in-law that their own son or daughter cannot help, paradoxical as it may sound, but react with jealousy to the chosen one. This may ultimately lead to unexpected disenchantment and even to breaking up. As to the general attitude of parents toward the in-laws, which inevitably will influence the young couple's attitude toward them, we refer to the pertinent psychologic constellation and illustrations already provided.

CONCLUSION

The exploration of the preventive potentialities of formal education as seen from the genetic-analytic view will be postponed to the second volume on group-psychological prophylaxis, and this for the following reason: In school the child faces for the first time social demands and values not mediated to him by his parents, and moreover it takes place in a group situation. The question of how much truth there is to the presently popular view that schools, including those of higher learning, are teaching things basically removed from the realities of life and social issues will have to be answered, as well as what remedies genetic psychoanalysis is able to suggest on the strength of its findings.

The question of how values in general, and particularly those of a moral nature, are conveyed to and absorbed by youth, not only within the family but in society, in our view strikes at the core of the problem of prevention. To the realm of group psychology also belong the exploration of communal child-rearing like that in the Kibbutz where the triadic setting is only minimally retained, as children are raised largely by professional personnel rather than by parents. To what degree and in what respects such a collective approach offers a better preventive outlook will be gone into on the basis of what several decades of experience seem to suggest.

In respect to the issue of moral and social values, I feel that the attitude of psychoanalysis toward the problems of society and mankind in general deserves an objective evaluation. Voices are raised from time to time to the effect that any judgment about the difficulties besetting society is beyond the competence of the analyst: this is not the only example of analysts' making vice into a virtue. Still Freud himself, though he made no special effort to deal with the topic of psycho-

339

analytic prevention on a collective level, did devote three of his most original and thought-provoking monographs to the study of collective irrationality. (Group Psychology and the Analysis of the Ego (1921), The Future of an Illusion (1927) and Civilization and its Discontents (1930).)

On the whole it is my firm belief that in studying the problem of psychic prevention it is a grave omission to neglect the interrelationship between individual psychology and the manifestations of collective life (social, political, cultural and racial), i.e. not to deal with rational and irrational *group* psychology. *The major source of man's anxiety and suffering,* both physical and moral, is *other human beings,* especially those organized in religious, ethnic, racial and national groups up to the so-called "power blocs." If an analyst who daily treats mental and emotional disorders does not feel compelled to take a stand on predicaments arising from the *summation* of individual psychopathology, he will continue to be justly criticized for living in the ivory tower of an unrealistic overconcentration on the individual microcosmos. He will also run the risk that what appears to be his self-protective "tower" will be blown away under his feet without his having made the slightest attempt to prevent it.

But there is even a moral aspect to this issue. A world-renowned pediatrician felt it his duty to take to the streets to convey his views on war and peace and on political matters in general, sharing with youth both their idealism and the risk of being called naïve. The least, therefore, that a physician-analyst, working day in and day out with men's irrationality, could do would be to advance, on the basis of his experience, suggestions which could ameliorate the human condition, both ours and our offspring's. Even if my counsel were to prove unworkable, I fail to see any reason why it should not be offered. Indeed, I hope to be able to bring convincing evidence that the reason for the agnosticism and abstention of analysts, concerning the most important issues facing humanity, is at the core of our basic proposition relevant to the triadic principle of maturation.

Regarding the point of departure for my investigative study of the avenues of individual and collective mental prophylaxis, I would like to state that the uncontested reversibility of psychic disorders has always kept alive my deep conviction of the therapeutic efficacy of psychoanalysis. I have been vindicated in this because the analytic method has been proven the most effective and dependable of available psychotherapies, provided it is implemented in accordance with the exigencies of our principle of maturation. This very same principle, I am equally convinced, will show itself capable of insuring effective psychic prevention.

If on the basis of this understanding we succeed in properly discharging our responsibility toward the coming generation, we may ultimately achieve a radical change of the condition, as paradoxical as it is tragic, in which humanity finds itself: On the one side we witness the enormous breakthroughs in physical, chemical, biological and medical science which promise to eliminate the major sources of man's miseries (want, physical illness, premature aging and untimely death). On the other, we must sit by and watch the deadly spiraling of the nuclear arms race which threatens ultimately to extinguish life on our planet altogether. Pertinent to the latter is the tendency to use war as a means of settling accounts. Among these are both the account between affluence and poverty, when shortsightedness and bigotry prevent a more sensible *distribution of goods,* and the elimination of the spectre of *population explosion.* Both these factors represent the major sources of dangerous aggravation of the consequences of economic privations, among which are physical and psychic maladies and the fatal, because easily exploitable, ignorance of the masses.

The second volume will explore precisely how preventive education based on the principle here proposed may act also as a radical *long-range* preventative for collective irrationality. It will also deal with the repercussions of individual irrationality on group formation and choice of political leaders and conversely, repercussions of groups and leaders, through feedback, on the moral standards of the individual. Finally, until the more causal and long-range intervention proposed can be implemented, we will consider *interim measures* to offset the nefarious consequences of immorality of political life on one side, and on the other the increase of individual and collective disregard for social institutions which convulses so many leading nations.

In other words, we will consider possible measures to counteract the impending danger to the evolutionary product of nature's experiment of a million years. We mean the human race, which may come to a sudden end only because this same nature, by a fatal fluke, has endowed us with immense technical power but with too little emotional maturity to use it wisely.

BIBLIOGRAPHY

Bach, G. R. and Wyden P. (1969) *The Intimate Enemy.* New York, William Morrow & Company.

Fenichel, O. (1945) *The Psychoanalytic Theory of Neurosis.* New York, W. W. Norton.

Ferenczi, S. (1916) *Contributions to Psychoanalysis.* Boston, Richard C. Badger.

———— (1950) The Ontogenesis of the Interest in Money. *Sex in Psychoanalysis.* New York, R. Brunner.

Flescher, J. (1945) *Psicoanalisi della Vita Istintiva.* Rome, De Carlo.

———— (1946) L'infanzia come destino dell'umo (Childhood—destiny of the adult). Riv. d. Psa. II.

———— (1949) *Psicoanalisi della Vita Istintiva, Profilassi Psichica* (third and expanded edition), Rome, Scienza Moderna.

———— (1949) Political Life and Super-Ego Regression. Psa. Review, 36.

———— (1951) *Mental Health and the Prevention of Neurosis.* New York, Liveright Publ. Corp.

———— (1953) The "Primary Constellation" in the Structure and Treatment of Psychoses, Psa. Rev. Vol. 38.

———— (1953 a) On Different Types of Countertransference, Int. J. Group Psychotherapy, 3.

———— (1955) A Dualistic Viewpoint on Anxiety, J. Am. Psa. Ass. 3.

———— (1958) The "Dual Method" in Analytic Psychotherapy. *Frontiers in Child Guidance.* New York, Int. Universities, Press.

———— (1959) On Regression and its Therapeutic Management. (Read at the 46th Annual Meeting of the Am. Psychoanalytic Ass., Philadelphia—unpublished.)

———— (1966) *Dual Therapy and Genetic Psychoanalysis.* New York, D.T.R.B. Editions.

———— (1966 a) Conjoint Therapy. The Psychoanalytic Forum 1:4.

———— (1968) Dual Analysis. *Current Psychiatric Therapies.* New York, Grune & Stratton, Inc.

———— *Anxiety, Guilt and Aggression:* A Dualistic Inquiry into Human Psychopathology (in preparation).

———— *Prevention of Collective Irrationality* (in preparation).

Freeman, W. (1967) Psychiatrists who kill themselves. A Study in Suicide, Psychatric Spectator.

Freud, A. and Burlingham, D. T. (1943) *War and Children.* New York, Int. Universities Press.

Freud, S. (1905) Jokes and their Relation to the Unconscious Standard Ed. 8.

———— (1921) Group Psychology and the Analysis of the Ego. Standard Ed. 18.

———— (1926) Inhibitions, Symptoms and Anxiety. Standard Ed. 20.

———— (1927) The Future of an Illusion. Standard Ed. 21.

———— (1930) Civilization and its Discontents. Standard Ed. 21.

———— (1937) Analysis Terminable and Interminable. Standard Ed. 23.

———— (1938) An Outline of Psychoanalysis. Standard Ed. 23.

Gesell, A. and Ilg, G. (1943) *Infant and Child in the Culture of Today.* Harper.

Ginott, H. G. (1965) *Between Parent and Child.* New York, The Macmillan Company.

Greenacre, P. (1950) General Problems of Acting Out. Psa. Quarterly, 19.

———— (1966) Overidealization of the Analyst and of Analysis: Manifestations in the Transference and Countertransference Relationships. *Psychoanalytic Study of the Child.* New York, Int. Universities Press, Vol. 22.

Grotjahn, M. (1969) Das analytische Gruppenerlebnis im Rahmen der psychotherapeutischen Ausbildung. Dynamische Psychiatrie, Vol. 2, June.

Haas, W. (1968) The Intergenerational Encounter: A Method in Treatment. Social Work.

Hawkins, Mary O'Neil (1952) The Panel on the Use and Abuse of Psychoanalytic Principles in Education. *The Annual Survey of Psychoanalysis.* New York, Int. Universities Press, Vol. 3.

Hoffer, W. (1945) Psychoanalytic Education. *Psychoanalytic Study of the Child*. New York, Int. Universities Press, Vol. 1.

Hunter, E. (1968) *Last Summer*. New York, Signet Books.

Jones, E. (1955) *The Life and Work of Sigmund Freud*. New York, Basic Books, Inc. Vol. II.

Liss, E. (1952) The Panel on the Use and Abuse of Psychoanalytic Principles in Education. *The Annual Survey of Psychoanalysis*. New York, Int. Universities Press, Vol. 3.

Nowlan, J. B. et al. On the Physiologic Response: Active and Passive Participation in a Two Person Interaction. Psychosomatic Medicine, 1968:30.

Peller, L. E. (1946) Incentives to Development and Means of Early Education. *Psychoanalytic Study of the Child*. New York, Int. Universities Press, Vol. 2.

Spitz, R. (1945) Hospitalism. An Inquiry into the Genesis of Psychiatric Conditions in Early Childhood. *The Psychoanalytic Study of the Child*. New York, Int. Universities Press, Vol. I.

———— (1946) Anaclitic Depression. *The Psychoanalytic Study of the Child,* New York, Int. Universities Press, Vol. II.

Sterba, E. (1945) Interpretation and Education. *Psychoanalytic Study of the Child*. New York, Int. Universities Press, Vol. 1.

Stone, L. (1954) The Widening Scope of Indications for Psychoanalysis. Journal A.P.A. 2.

———— (1961) *The Psychoanalytic Situation*. New York, Int. Universities Press.

INDEX